The
Social Origins of the
French Revolution

PROBLEMS IN EUROPEAN CIVILIZATION

Under the editorial direction of
John Ratté
Amherst College

The Social Origins of the French Revolution

The Debate on the Role of the Middle Classes

Edited and with an introduction by

Ralph W. Greenlaw

North Carolina State University

D. C. HEATH AND COMPANY
Lexington, Massachusetts   Toronto   London

75-527

International Standard Book Number: 0-669-91116-X

Library of Congress Catalog Card Number: 74-15183

CONTENTS

IV WHO INTERVENED IN 1788? A CASE STUDY IN THE ORIGINS OF THE FRENCH REVOLUTION

INTRODUCTION

They are at it again in France. Although, as one leading scholar of the French Revolution sorrowfully noted, the study of the great Revolution has been losing its appeal to new generations of students who seem to find more recent events in other areas of the world more relevant, it has once again become a focal point of controversy revolving around not only scholarly, but also, and perhaps even more intensely, political and ideological differences. Certain members of the current scholarly historical "Establishment," which to a very large degree determines what is acceptable historical truth at the university level, have charged other scholars who dare to deviate from a basically Marxist interpretation of the Revolution with being guilty not only of promulgating bad history, but of being both unpatriotic and anti-Soviet as well. They further accuse these critics of being the prisoners or dupes of bourgeois or even more reactionary ideologies, and either conscious or unconscious supporters of the anti-Soviet feelings generated by the Cold War. These critics strike back by charging the orthodox Establishment group with being the prisoners of an outmoded ideology that refuses to countenance any fundamental deviation from the sociological and economic theories enunciated by Marx and Engels over a century ago.

With the publication of charges and counter-charges on both sides, tempers have risen and voices have become more strident. At the moment it seems as though the temperature will probably continue to rise and the heated controversy about the causes, character, and results of the Revolution which has been going on for two hundred years seems likely to continue for a few more decades at least.

But why this revival of controversy at this time? Aside from the well-known fact that each generation of historians feels compelled to revise the traditional interpretations it has received from its masters, the intensity in this instance may perhaps reflect a heightening of political feeling within the scholarly community as a residual effect of divisions created during the French student uprising of 1968. There has been a long-standing tradition in France (as in other countries, but perhaps most strongly in France) for historians to openly associate contemporary political viewpoints with particular interpretations of the past. This has been especially true of historians of the French Revolution. Thus Michelet has traditionally been associated with the republicanism of 1848; Taine with the conservatism of the post-1870 period; Aulard with the defense of the Third Republic and Jaurès and Mathiez with the rise of socialism in the early twentieth century.

With victory in World War I and the firm establishment of the Third Republic, controversy diminished somewhat because, however violently Aulard and Mathiez may have berated each other over the relative merits of their heroes, Danton and Robespierre, they were in complete agreement on two crucial points. First that the Revolution had been a "good thing" for France and the world; and secondly, that it had been initiated and carried through by a bourgeois class that had merely taken over the political power to which, as Abbé Sieyès had pointed out in 1789, its wealth, intelligence and general capabilities entitled it. Because it is, of course, a fundamental tenet of classical Marxism that a bourgeois revolution has to precede the ultimate socialist one, it was possible at this point for bourgeois republican and socialist historians to co-exist very comfortably and to join in a kind of popular front against reactionary and totalitarian threats.

After the appearance of Jaurès' scholarly and fully articulated socialist interpretation of the Revolution, revolutionary scholars, including many who were not Marxists in the doctrinaire or philosophical sense, began to put increasing emphasis on research into the social and economic aspects of the Revolution.

One such scholar was Georges Lefebvre whose study of the peasants of northern France during the Revolution became renowned as a model for investigations of social and economic history. But perhaps Lefebvre's even more remarkable accomplishment was a general history of the French Revolution published in 1931 in which he incorporated the results of three decades of study and research into the social and economic aspects of the Revolution. Then in 1939 at the request of the government he produced a small volume entitled *Quatre-vingt-neuf* [1789] in celebration of the sesqui-centennial of the opening of the Revolution. If the new social and economic research had proved anything beyond dispute, it was the variety and complexity of practices, customs, traditions, institutions, attitudes and modes of life in the France of the Old Regime. Finding it impossible to sustain the older traditional view of a monolithic bourgeois class rising up and overturning a weakened and degenerate nobility and a monarchy that represented its interests, Lefebvre, in a remarkable piece of historical synthesis, undertook to explain the Revolution which arose out of the infinitely complex Old Regime as arising from the interaction of four discrete social groups: the nobility, the upper bourgeoisie, the lower bourgeoisie (including artisans and day laborers), and most importantly, the peasantry. Both in this and later works Lefebvre took pains to point out the fact that both before and after the events of 1789 these groups made evident in both speech and actions their deep-seated antipathy, not only toward the nobility but toward other groups. He carefully pointed out peasant hostility toward bourgeois capitalistic land-owners as well as toward the generally noble recipients of the remaining seigneurial dues. He also pointed out the continuing bases for tensions between upper and lower bourgeoisie. Although the Marxists have always maintained that in this brilliant tour de force Lefebvre succeeded in preserving the basic theory of the Revolution as a "bourgeois revolution" (and Lefebvre certainly believed he had), it might well seem to an impartial observer that, although much of the structure remained intact, so many of the old supports had to be modified that it was in some danger of crashing completely.

In spite of his modification of traditional doctrine, Lefebvre has been cordially embraced by the Marxists and is claimed by them as one of the foremost supporters of their theories. Some of these who are perhaps more sensitive to the implications of Lefebvre's thesis have celebrated his contribution as having required a shift from a "simplistic" Marxism to a more sophisticated variety. By this they seem to mean one in which the tremendous variety of groups and subdivisions within both the noble and bourgeois class are recognized, but without accepting the further conclusion that this requires any serious modification of the overall view of the Revolution of 1789 as a "bourgeois revolution."

Only in the years following World War II did Lefebvre's interpretation become generally known both in Europe and America (the original 1939 edition had been confiscated by the Vichy government), but it held the field almost unchallenged. Lefebvre was soon appointed to the chair of French Revolutionary History at the University of Paris and was generally looked to as the dean of revolutionary studies. Perhaps because of his domination of the field in France the first serious challenge to his Marxist-republican viewpoint came from across the Channel. In 1955 in his lecture on the occasion of the inauguration of a chair in French Revolutionary History at the University of London, the late Alfred Cobban, an established scholar in the field, proposed the daring thesis that the Marxist-Lefebvrian view that the Revolution was primarily a social and economic revolution, both in its origins and its effects, was nothing but a myth. He, in effect, called for a return to an earlier view of the Revolution as a fundamentally political revolution with some obvious social and economic effects, but more limited than generally thought. The lecture when published provoked some response from the French side, but it was not until the publication of his Wiles lectures in 1965 under the title *The Social Interpretation of the Revolution* that the disciples of Lefebvre of all nationalities, as well as the Marxists, took after Cobban in full cry. Since they hold that any true revolution *must* be *primarily* social and economic in character, they rightly judged that Cobban's thrust could be fatal if it were not countered.

Unfortunately Professor Cobban died in 1968, and so other scholars have had to carry on the controversy. He had had some support even before his death, however. In the early sixties a compatriot, Ms. Betty Behrens, had published a long article on the tax status of the nobility at the end of the Old Regime and in it showed how little the situation conformed to the Marxian-Lefebvrian stereotype. In an article published in 1965 and reproduced in this volume she raises further pertinent questions about the validity of interpreting the events of 1789 as a "bourgeois revolution." In the sixties Cobban also received some support from two American scholars. One of these was Professor George Forster whose meticulously detailed analysis of property, wealth and social status in the area around Toulouse on the eve of the Revolution seems to make necessary a reexamination of traditional generalizations about the respective economic roles and viewpoints of groups and individuals designated either as noble or bourgeois in eighteenth-century France. The other was Professor George V. Taylor whose extensive research into the development of French capitalism during the Old Regime ended by convincing him of the inadequacies of the current orthodox Marxist framework. At about the same time another American, Ms. Elizabeth Eisenstein, in an article published in the *American Historical Review,* made the first and most direct attack on a major component of the Lefebvrian thesis with respect to the coming of the Revolution by questioning Lefebvre's assertion that the bourgeoisie took control of the revolutionary movement in the fall and winter of 1788–1789.

But what about the French? Might this not seem to them to be some kind of a foreign plot to denigrate the great Revolution? Although in the fifties and sixties there had been numerous monographs and studies that seemed to make necessary some modifications, or perhaps a further elaboration or sophistication of the orthodox view, it was not until the publication of a general interpretive synthesis by François Furet and Denis Richet that there was any serious challenge to the Establishment view. On the surface it is difficult to see why this general work evoked such a strong reaction from the defenders of orthodoxy. In its discussion of the Old Regime and the origins of the Revolution it seems to conform to the Lefebvrian pattern in seeing multiple groups interacting to bring about the Revolution in 1789. It does, however, depart from orthodoxy in two main ways. The authors do not interpret the outbreak of war in 1792 as a predictable attempt by a "naturally" aggressive and now dominant bourgeoisie to embark on imperialist ventures intended to serve their economic interests. But more importantly, Furet and Richet describe the radical-republican phase of the Revolution as a point at which it went "off course." For the Marxists to accept this view would require that they relinquish their view that the radical phase of the Revolution in some of its aspects at least represented a natural and logical foreshadowing of the greater proletarian revolution to come, and accept it as being simply the result of accident or chance. Furthermore this would not only seem to tarnish somewhat the traditional aura of glory of the radical phase of the Revolution by making it a mere chance event, but it also suggests that the two authors look upon the elitist and moderate bourgeois revolution of 1789–1792 as the norm, and in so doing reveal their secret bourgeois bias.

Whether or not these were the real reasons, Furet and Richet's work received an extremely critical review in the leading Establishment journal of revolutionary history, and this was followed by a long polemic directed not only against Furet and Richet, but also against a number of other challengers of the Marxist viewpoint, such as Alfred Cobban and E. Rostow. Both the review and the polemic were written by an ardent Marxist defender of orthodoxy, Claude Mazauric. The fact that M. Mazauric is not expressing an individual or eccentric viewpoint but speaks with authority is shown by the fact that his work was given specific approval in its preface by Professor Albert Soboul, who in orthodox and Marxist circles is now generally looked upon as the heir of Lefebvre's mantle as dean of revolutionary studies as well as of his chair at the University of Paris.

After the publication of M. Mazauric's intemperate and, in M. Furet's view, unprovoked attack, the latter felt that he had no alternative but to respond. He did so in the spring of 1971 in the leading periodical of social and economic history, the *Annales*. Following the principle that a good offense is the best defense, M. Furet in this article turned his attack on the most recent work on the pre-Revolution by M. Soboul, the foremost representative of the currently orthodox Marxist viewpoint. With this response the battle is now fully joined.

In order to enable the student to establish his own position in this controversy, selected excerpts from the works of many of these scholars who have written on both sides of the question of the social origins of the Revolution are reproduced in the text that follows. They are intended to enable the student to follow—and hopefully in many instances to judge critically—the arguments and evidence presented by both sides. To save space all footnote references, except for a few explanatory notes, have been omitted.

The first excerpts are intended to present as succinctly and fairly as possible what the editor feels may properly be called the orthodox or Establishment view of the role of class in the initiation of the French Revolution. Because of the dominant position of Professor Georges Lefebvre in this field since World War II, one may be surprised not to see his classic work on 1789, translated into English by Professor R. R. Palmer under the title of *The Coming of the French Revolution,* included in this group. Since it is generally so well known to American students and is easily available in a paperback edition, the editor is assuming that students reading this book will already be familiar with the Lefebvre classic, or can easily obtain it and familiarize themselves with it concurrently. It will be especially useful to have read at least the sections dealing with the role of the bourgeoisie in the fall and winter of 1788–1789 before reading the selection by Ms. Eisenstein included below. And, of course, it is still true that Lefebvre's interpretation of the events of 1789 is looked upon as providing the cornerstone for the orthodox interpretive structure.

It may seem strange that the first selection is by an Englishman rather than a French representative of the orthodox position. The choice was deliberate. Professor George Rudé has worked extensively in France using new archival resources, but more importantly is a scholar with an independent mind who, although he seems to adhere generally to the orthodox position, does not hesitate to deviate from the stereotypes of the Marxist school if he feels impelled to do so by the evidence. He might be described as a "sophisticated" economic determinist, and by giving prominence to his views the editor hopes to avoid the accusation of having set up a kind of simplistic version of the orthodox view that might seem to present too easy a target for the criticism that follows. Furthermore, Rudé's brief article provides an excellent summary in English of what might be described as an updating of the Lefebvrian thesis. Even as Lefebvre did, Rudé recognizes the importance of bourgeois and even noble leadership, while at the same time emphasizing the critical role of the urban and rural masses. His sensitivity to the complexities of class and group motivation and interaction might lead one to believe that Professor Rudé would find it difficult to accept any monolithic concept of a "bourgeois" revolution, but he gives little or no evidence of discomfort in remaining within the traditional framework. The reader can decide for himself whether, after being made so acutely aware of the social complexity of the opening phase of the Revolution, the term "bourgeois" revolution still has meaningful validity for him.

As was indicated earlier the Lefebvrian mantle has now been

formally assumed by Professor Albert Soboul. His view of his relationship to the work of Georges Lefebvre is perhaps best illustrated
by the fact that when a new edition of Lefebvre's *Quatre-vingt-neuf*
was published in 1970 by the Marxist press, Editions Sociales, Professor Soboul contributed both a preface and a postface. In the
latter, from which the excerpts included here are taken, he states in
pure classic form a Marxist analysis of the character of the Old
Regime and the causes for its overthrow. Since in some of his works
he has had no qualms about departing from traditional Marxist views
when the evidence seemed compelling, one can only reasonably assume that even though obviously hindered by lack of space from
qualifying his remarks in detail, the views set forth in his postface
express his reasoned personal conviction. A further insight into his
views with respect to those who challenge and criticize the fundamental Marxian framework is given in his preface to the polemical
attack on the opponents of orthodoxy written by M. Mazauric. This
preface is also included following M. Soboul's postface to the Lefebvre work.

The excerpt from M. Mazauric, who is the final spokesman for
orthodoxy, is particularly valuable not only because of the detailed
analysis which it gives of the Marxist position on many issues relating
to the Revolution, but also because of the insight which it, along with
the excerpts from Professor Soboul, gives us into the tone and temperature of the debate. In his preface M. Mazauric declares his intention to be avowedly polemical, and that quickly becomes obvious.
The excerpts included below start with his preface, in which he tries
to justify his polemical approach. This is followed by an excerpt in
which he presents a detailed basic statement of the Marxist interpretation of the Revolution in general, and of its origins in particular.
It is hoped that this analysis will make it easier for the reader to
understand his specific criticisms of the Furet–Richet book, which
are presented in the last excerpt. The reader will probably quickly
recognize that the origins of the Revolution represent only one
phase of the revolutionary movement, and that much of Mazauric's
general discussion refers to later phases of the Revolution. In spite
of the traditional requirement of looking at the Revolution as a block,
it would seem legitimate to follow the example of the master, Georges
Lefebvre in his famous *Quatre-vingt-neuf,* and focus attention on its
social origins.

The first excerpt challenging the orthodox Establishment viewpoint is by the prominent French scholar, François Furet. In it he makes the most systematic and detailed attack on the defenders of orthodoxy to appear thus far. Unfortunately it was not possible to include any material from the original Furet–Richet volumes which so aroused M. Mazauric. In the article included here, however, M. Furet indicates the general interpretive positions that he and M. Richet took. Assuming an offensive stance, much of the article takes the form of a critique of a recent work of Professor Soboul. In this critique M. Furet makes effective use of his extensive knowledge of the most recent and most significant monographic work on various aspects of the Old Regime. A small portion of the article dealing with later stages of the Revolution has been omitted. Although M. Furet counterattacks with brilliance, vigor and effective irony, he also seems to be making an effort to moderate the degree of emotion and to avoid ad hominem accusations. One gets the feeling that M. Furet writes more in sorrow than in anger, because he and his associates have generally had only the greatest of respect for the work of many of the scholars of the orthodox viewpoint, whose common interest in social and economic history they share. Furthermore, neither M. Furet nor M. Richet had ever considered himself to be an anti-Marxist in the crude, undiscriminating Cold War sense of that term, and obviously were shocked to find themselves so designated. But having been attacked, the two men quite naturally felt justified in defending themselves.

The third group of excerpts from the work of other critics begins with one from Alfred Cobban, taken from his book dealing with the social interpretation of the history of the French Revolution published in 1964. As indicated earlier, Cobban was the first and initially most serious challenger of the orthodox position. Because he rightly saw that his disagreement was fundamentally with the orthodox view of the nature of social history, he devotes his opening chapters to that problem. He then goes on to illustrate his specific points of disagreement by using examples taken from the social history of the Old Regime and the Revolution. The excerpt included here is limited to those points relating primarily to the initial stages of the Revolution.

The eminent Professor Jacques Godechot reviewed Cobban's book for the *Revue Historique,* and his review follows the Cobban excerpt. While he pays tribute to the value of Cobban's work as requiring scholars to reconsider certain formerly accepted views, Godechot seems to find few, if any, of his points convincing. There does seem to have been a real problem in communication here, as well as a difference in fundamental philosophy. This is indicated in the final selection from Cobban's work which is his detailed reply to Godechot's critical comments.

While Professor Cobban's assault on orthodoxy seems to be more philosophically or ideologically based, Professor George V. Taylor dares to challenge the orthodox on their own turf, the field of economic history. The excerpt from one of his articles, which is included here, represents only the tip of an iceberg. Beneath it lies years of research in both archival and printed sources and wide reading in relevant monographic literature. His findings have been published in several articles, and the excerpt included here represents only the concluding portion of a paper presented at a meeting of the American Historical Association in 1965 and published in the *American Historical Review* a year later. It directly questions the traditional Marxist reading of the economic history of the Old Regime, particularly where it relates to the respective roles and attitudes of the bourgeoisie and the nobility. Since for the Marxist, history is economically determined, the charge that they do not have their economic history straight potentially threatens their whole structure. In spite of the fundamental character of its challenge, however, there is little evidence that Professor Taylor's observations have had any great notice in France, much less any effect.

The final selection in this section is a review article from the Cambridge *Historical Journal* by an English scholar, Ms. Betty Behrens, in which she discusses books by three members of the revolutionary Establishment, Messrs. Soboul, Godechot and Méthivier. While these three scholars as well as other supporters of orthodoxy certainly would not agree, this editor finds Ms. Behrens' conclusions regarding the state of the question at this time to be both appropriate and perceptive:

> So much confusion has recently been introduced into French eighteenth-century history that the central doctrine of the class struggle between bourgeois and aristocrats can now only be accepted as an act of faith; for no two people can agree on who the bourgeois and the aristocrats were; no one can formulate (and few ever try to formulate) a criterion

for distinguishing between them that can be followed consistently, and every argument is thus liable to be at variance with ascertainable facts.

Her article includes much evidence in support of this conclusion. It was indicated above that Georges Lefebvre's work has generally been highly esteemed by all French scholars of the Revolution and only indirectly challenged by Alfred Cobban. But Ms. Elizabeth Eisenstein, an American scholar who was investigating the role of the printing press in the fermentation of the Revolution, turned to Lefebvre's treatment of its opening phases to try to find out precisely who the revolutionary leaders were at the critical moment when, according to Lefebvre, leadership went from the noblemen who had led the aristocratic revolt of 1787–1788 over to members of the bourgeois class that was to complete the Revolution and become its principal beneficiary. Ms. Eisenstein was annoyed to find not only relatively little solid factual information on this critical point, but what she did find she felt hardly seemed adequate to support Lefebvre's broad conclusions. The result was the article reproduced here, in which she questions not only Lefebvre's conclusions on this point, but also by implication the whole tradition of the role and responsibility of the bourgeoisie in the initiation of the Revolution. A discussion of the specific question raised by Ms. Eisenstein provides an excellent case study of a specific phase of the broader question of the role of the bourgeoisie.

Because precise evidence is so crucial in attempting to establish the validity of Ms. Eisenstein's questions about the leadership of the Revolutionary movement in the fall and winter of 1788–1789, an excerpt has been included from Professor Jean Égret's comprehensive and solidly researched study of the complex events of the two years preceding the meeting of the Estates-General. It is a history of events—and primarily political ones—of the traditional kind, but Professor Égret digs far below the surface to try to discover the underlying factors and forces influencing the direction of the revolutionary movement. His discussion of the background and activities of the leaders in the fall of 1788 represents an invaluable first step toward providing the essential factual data for a verification of Lefebvre's thesis about the transition from noble to bourgeois leadership. While it seems to be accurate to say that the results of all Professor Égret's extensive work on the pre-history of the Revolution

in all parts of France seem to fit generally into the traditional Lefebvrian structure, it would seem that his primary concern in his
work has been to establish as firmly as possible our detailed knowledge of the course of events in the many areas of revolutionary
ferment, rather than to present any new interpretation of the broader
significance of these events. Thus, although it probably would be
proper to include Professor Égret in the Establishment, his clear
commitment to traditional empirical history suggests that it might be
more appropriate to class him as an independent scholar.

Although the French have been silent, some American scholars
who read Ms. Eisenstein's article felt impelled to come to the defense of the Old Master and the orthodox view of the origins of the
Revolution. Their reply to Ms. Eisenstein also appeared in the *American Historical Review*. The first defender, Professor Jeffry Kaplow,
attacks Ms. Eisenstein's analysis on several points of both definition
and interpretation, and ends by reasserting the validity of the concept of a bourgeois revolution, so long as the term is qualified in
certain obvious, but to him noncontroversial, ways. The second
American defender, Professor Gilbert Shapiro, a sociologist, became
interested in the French Revolution as a result of participation in a
project to make a computerized analysis of the *cahiers* of 1789. Professor Shapiro broadens his critique of Ms. Eisenstein's article by
also including some comments on Cobban's book on the social interpretation of the Revolution. He criticizes both of them for what he
feels is a simplistic misunderstanding of the refined neo-Marxism,
which he implies represents the true viewpoint of those who defend
the Lefebvrian position. In her response to these two critics, Ms.
Eisenstein defends her original position with vigor, having found
nothing in the remarks of the two critics that she felt compelled any
serious alteration of her views.

In summary it would seem justified to say that the case study, as
well as the points made by the other critics of the orthodox interpretation of the reasons for the revolutionary overthrow of the Old
Regime, apparently indicate the need for extensive reconsideration
of the whole question—and possibly its reformulation. Perhaps students reading this book will be inspired to join in the effort to complete this important and difficult task, for it seems that after nearly
two hundred years, we are still very far from certain about who or
what caused the Revolution, or why it took the course it did.

Conflict of Opinion

The present study...attempts to place the revolt of the privileged orders and the parlements (the *révolte nobiliaire*) and the revolutionary action of the bourgeoisie in the crisis of 1788–1789 in their correct historical setting; but above all, it is concerned to trace the main stages and currents of the popular movement during the last years of the Old Regime up to the point where its "merger" with that of the bourgeoisie touched off the revolutionary explosion.

GEORGE RUDÉ

The Revolution of 1789–1794 marked the advent of modern bourgeois and capitalist society in the history of France. Its most important characteristic was its achievement of national unity for the country by the destruction of the seigneurial regime and the "feudal" privileged orders.

ALBERT SOBOUL

Under the pretext of not neglecting the new methods of history, or the new influences of particular sciences, certain historians recently have by their theories tended to minimize the importance of the Revolution. They do this by retrospectively putting on trial the classical historians of the Revolution and particularly those progressive or Marxist historians such as Jaurès, Mathiez, Lefebvre and their disciples.

It is with Albert Mathiez—although hardly in a direct way—then with E. Labrousse, Georges Lefebvre and their French and foreign pupils, that a history of truly Marxist direction or inspiration was implanted in France. It has served as guide in the opening of new sectors of research and at the same time has provided new means of deepening the knowledge of the Revolution as a bourgeois, antifeudal and mass revolution as Marx understood it.

CLAUDE MAZAURIC

The interpretation of the French Revolution, for example, has gained neither richness nor depth by the constant, implicit attendance of the history of the Russian Revolution: such preoccupation with the future has proliferated like a cancer within the vitals of historical analysis to the point of obliterating all complexity, and even all significance. . . . One result is the substitution of an extraordinarily simplified and oversimplifying Marxism for the few sometimes contradictory analyses of the French Revolution which Marx and Engels have left us. What is substituted is a simple linear pattern of history in which the revolutionary bourgeoisie, with the support of the peasantry and the urban masses, permits the passage from a feudal to a capitalist mode of production.

Thus, the key to the politico-social crisis of the eighteenth century is neither a hypothetical closing of the nobility, nor its gross hostility to the bourgeoisie in the name of an imaginary "feudal system." On the contrary, it is the opening of the noble estate: too broad to maintain

xix

the cohesion of the order, and too narrow for the prosperity of the century. The two great heritages of the history of France, a society of orders and absolutism, entered into a conflict without issue.

FRANÇOIS FURET

There is really no alternative to accepting what every historian who had looked at the evidence would have been bound to have accepted if it had not been for intellectual enslavement to a theory. The abolition of seigneurial dues was the work of the peasantry, unwillingly accepted by the men who drew up the town and *bailliage cahiers,* and forced on the National Assembly through fear inspired by a peasant revolt. It follows that the "overthrow of feudalism by the bourgeoisie" takes on very much the appearance of the myth I suggested it was in a lecture some eight years ago.

ALFRED COBBAN

If the Revolution put an end to a regime, it was certainly to the "feudal regime," and the arguments advanced by Alfred Cobban against the evidence, although they are interesting and clever, will not persuade those who have worked to any extent in the documents of the time.

JACQUES GODECHOT

The error does not lie in seeing the Revolution as a political struggle for power, but in taking the political division as the basis for social history. The result is, inevitably, the kind of history which is irreconcilable with any serious social analysis.

ALFRED COBBAN

There was, between most of the nobility and the proprietary sector of the middle classes, a continuity of investment forms and socioeconomic values that made them economically a single group. In the relations of production they played a common role. The differentiation between them was not in any sense economic; it was juridical. This situation in the historiography of the Revolution, has received practically no serious attention and remains, in Orwellian language an "unfact." The reason for that is that it contributes nothing to what Cobban rightly calls "the established theory of the French Revolution," the theory that the Revolution was the triumph of capitalism over feudalism.

GEORGE TAYLOR

On "the debated question of who started the Revolution" then, the author's [Lefebvre's] evidence suggests that the initiative came, beginning with the first Assembly of Notables called by Calonne in 1786, through the stormy year of 1789 and beyond, from a loose coalition of like minded men drawn from all three estates. No conventional social nomenclature appears applicable to this group whose collective biography remains to be written.

ELIZABETH EISENSTEIN

What Lefebvre and his followers have undertaken to prove is that the French Revolution was a bourgeois one, in that it was made by the bourgeois for the benefit of the bourgeoisie—or, if you will, in the name of an ideal formulated by the bourgeoisie and identified with the well being of humanity as a whole.

JEFFRY KAPLOW

I suggest that ... both contemporaries and Marxists have generally meant by the "bourgeoisie" nothing more complex, nor better defined, than the "upper levels of the Third Estate," which is to say the wealthier, more urban, more educated, less privileged members of the society. ... One can readily see their very minor role in the *leadership* of the movement that intervened in the conflict between the aristocracy and the monarchy in the winter of 1788 to insist upon the doubling of the representation of the Third Estate. But this does not mean that they did not play an important role.

GILBERT SHAPIRO

I THE ESTABLISHED OR ORTHODOX VIEWPOINT

George E. Rudé

THE OUTBREAK OF THE FRENCH REVOLUTION

Although George Rudé (b. 1910) is best known among French revolutionary scholars for his pioneering studies of crowds in the French Revolution, he also has written several general interpretive studies of the revolutionary period both inside and outside France. The article which follows reflects the general interest of his scholarly generation in the formerly little-studied and therefore silent masses. While Professor Rudé for the most part seems to adhere to the currently orthodox view of the primacy of social and economic factors in history, he does not hesitate to reject a rigid determinism in this area and seems willing to accept modification of the orthodox position where evidence seems to require it. Professor Rudé has been associated with several universities in the British Isles and the Commonwealth and at present is professor of history at Sir George Williams University in Montreal.

Although there is a tendency to reopen the debate on the causes of the French Revolution, most reputable historians of the event have by now accepted the thesis that the Revolution was the product of a conflict of social classes rather than the outcome of a conspiracy hatched by *philosophes,* lawyers, disgruntled officials or Freemasons. Since the publication of Jaurès' *Histoire Socialiste* at the turn of the century, a serious effort has been made, as well, by a number of historians to treat the problems, aspirations and movements of the peasant and urban masses in their own right instead of as an echo or reflection of the speeches and actions of the revolutionary leaders in Paris.

Such studies have, of course, done more than merely throw a fresh light on the general causes and course of the Revolution; they have made it possible to measure with greater accuracy the point of revolutionary outbreak and the part played by the masses of town and countryside in relation to it. The revolutionary explosion, therefore, no longer appears as a more or less fortuitous climax to a series of purely political, though interrelated, crises—the rejection

From George Rudé, "The Outbreak of the French Revolution." World copyright © the Past and Present Society, Corpus Christi College, Oxford. This article is reprinted with the permission of the Society and the author from *Past and Present, a journal of historical studies,* no. 8 (November 1955), pp. 28–42. Footnotes omitted.

of Calonne's proposals by the Notables, the convocation of the States General, the dismissal of Necker, etc.—but as the sharp collision of a complex of social forces at a moment of acute revolutionary crisis.

Even when this is accepted, however, the picture may still become lop-sided if one or other of the social forces, whose coming together—either in alliance or in opposition—provoked the revolutionary crisis, is not seen in its proper perspective. The most familiar distortion of this kind is that which presents the revolutionary action of the peasant and urban masses as "waiting upon" that of the bourgeoisie, or even of the privileged orders themselves. Mathiez, in particular, has made us familiar with the picture of the origins of the great Revolution as a gradual "unfolding" of minor revolutions— first the *"révolte nobiliaire"*; then the *"révolution bourgeoise"*; and, finally, the popular revolution. While such a presentation is convenient and has more than a grain of truth in it, it tends to reduce the intervention of the masses to one of secondary importance and fails to show that the popular movement, while intensified and accelerated by the revolutionary crisis, had its origins in the Old Regime and, in fact, preceded by many years the revolutionary activity of the bourgeoisie.

On the other hand, writers like Daniel Guerin have gone to the opposite extreme by exaggerating the independence and the degree of coherence and political maturity of the popular movement, and particularly emphasizing those aspects of it which appear to look forward to the working-class movements of the nineteenth and twentieth centuries. In the view of such historians, of course, it is not the wage-earners or *sans-culottes,* but the bourgeoisie itself which ceases to be a revolutionary force.

Yet another tendency has been to present the revolutionary crisis almost exclusively in terms of more or less short-term economic factors, particularly of rising or falling prices. No one will deny the great contribution made to our knowledge of the origins of the Revolution by Ernest Labrousse: before his work appeared, little was known of the movements of prices and wages in eighteenth-century France, particularly in the crucial years preceding the revolutionary outbreak. Labrousse's insistence, however, on the primacy of "natural" (i.e. uncontrollable economic) over "anthropomorphic" causes has the effect of reducing the popular movement to the automatic product of purely economic factors.

The present study introduces new material to illustrate the range and diversity of the movement in town and countryside—particularly in the Paris region—in the years leading up to the Revolution; it also attempts to place the revolt of the privileged orders and the Parlements (the *"révolte nobiliaire"*) and the revolutionary action of the bourgeoisie in the crisis of 1788–1789 in their correct historical setting; but, above all, it is concerned to trace the main stages and currents of the popular movement during the last years of the Old Regime up to the point where its "merger" with that of the bourgeoisie touched off the revolutionary explosion.

Let us begin with the year 1775. There had, of course, been numerous other movements provoked by hunger and the high cost of bread in earlier periods of the century—as, for example, in 1725, 1739–1740, 1752 and 1768; but that of 1775 is not only the nearest to the point of revolutionary outbreak, but the most extensive, the best documented and that which bears the closest resemblance to the popular movements of the Revolution itself. Turgot had been appointed Comptroller-General in August 1774. He started with no particular record of unpopularity as far as the common people were concerned: at any rate, his predecessor and most vocal opponent, the Abbé Terray, was, soon after his appointment, burned in effigy in the Faubourg St. Antoine. Yet, to the delight of his enemies at Court, he was soon to lose any semblance of popular favor by his over-haste in applying Physiocratic doctrine to the grain-trade: an *arrêt* of 13 September restored freedom of trade in grain and flour. This, combined with a bad harvest, led to a shortage and a rapid rise in the price of corn, flour and bread in the following spring and summer. The price of the 4-lb. loaf in Paris (normally 8–9 sous, though, in recent years, more often 10–11 sous) rose to 11.5 sous in early March and to 13.5 sous at the end of April. Grain riots had already broken out in Dijon, Tours, Metz, Rheims and Montauban—and, in their wake, sprang up that particular series of riots, centered in Paris and its adjoining provinces, known to history as *"la guerre des farines."* The movement spread from market to market and took the form of a popular price-control of wheat, flour and bread—the price of bread being generally fixed at 2 sous per pound, that of flour at 20 sous a bushel and wheat at 12 francs a setier (2 quintals). Starting on 27 April at Beaumont-sur-Oise, twenty miles north of Paris, it reached Pontoise on the twentieth, St. Germain on 1 May, Versailles on the second and Paris itself on the third. It then spread eastwards and southwards up the valleys of the Seine and Marne, lingered for several days in the markets and villages of Brie, reached Beaumont-sur-Gatinais (50 miles south of Paris) on the ninth, and petered out somewhere near Melun on the tenth.

It is instructive to note the main features of this remarkable movement. It was essentially a spontaneous movement—in spite of some historians' claim to the contrary—provoked by hunger and the fear of shortage. It saw the massive invasion of markets and farms by urban poor, farm-laborers, village artisans, and even occasional farmers and well-to-do bourgeois. It was directed, in the main, against farmers or prosperous peasants (*laboureurs*), grain-merchants, millers and bakers; and aroused some sympathy among other classes—certain priests, for example, either encouraged, or did little to restrain, their parishioners from taking part in the movement, and more than one market official helped it along by himself fixing a "just" price for grain or flour.

Why, then, did a movement of such magnitude and bearing striking similarities with certain movements of the Revolution yield no tangible result? In the first place, the food crisis itself, though protracted, was overcome by the end of the summer: prices began to fall in October. Secondly, Turgot managed to crush the movement by a combination of propaganda—via the Bishops—and the use of troops, who remained entirely loyal to the government. More important still, the bulk of the peasantry was not involved: the question of tithes, feudal dues or game laws did not arise. Lastly, and perhaps most important of all, the bourgeoisie had not yet begun to challenge the existing order and, in any case, were bound to be hostile to a movement directed against members of their own class and against a Minister, whose accession to office they had hailed with enthusiasm and whose reforms—including that of free trade in grain—they actively supported: in several towns, in fact, the *milice bourgeoise* was mustered in order to crush the riots. The main lesson of 1775 was, in short, that, in the conditions of eighteenth-century France, no isolated movement of wage-earners, artisans and village poor could hope to yield revolutionary results. This truth was to be realized on more than one occasion both before and during the Revolution.

The twelve years that followed (1775 to 1787) were, despite a general sharpening of the longer-term economic crisis, years of comparatively stable food prices and social peace. In Paris, at least, the price of bread remained remarkably steady: from the manuscript Journal of the Parisian bookseller Sébastien Hardy we learn that, whereas in the period of 1767-1775, the price of the 4-lb. loaf rarely fell below 11 sous (and, for a few days in November 1768, actually reached 16 sous), in the later period, the normal price was 8 or 9 sous, and it only rose to 10.5 or 11 sous for very brief spells in 1784.

Popular movements during these years were scattered and sporadic, arising on a number of separate issues. In June 1778, bread riots took place in Toulouse and Grenoble; in both, rioters were fired on by troops. In 1784 and 1786, there were protest movements in Paris against the *barrières,* or ring of customs posts, recently erected by the Farmers-General to tax livestock, meat, wine, firewood and other commodities entering the capital; and, also in 1786, Hardy noted protests against the cost of meat and firewood. In Paris, too, there appears to have been a resurgence of anticlerical feeling among the people: Hardy recorded a number of incidents between 1783 and 1789 that are reminiscent of the hostility to Jesuits in the 1720s and to the Archbishop of Paris over the *billets de confession* in 1752.

More remarkable perhaps is the number of strikes, involving the journeymen in a number of trades and, in the case of the Lyons silk workers, assuming almost insurrectionary proportions. Jules Flammermont may be right in attributing these, in part at least, to the special penal measures in restraint of combination introduced in August 1776 and to the anger of the workers at the reversal of the decision to abolish the guilds; but it is worth observing that, in eighteenth-century France, a crop of strikes usually coincides, as here, with a period of comparatively stable prices. In 1776, a general strike broke out among Parisian bookbinders who were demanding a 14-hour day. In July 1785, there was a large-scale and successful strike of Paris building-workers against a wage-cut imposed by the employers; in March 1786, the carpenters were on strike again and, this time, Hardy reported *"une espèce de fermentation"* among the journeymen of several trades. In January of the same year, the carriers and porters of the capital struck against the institution of a rival monopoly by Court favorites, and seven to eight hundred of them marched to Versailles to see the King. In Lyons, the strikes of the silk-weavers led to widespread rioting and bloodshed. Yet, with the exception of the movement in Lyons, which had its sequel in the domination by the *maitres-ouvriers* of the meetings called to draw up the *cahiers de doléances* for the silk industry in 1789, it is doubtful if these labor disputes gave an appreciable impetus to the widespread and varied popular movement that was to arise in the period of revolutionary crisis.

The year 1787 saw the opening of the *"révolte nobiliaire"* which served as a curtain-raiser to the revolutionary crisis of 1788–1789. In February, an empty exchequer and mounting deficit forced the government to convene the Assembly of Notables. Calonne, as Comptroller-General, proposed a number of stopgap measures to meet the crisis, including a stamp duty and a tax on landed estates. The privileged orders refused to cooperate. Calonne was dismissed on 8 April and succeeded by Loménie de Brienne, Archbishop of Toulouse. Brienne's proposals being no more acceptable than Calonne's, the Notables in turn were dismissed on 25 May, and the *"révolte nobiliaire"* began. The opening shot was fired, as so often in the past, by the Paris Parlement which, while accepting Brienne's plan to relax controls on the sale and export of grain and protesting against the stamp duty, refused absolutely to register the decree on the land tax and demanded that the States-General be convened to deal with the matter. When the decrees were, nonetheless, promulgated in a *lit de justice* in August, the provincial Parlements rallied to the support of Paris, and Brienne was forced to capitulate; the decrees on the land tax and stamp duty were withdrawn on 21 September and the Paris Parlement was reinstated a few days later.

The return of the Paris Parlement from exile was the occasion of wild scenes of jubilation in the Place Dauphine, the rue du Harlay and other approaches to the Law Courts. Calonne was burned in effigy, bonfires were lit on the Pont Neuf, fireworks and squibs were let off at the Guards. From Hardy's description and from the arrests made on 28 September (the climax of the disturbances) it is clear that the shock-troops in these riots were formed by the clerks of the Palais—*"une jeunesse effrénée"* Hardy calls them—and the apprentices and journeymen of the luxury trades in the Place Dauphine; the "populace" of the surrounding quarters joined them but played only a subordinate part. The bourgeoisie was as yet uninvolved.

In the months that followed it was the economic crisis, above all, that brought the "fourth estate" once more into the picture, either on their own account or (as in Paris) as the temporary ally of the dissident privileged orders. Brienne's return to the "free trade" measures of Turgot had led to a sharp rise in the price of grain; by July 1788, in the North at least, speculators were at work again and widespread complaints were voiced against forestalling and hoarding. At Troyes, the *milice bourgeoise* was already mustered in April to overawe the textile workers; and, in Paris, as we shall see, the high price of bread was to contribute to a popular outbreak in the late summer. Peasant revolt, however, lay dormant until the following spring, when long-simmering discontent with food-prices and seignorial exaction was to be touched off into violent outbreak by the political ferment emanating from the local electoral assemblies.

Meanwhile, the political crisis had sharpened. Brienne had fallen back on the expedient of raising a loan, which the Paris Parlement was willing to accept, provided the States-General should be summoned. But negotiations broke down again in November; the Duke of Orléans and two *conseillers* were exiled; and, in May 1788, the Parlement issued a declaration, condemning the whole system of arbitrary government, including the *lettres de cachet.* The Government riposted by ringing the Palais with troops, forced the *Parlementaires* to surrender their ringleaders to royal justice and promulgated six edicts, prepared by Lamoignon, the *garde des sceaux,* which restricted the jurisdiction of the Parlements and vested the royal courts and officials with greater powers. A new phase of violence followed: there were mass riots in Grenoble and Rennes in June; in the Dauphiné, nobility and Third Estate joined forces against the Crown in July. In early August, troops were concentrated around the capital for fear of an "insurrection," not so much of the Palais clerks and apprentices as of the *menu peuple* of the markets and the Faubourgs St. Antoine and St. Marcel.

These fears proved well-founded. The government was compelled to bow before the storm and promised that the States-General would be called in May 1789; on 24 August, Brienne was replaced by Necker and the Parlement was recalled soon after. The news was greeted with another outburst of celebrations in the Place Dauphine and the approaches to the Palais: bonfires were lit and the occupants of coaches crossing the Pont Neuf were compelled to bow low to the statue of Henri IV and to shout "A bas Lamoignon!" A new factor, however, was to extend these disturbances far beyond the scope and limits of those of the previous year. On 17 August, the price of the 4-lb. loaf, after remaining at 9 sous, rose to 9.5 sous, on the twentieth to 10 sous, on 2 September to 10.5 sous, and on 7 September to 11 sous. Under this stimulus, the inhabitants of the Faubourgs joined in the riots on the third day (29 August) and changed their whole character: they spread to the markets and University quarter, continued—with short lulls—until the end of September and took a heavy toll in casualties and arrests; the latter were mainly composed of craftsmen and wage-earners of widely scattered districts. The Parisian *sans-culottes* had entered the arena as a decisive force, but not yet as the ally of the bourgeoisie; the real revolutionary crisis was yet to come.

This developed in the winter of 1788–1789 and was to bring about a radical realignment of classes. The harvest was generally bad, and, in the Paris region, crops had been flattened by a freak hailstorm in July. There followed a winter of phenomenal severity which threw thousands out of work and brought further thousands of villagers flocking to the capital; in December, Hardy wrote of 80,000 unemployed. The price of the 4-lb. loaf in the Paris markets rose to 12 sous on 8 November, to 13 sous on the twenty-eighth, to 14 sous on 11 December and, finally, to 14.5 sous on 1 February; it was to remain at this level until after the fall of the Bastille. In April, in the grain-starved markets of the Paris region, the price of wheat rose to the fantastic sum of 40–44 francs the *setier*. Meanwhile, the crisis in industry—itself the offshoot of the agrarian crisis, though doubtless aggravated by the results of the Commercial Treaty with England in 1786—had thrown thousands out of work in every textile center: according to the reports of the industrial inspectors for September 1788 to January 1789, there were 46,000 unemployed in Amiens, 10,000 in Rouen, 8,000 in Falaise, 30,000 in Carcassonne, 25,000 in Lyons; while at Troyes and Sedan half the looms were idle. It was against this economic background that the bourgeoisie made its entry on the revolutionary stage. The cause of conflict had its roots deep in the Old Regime: while colonial trade, land values and luxury spending had enormously increased in the course of the century, capital investment and expansion of manufacture were everywhere impeded by the restrictions imposed by privileged corporations, feudal landowners and government on the elementary capitalist freedoms—the freedom to hire labor, the freedom to produce and the freedom to buy and sell. Yet, while the ensuing conflict owed its eventual sharpness and finality to these deeper social antagonisms, the clash between the bourgeoisie and the privileged orders arose, in the first instance, over representation and voting in the States-General. Already in September, the Paris Parlement had shattered its reputation as the spokesman for "popular liberties" by demanding that the States-General be constituted as in 1614—i.e. that each order should have equal representation and vote separately. An even more forthright insistence on the maintenance of privilege was voiced in the Manifesto of the Princes of the Blood in December. Necker, however, persuaded the Council to allow the Third Estate double representation; but the question of voting "par téte" (as demanded by the bourgeoisie) or "par ordre" (as insisted by the nobility and clergy) remained open and led to bloody clashes between nobles and commoners at Rennes. By January, the new alignment of forces was becoming clear and Mallet du Pan noted that it was no longer a question of a constitutional conflict between the King and the *privilégiés* but a "war between the Third Estate and the two other orders." In February, the conflict was raised to a higher pitch by the publication of the Abbé Sieyès' pamphlet *Qu'est-ce que le Tiers Etat?*, in which the bourgeoisie, for the first time, laid claim to control the destinies of the nation irrespective of the wishes or privileges of the other orders.

It is not surprising that, with these developments, the winter of 1788–1789 should see the beginnings of a popular movement of an altogether vaster scope and intensity than those of the preceding years. This movement had other, even more significant, features: it became a continuous movement that did not cease until after the point of revolutionary outbreak; it grew from a movement concerned, in the first place, with purely economic ends into one with more or less clearly defined political aims; it developed a common bond of interest between the wage-earners, craftsmen, wine-growers, and small tradesmen of town and countryside against monopolists, hoarders and grain speculators; this movement, in turn, began to "merge" with that of the small peasant proprietors against feudal game laws, tithes and dues; and, finally (though not always in point of time), the movement of townsmen and villagers "merged" with the political action of the bourgeoisie against feudal privilege and the whole apparatus of government of the Old Regime.

The revolt against shortage and rising prices started in the last days of December 1788 and is recorded in the reports of the Intendants (or their *sub-délégués*) of several provinces. It variously took the form of pillaging of grain-boats and granaries; of enforcing price-control of bread, flour and wheat; of rioting in bakers' shops and markets, and at town halls; of assaulting customs officials, dealers and farmers; and the widespread destruction of property. In December and January, such reports come in from Brittany and Touraine; in March and April, from Burgundy, the Ile de France, Languedoc, Nivernais, Orléanais, Picardy, Poitu, Provence and Touraine; in May and June, from the Limousin and Lyonnais; in July, from Champagne and Normandy. Hardy records bread riots at Rheims in March and at Nancy and Toulouse in April.

In the Faubourgs and markets of Paris, the high cost of meat and bread provoked a mounting wave of anger which broke out into destructive violence in the Réveillon Riots in the Faubourg St. Antoine at the end of April. Ten "smugglers" were arrested at the *barrières* in early May; this movement reached its climax on 12–14 July, when 40 of the 50-odd customs posts ringing the capital were burned down.

In the country north of Paris, the fight against famine developed into a movement against the game laws and the hunting rights of the nobility. On the estates of the Prince de Conti at Cergy, Pontoise, l'ile Adam and Beaumont, peasants and land-workers, having reaped no harvest owing to the ravages of hail, set out to trap and destroy the rabbits that infested their fields. The movement spread in the spring to Conflans Ste. Honorine and adjoining villages, and led to clashes with the *maréchaussée*. At Oisy, in the Artois, the peasants of a dozen villages banded together to exterminate the Count of Oisy's game and refused in future to pay him the traditional *siyeté*, or *terrage*. More violent clashes occurred near Corbeil and at Chatou; south and west of the capital, whole parishes, suspected of large-scale poaching on royal and aristocratic preserves, were disarmed in June. In Lorraine and the Hainaut, landless peasants and small *laboureurs* joined forces in opposition to enclosure edicts and land clearance schemes. Meanwhile, peasant revolt against royal taxes and seignorial exactions had broken out in Provence in March, at Gap in April, and in the Cambresis and Picardy in May. This movement led, in turn, into that far vaster movement of July and August which, spreading over regions as widely scattered as Alsace, Normandy, the Hainaut, Mâconnais and Franche-Comté, left in its trail the widespread destruction of *chateaux* and manorial rolls. Yet peasant hostility to enclosure and encroachment on rights of pasture led also to attacks on capitalist farmers; and in more than one case again, the *milice bourgeoise* joined forces with the *maréchaussée* to repress peasant disorder.

Yet, in spite of such contradictions, as the crisis deepened, bourgeois and *sans-culottes* were drawn into closer partnership in opposition to the privileged orders and the feudal regime. The urban and peasant masses were never to be fully won for the bourgeois conception of "freedom"—this was to remain a cause of division throughout the Revolution—but it was in their common interest to remove the fetters on production and the high cost of food occasioned by internal customs duties and fiscal charges; to clip the wings of (if not to dispossess entirely) the tithe-owner and the extractor of feudal *rente* and *champart;* to reduce taxes and the ruinous costs of government; to compel the privileged orders to make a fair contribution to the national exchequer; to curb the monopolists and Farmers-General; to destroy such relics of ancient tyrannies as the Bastille, the *lettre de cachet* and the vexatious inquisitions of the Parlements. It is precisely such demands that we find voiced most frequently in the *cahiers de doléances* which began to be drawn up in the early months of 1789—usually drafted, it is true, by the professional bourgeoisie, but often endorsed by meetings of peasants, small tradesmen and workshop masters, and even, though more rarely (as at Rheims, Marseilles, Troyes and Lyons) by guilds of journeymen or *maitres-ouvriers*.

And the States-General roused such ardent hopes—"la grande esperance," Georges Lefebvre has called it—because it was widely believed that, cleared of the obstruction and domination of the privileged orders, it could realize a radical program of this kind.

From these hopes stem the enthusiastic adoption of the slogan, *"Vive le Tiers Etat!"* (which is certainly thought to include the "Fourth Estate" as well), and the passionate belief, once the Court Party began to threaten to dash these hopes to the ground, in the existence of an "aristocratic plot." It was in direct response to this stimulus that the Parisian journeymen, laborers, workshop masters and shopkeepers—already roused to action by the ruinous cost of bread, meat and wine—rallied to the call of the revolutionary leadership installed at the Palais Royal and—less certainly—to that set up by the Electors of the Paris Third Estate at the Hôtel de Ville; it was also this conviction that the Court Party was preparing to disperse the States-General and to subdue Paris with the aid of foreign troops, far more than the gold of the Duke of Orleans, that won over the main body of the Paris garrison, the Gardes Françaises—so recently engaged in shooting down the Réveillon rioters—to the side of the Revolution. When Necker, the popular Finance Minister, was dismissed by the King on 12 July, the people of the Faubourgs and the markets joined with the bourgeois revolutionaries and the disaffected troops in carrying through the Paris insurrection—the first great armed uprising of the Revolution. The gunsmiths, arsenals and religious houses were raided for arms, the hated *barrières* were destroyed, a *milice bourgeoise* (including journeymen, but excluding "vagrants" and unemployed workers) was organized, a revolutionary government was installed at the Hôtel de Ville, and, finally, the Bastille was taken by storm. The popular movement had fully "merged" with that of the revolutionary bourgeoisie; the example was quickly followed in other parts of France.

Labrousse tells us that the Bastille fell on the very day when the price of grain throughout France reached its cyclical peak. This is no doubt significant, but it would be a mistake to attempt to explain the revolutionary crisis wholly in such terms. To do so would be to discount entirely the revolutionary action of the bourgeoisie and the permeation of the Parisian *menu peuple* with the political ideas and slogans of the Third Estate. It is evident that the basic motive prompting popular action was the high cost of food and the fear of famine. This continued to be so and is the most constant element in the repeated upsurge of the popular movement during the years of the Revolution—in August–November 1789, in the years 1792–1793 and, above all, in 1795. Yet there was a similar fear of famine in 1768; and, in 1775, as we have seen, the fears thus aroused led to a massive movement of popular protest; yet in neither case did a revolutionary outbreak result. This was because the economic and political crisis as a whole—and not one single aspect of it, however important—had not fully matured and because the conflict of social classes which it occasioned was as yet only one-sided and partial; above all, it was because one of these classes, the bourgeoisie, although dissatisfied with the inequalities, the corruption, the extravagance and the restrictions of the Old Regime, had not yet begun seriously to challenge the absolute monarchy or the privileged orders, or the social system on which they depended. It was only when the bourgeoisie entered the revolutionary struggle, as it did in the winter of 1788–1789, that the popular masses were able to acquire a political direction and a set of political aims and concepts—such concepts as Third Estate, Nation, *"complot aristocratique"* and the Rights of Man—without which they would have expended their energies on actions limited to economic ends. This is not to underrate the importance of their contribution; without their intervention, the bourgeois revolutionaries of July 1789—many of whom were stricken by panic at the crucial moment of insurrection —would have been doomed and the recently constituted National Assembly dispersed by royal troops. Yet, for all their vacillations and fears—fears of the Court Party and of the masses themselves— in the social conditions of the day, the insurrection would not have been successfully carried out without the direction and political guidance of the deputies, journalists, pamphleteers and Electors of the Third Estate.

It was, in fact, to be one of the great lessons of the French Revolution that the popular movement, however militant and widespread, could only succeed and survive as an effective revolutionary force as long as it was allied to an important section of the bourgeoisie; conversely, that the bourgeoisie could only carry out its historical task of destroying feudal property relations as long as they, or a substantial part of them, maintained their links with the broad masses of town and countryside. Nothing is to be gained by omitting one side or other of this picture, as some historians have done. In July 1789, as we have seen, at the moment of revolutionary crisis, the immediate interests of the masses coincided with those of the main body of the bourgeoisie and even of a minority of the privileged class itself. In the following autumn, as so often in the course of the Revolution, the preoccupation of the Parisian *menu peuple* with the problems of high prices and shortage threatened to disrupt the alliance by directing their main fury against the monopolists and the newly constituted city authorities; and it was only by the harnessing of this movement to the political tasks set by the Constitutional Monarchists that the Royal Family was brought to Paris and the National Assembly was once more saved. Similar situations arose—though with changing forms of alliance, as the bourgeois-democratic revolution advanced—in the years 1791–1794; but, in the summer of 1794, when the Revolutionary Government was compelled by its own contradictions to sacrifice the interests of the *sans-culottes,* the alliance was broken and Robespierre fell an easy victim to the intrigues of his enemies. In the spring and early summer of 1795, attempts were made to reconstitute it at the time of the massive popular insurrections of *Germinal* and *Prairial;* but, at the crucial moment, the radical wing of the bourgeoisie deserted, either from weakness or from fear of the masses, and the popular movement was finally crushed. It was only to rise again—and under very different conditions—in 1830.

Albert Soboul

THE SOCIAL AND ECONOMIC CHARACTER OF THE FRENCH REVOLUTION: ITS RELEVANCE IN THE MODERN WORLD

Albert Soboul (b. 1914) was born in Algiers, the son of an artisan, and worked his way up through the French university system to receive his doctorate after presenting his now classic study of the sans-culottes *(workingmen) of the section of Paris in the Year II (1793–1794). He has openly associated himself with the Marxist interpretation of the revolutionary episode, and his appointment to the chair of Revolutionary History at the University of Paris*

From Albert Soboul, "Postface" to *Quatre-vingt-neuf* by Georges Lefebvre (Editions Sociales, 1970), pp. 246–263 and 271–274. Reprinted by permission of the publishers and Professor Soboul. Footnotes omitted. Editor's translation.

in 1968 and his assumption of the editorship of the leading journal on revolutionary history provide striking evidence that the Marxist view of the Revolution is now generally accepted as the orthodox viewpoint in French circles. Professor Soboul has published several general histories of the Revolution as well as his special works on the sans-culottes. *The first excerpt presented here is taken from the postface to a recent new edition of Georges Lefebvre's classic,* Quatre-vingt-neuf, *and the second is a preface he contributed to the recent Marxist polemic published by a fellow Marxist, Claude Mazauric.*

Postface to *Quatre-vingt-neuf*

The Revolution of 1789–1794 marked the appearance of modern bourgeois and capitalist society in the history of France. Its most significant aspect was its achievement of national unity for the country by its destruction of still existing elements of the seigniorial regime and the "feudal" privileged orders. According to Tocqueville in *The Old Regime and the French Revolution,* "the real objective of the Revolution was to abolish completely the vestiges of the institutions of the Middle Ages." The fact that the French Revolution ended finally in the establishment of liberal democracy adds another dimension to its historical significance. From the point of view of these two achievements as well as from that of world history . . . , it deserves to be considered the classic model of a bourgeois revolution.

The comparative study of the French Revolution accordingly poses two series of problems.

The first are problems of a general kind. They relate to the historical laws governing the transition from feudalism to modern capitalism. Summarizing the problem as it is presented by Marx in Book Three of *Das Kapital,* this transition can be effected in two ways: either by the total destruction of the former social and economic system, "the true revolutionary way," or by preserving the former mode of production within the new capitalist society, the way of compromise.

Secondly there are problems of a specific kind: those having to do with the precise structure of French society at the end of the Old Regime, and those dealing with the particular characteristics of the French Revolution as they relate to other instances of bourgeois revolution.

Viewed in this double perspective, the history of the French Revolution cannot be isolated from that of Europe. In all the countries of Europe, the prototype of modern society was sketched out within the very breast of the preceding social and economic system with its vestiges of feudalism, and at its expense. In all the countries of Europe this evolution took place to the benefit of the bourgeoisie in varying degrees. The French Revolution was not even the first one from which the bourgeoisie profited. Before it the Dutch revolt in the sixteenth century, the two English revolutions in the seventeenth, and the American Revolution in the eighteenth prefigured its development. Still one must understand the unique character of the French Revolution.

At the end of the eighteenth century France and most of Europe were organized according to a pattern which has since been called the *Ancien Régime* [Old Regime]. Socially its structure was characterized by aristocratic privilege, and politically by divine-right royal absolutism.

The aristocracy, whose role had been declining since the Middle Ages, nevertheless remained at the top of the social hierarchy. The social structure of France was still essentially aristocratic. It had retained the characteristics of the period in which it had its origin, a period when land constituted the sole form of social wealth and conferred power on those who possessed it over those who tilled it. The Capetian monarchy had succeeded by dint of long effort in depriving the *seigneurs* of their regalian rights and the nobility and the upper clergy of all political influence. But even though they had become subjects, the nobility and clergy nevertheless continued to enjoy privileges. The *seigneurs* held on to their social and economic privileges, and their seigniorial rights continued to make evident the subjection of the peasants.

Socially privileged but politically degraded, the aristocracy never forgave the absolute monarchy for having despoiled them of all political authority. It denounced despotism, and called for freedom, but its real aim was to share power with the sovereign. Its ideal of limited or mixed monarchy was inscribed in the frame of a theory of historic or traditional rights. It was affirmed at the end of the reign of Louis XIV particularly by Bishop Fénelon whose political ideas are not only implicit in the allegories of *The Adventures of Télémaque* (1699), but are set forth even more clearly in *The Plans of Government...to Be Proposed to the Duke of Burgundy* which he published in 1711 under the title *Tables of Chaulnes*. This aristocratic reaction against absolutism divided during the first half of the century into two streams. One of these represented a feudal reaction which accorded with the interests of the nobility of the sword [or blood] and for which the Count Boulainvilliers was the principal representative.[1] The other was the juridical reaction of the Parlements which supported the interests of the nobility of the robe [so-called from the robes worn by the judges and officials] and whose position was set forth in 1732 in the publication of the *Judicium Francorum*.[2] The theories of these parlementary and feudal reactions were repeated again in the middle of the century, no longer by obscure pamphleteers, but by Montesquieu in 1748 with the publication of his *Spirit of the Laws*. This aristocratic justification of liberty as opposed to monarchical absolutism was, as Georges Lefebvre noted, only a "vestige of the past."

The revival of commerce and the development of handicraft production had, however, beginning in the tenth and eleventh centuries, created a new form of wealth, moveable wealth. The result was the birth of a new class, the middle or bourgeois class whose admission to the Estates-General at the beginning of the fourteenth century confirmed its new importance. Within the framework of feudal society, it progressed in rhythm with the development of capitalism, stimulated by the great discoveries of the fifteenth and sixteenth centuries, by the opening of colonial territories, and by the financial operations of a monarchy perennially in need of money. By the eighteenth century the bourgeoisie were dominant in finance, commerce and industry. They provided the monarchy with its administrative officials as well as the resources required for the progress of the state. Then, even as the aristocracy solidified into a caste, the bourgeoisie increased in numbers and economic power, as well as in culture and knowledge. The progress of the Enlightenment under-

---

[1] Henri Boulainvilliers (1658–1722) became famous as the author of a political treatise published after his death which professed to show that the nobility of his period legitimately possessed their rights and privileges because they were the lineal descendants of the Franks who had conquered Gaul in the fifth century.—Ed.

[2] The *Judicium Francorum* was a famous pamphlet which claimed that the Parlements, or highest law courts of France, as a corporate body were the heirs to the power of the defunct Estates-General and that royal laws which were not registered (in effect sanctioned) by these courts, and especially the most important one, the Parlement of Paris, had no legal validity.—Ed.

mined the ideological foundations of the established order at the same time it strengthened the class consciousness of the bourgeosie. It had a good conscience too, because as a rising class believing in progress, it was convinced that it represented the interests of the whole nation, for which it was willing to accept responsibility. As the progressive class it exerted a powerful attraction over the masses of the population just as it did over dissident segments of the nobility. But the ambition of the bourgeoisie, although based on social and economic realities, found itself checked by the aristocratic structure of the laws and institutions.

The bourgeoisie, like the aristocracy, hoped to see itself associated with royal power and in opposition to absolutism it called for liberty. But instead of justifying this by appealing to historic rights, it based its claim on natural rights. Society, it said, is based on a free contract between its members and government; on a free contract between the sovereign and those who are governed according to the terms of which power can rightfully be exercised only for the benefit of the community and in support of the rights of its citizens. In 1724 appeared the first French translation of Locke's *Treatise on Civil Government* which had been published in 1690. This work provided inspiration for the whole century. Theoretician of the English Revolution of 1688–1689, Locke gave expression to the bourgeois ideal, in a way that might be said to have transformed "an historical accident into an event called forth by human reason." The fundamental reason for the great influence of his political ideal was that it coincided with that of a rapidly rising bourgeois class. It presented a complex amalgam of empiricism and rationalism which defended property and the established social order, but in moral terms; which provided for effective power, but with the necessity of consent; and for individualism but with recognition of the principle of majority rule.

Political freedom was demanded, assuredly, but even more importantly it called for economic freedom, especially of initiative and profit. Capitalism required liberty becaused it needed to ensure its progress. It needed all forms of freedom: freedom for the individual; freedom to establish wages and working conditions; freedom for property so essential to its mobility; and freedom of inquiry as an essential condition for research and scientific and technical discovery.

The bourgeoisie did not, like the aristocracy, demand only power and freedom; they undertook to suppress privilege and acquire equal rights. In the second half of the eighteenth century, the bourgeoisie found themselves, in effect, at odds with the aristocracy. For centuries, the bourgeoisie had dreamed only of gaining noble status. Purchase of offices had provided the means. Ever since the sixteenth century the monarchy had drawn off a part of bourgeois wealth by putting on sale certain government offices which were made more attractive by carrying with them certain corporate privileges as well as either personal or hereditary nobility. And so, while many bourgeois families had infiltrated directly into the aristocracy, they constituted a nobility of the robe which, although it moved them closer and closer to the aristocracy of birth, remained nevertheless bourgeois in its characteristics—especially in the administration of its property. But in the eighteenth century the nobility of the robe like the aristocracy tended to close its ranks so that the bourgeoisie remaining outside were too numerous to be able to hope to all be admitted. "In one way or another," writes Sieyès in his pamphlet entitled *What Is the Third Estate?*, "all the branches of executive power have also fallen to that caste which includes the clergy, the nobility of the robe and the nobility of the sword. A kind of spirit of brotherhood causes noblemen to give preference to each other in everything before all the rest of the nation. The usurpation is complete, they reign in truth." [3] The bourgeoisie call for the suppression of privileges and equality of rights.

In France, then, in the second half of the eighteenth century, the rise of a capitalistic economy, on which base was built the power of the bourgeoisie, finds itself held back by the feudal structure of society and by the traditional organization and regulation of property, of production and of trade. "It was necessary to break these chains," wrote the authors of the *Manifesto,* and "they were broken." Thus was posed the problem of moving from feudalism to capitalism. It did not escape the more farsighted men of the period. Far from being inspired by an abstract individualism as Taine has maintained, the bourgeois revolutionary had a definite consciousness of the

---

[3] Perhaps the most famous and influential pamphlet published during the controversy over voting procedure in the Estates-General of 1789. Sieyès argument provided a philosophical basis for the demand of the Third Estate for at least equal representation in the Estates-General.—Ed.

economic reality which provided his strength and made inevitable his victory.[4] Barnave first formulated, more than a half century before Marx, the theory of the bourgeois revolution. In his *Introduction to the French Revolution* written in 1792, Barnave posed the principle that property-holding influences institutions.[5] "The rule of the aristocracy lasts as long as the rural population continues to ignore or neglect the crafts, and the ownership of land continues to be the sole basis of wealth." "When handicrafts and commerce take hold among the people and create a new source of wealth benefiting a new class of working people, this paves the way for a revolution in political structure. A new distribution of wealth opens the way to a new distribution of power. In the same way that the possession of land creates an aristocracy, industrial property increases the power of the people; it provides the means to achieve its freedom." It should be understood that when Barnave refers to the people he means the bourgeoisie.

The Dutch and English revolutions had earlier demonstrated that the underlying causes of the bourgeois revolution are to be found in the vestiges of feudalism and the resultant contradictions within the preceding regime. But this does not completely explain the character of the French Revolution. The reasons that this, by its very violence, constituted the most striking episode in the long class struggle which carried the bourgeoisie to power, are to be found in certain specific traits of French society of the Old Regime.

The bourgeoisie would undoubtedly have been contented with a compromise which would have associated them in power, following the pattern of the English oligarchy in the eighteenth century. But the aristocracy obstinately refused. All compromise broke down on the issue of feudalism. The peasant masses would not tolerate its retention, nor would the nobility as a whole accept its suppression since this would seal their doom. On the basis of the social and economic compromise affected by the redemption of feudal obligations decreed in principle on the night of August 4

---

[4] Hippolyte Taine (1828–1893) wrote a famous history of the Revolution in which he blamed its failures and its excesses on the abstract theorizing of the philosophes. He argued that when the revolutionaries tried to apply their theories from 1789 to 1799 the results were disastrous.—Ed.

[5] Antoine P. J. M. Barnave (1761–1793) was extremely active and prominent in the Revolution from its beginning. Because of his firm attachment to the principle of monarchy, however, he was denounced and executed during the Terror.—Ed.

and enacted into law on March 15, 1790, the bourgeoisie of the Constituent Assembly for a long time sought a political compromise with the aristocracy. The obstinate resistance of the mass of petty noblemen, who lived for the most part on income from their lands, and the stubborn and aggressive determination of the peasants to have an end to the vestiges of feudalism made a policy of compromise and reconciliation impossible. In order to prevail, the bourgeoisie had to commit itself to alliance with the masses.

The mass of the people carried the whole weight of the Old Regime, and it had become insupportable for them.

The urban masses, artisans and shopkeepers, journeymen and apprentices, wage-earning clerks, and to a lesser degree handicraft workers, all were pushed to revolt by the aggravation of their living conditions. These have been revealed by the work of C. E. Labrousse.[6] From 1726–1741 to 1785–1789 a long-term rise in prices resulted in an increase in the cost of living of 62 percent. Bread on the average constituted about half the food budget for the masses; in 1789 seasonal variations in the price of grain brought it as high as 88 percent above normal. The nominal rise in wage levels, of about 22 percent on the average, did not keep up with rising prices. Wages, as usual, lagged behind prices without ever catching up with them. To be more specific, real wages declined by about 25 percent. This worsening of the living condition of the masses did not escape the most perceptive observers of the time. In 1766 Turgot set down one of the earliest formulations of the "Iron Law of Wages" in his *Reflections on the Formation and Distribution of Wealth*.[7] The urban masses were more concerned about their daily bread than their freedom: they gave top priority to the question of subsistence. To the demand for economic freedom they opposed the right to existence, or more specifically to the taxation and economic regulation which would ensure it. To the equality of rights which the bourgeoisie demanded of the aristocracy they opposed "equality of satisfactions."

Among the real urban masses, soon to be designated by the term

[6] C. E. Labrousse, a contemporary French economic historian, has done the definitive studies of the movement of wages and prices in France in the eighteenth century.—Ed.

[7] A. R. J. Turgot (1727–1781) was an important writer on economic matters as well as holding responsible administrative offices. He was comptroller-general of France from 1774 to 1776 but failed in his attempt to introduce economic reforms.—Ed.

sans-culottes, class spirit was lacking. Isolated in numerous work-shops, not specialized as a result of the limited development of techniques, nor concentrated in large-scale enterprises or in industrial quarters, and generally little different from the peasantry, wage-earners, like the peasant, were incapable of conceiving of efficacious remedies for their misery. The weakness of organization of labor attests to this. Hate for the aristocracy, and implacable opposition to the rich and powerful provided the leaven for the unity of the laboring masses. When bad harvests and the economic crisis which inevitably followed them set the laboring masses in motion, they ranged themselves, not as a distinct class but as associates of the artisans, behind the bourgeoisie, and in this way delivered the most effective blows against the old society. But this victory of the masses could not be other than a "bourgeois victory" because the bourgeoisie accepted the alliance of the people against the aristocracy only because the masses remained subordinate to them. If it had been the other way, the bourgeoisie would understandably have repudiated the support of allies considered to be too threatening—as was the case in the nineteenth century in Germany and to a lesser degree in Italy.

The peasant masses constituted, however, the primary element of the French population with its numbers probably reaching as many as 22 or 23 million out of a total population of about 25 million. In 1789 the great majority of peasants had for a long time been free men with serfdom remaining only in a few isolated spots, primarily in the Nivernais and Franche-Comté. Feudal modes of production nonetheless prevailed in the countryside as evidenced by the seigneurial obligations and the ecclesiastical tithes. Certain historians have tended to minimize the burden of this feudal structure at the end of the Old Regime. Tocqueville has already answered them in a chapter of *The Old Regime and the French Revolution* entitled "Why Feudal Obligations Had Become More Disliked by the People of France than Anywhere Else." If the French peasant had not owned land he would have been less sensitive to the obligations imposed on landed property by the feudal system. Nevertheless, it would be appropriate in order to define the problem more precisely to establish the amounts involved in feudal dues in quantitative terms. For the three *élections* of Aurillac, Mauriac and Saint-Flour, according to fiscal records, these amounted to about 10 percent of the taxable product (by which is meant the average net product), not including the incidence of *lods et ventes,* of the *banalités* or the ecclesiastical *dîme.* But it is the total weight of the obligations supported by a piece of land in ratio to its product that must be determined. Only then can one get an accurate idea of the relative cost of the totality of the *complex of feudal dues.* In these same *élections* of upper Auvergne, these feudal obligations amounted in round figures to about a third of the income of the *seigneurie.* This percentage makes fairly predictable the resistance of the nobility of Auvergne to the abolition of feudal dues, its refusal of any compromise and, finally, makes it evident that the agrarian troubles of 1789, 1792 and 1793 were the result of counter-revolutionary efforts. "Imagine," wrote Tocqueville concerning the peasant in eighteenth-century France, "the condition, the needs, the character, the feelings of that man and calculate, if you can, the store of hate and envy amassed in his heart." To the hate of the feudal obligations one must add the hunger for land which gripped the peasants and which was made even more intense by the population increase that marked the eighteenth century. While about 130,000 members of the clergy shared, very unequally, about 10 percent of the land, and the nobility numbering about 350,000 held 20 percent, the bourgeoisie retained exclusively for itself about 30 percent of the total of landed property, and that part left over for 22 to 23 million peasants amounted to only 35 percent. The importance of the peasant question, because it is at the heart of the bourgeois revolution, cannot be overemphasized. For [some scholars], Jacobinism, which constituted the essence of the French Revolution, was characterized by the alliance of the bourgeoisie and the peasant masses.

The masses, peasant or urban, had a social ideal relative to the economic conditions of the time; their idea was to limit property rights and take counter-measures against concentrations of farmlands or business enterprises. Peasants and artisans, in order to establish free disposition of their persons and their work, first had to cease to be infeudated to others, that is, either attached to the land or imprisoned in the structure of a corporation. From this requirement arose their hatred of the aristocracy and the Old Regime. The masses have always provided the moving force behind the bourgeois revolution. But being actual producers, or dreaming of becoming such, peasants and artisans based property rights on

personal labor and dreamed of a society of small independent producers. In a confused way they understood how to prevent the
establishment of a monopoly of wealth, as well as of a dependent
proletariat. These deeper aspirations make understandable the social and political struggles of the Revolution both in their persistence
and their progress. From 1789 to 1793 one sees an intensification
of the struggle of the bourgeoisie against the aristocracy marked by
the increasing participation of the average citizen and the masses,
not a change in the nature of the class struggle. In this sense one
cannot speak of a "change of front" of the bourgeoisie after the fall
of Robespierre. After, just as before, the Ninth Thermidor, the aristocracy was not disarmed, it remained the primary enemy.[8] The law
of the Ninth Frimaire of the Year VI (November 29, 1797) inspired
by Sieyès is proof of this. It put the former nobles in the same situation as aliens. The French Revolution is indeed a "bloc"—it is
antifeudal and pro-bourgeois throughout its diverse history.

This rooting of the Revolution in French society, as well as its
continuity and its unity, were underscored by Tocqueville with his
customary lucidity when he noted its inevitability. "What the Revolution was less than anything else was a chance event. While it is
true that it took the world by surprise, nevertheless it was only the
culmination of a long period of travail—the sudden and violent
termination of an enterprise on which men had labored for ten
generations."

Foreword to *Sur la Révolution française*

The fact is now evident that for some time the period of the
French Revolution has been in disfavor among historians. There are
many reasons for this. In some instances the underlying ideological
reasons are evident, as in the case of the so-called theory of the
"Atlantic or Western Revolution" which appeared at the height of the
Cold War. More recently, certain individuals, seemingly more publicists than historians, and either ungrateful or renegade sons of "the

The following portion of this excerpt is taken, with permission of the publishers and
the two authors, from Professor Soboul's "Foreword" to Claude Mazauric's book,
Sur la Révolution française, Contributions à l'histoire de la Révolution bourgeoise
(Editions Sociales, 1970), pp. 5–9. Footnotes omitted. Editor's translation.

[8] The date of Robespierre's fall and traditionally thought of as marking the end of
the Reign of Terror.—Ed.

mother of us all," have attempted to place in question the achievements of more than half a century of historical study of the Revolution extending from Jean Jaurès to Georges Lefebvre. Under these circumstances one can only underscore the need for studies and essays in the polemical style such as these presented here by Claude Mazauric. While set forth in the polemical tradition of revolutionary historiography, there is more justification in this instance in that it is based on a solid foundation of erudition and critical analysis. Especially important are the innovations it proposes, and the new perspectives for research and historical consideration which it opens up. Examples of these in the collection of essays published here are those relating to the use of expressions *"régime féodal"* and *"féodalité"* during the French Revolution.

It is both good and necessary that a new generation molded in the social and political struggles of the second half of the twentieth century, and therefore attuned to the most recent problems and to more recent methods, is now in its turn taking up the study of the Revolution, and while doing so still holds true to that view which certain individuals, with the real purpose of denigrating it, call the "Jacobin" interpretation of the Revolution. This is a term which we do not repudiate, since we have been taught by our master, Georges Lefebvre, to understand it as standing for fidelity and devotion to the cause of the people by the historian, but without foregoing any of the essential requirements of the scholarly method or a proper critical spirit. To make it even more precise, we mean by this the progressive tradition of revolutionary historiography extending from Michelet to Lefebvre, and including Jaurès, Aulard and Mathiez. Whatever may have been the nuances or differences of opinion between these men, their interpretations are the only ones which, while holding fast to progressive principles, have been and continue to be scientific.

It is also good that research and reflection on the French Revolution has been renewed under the influence of methods which have been proved in other areas—such as linguistics—and that these sister-disciplines in coming to the aid of history allow the historian to get a new reading of the documents and a new perception of events. One should keep in mind, however, that the time for writing the history of the Revolution has been relatively short and that consequently, while wishing our history could be all inclusive, it ought to be first of all social and political, actual social conditions being only the effects of the contradictions and the class struggles which determine the complex unity (economic, political, ideological) of social structures.

For what will soon be two centuries, each generation has looked back in turn to the Revolution, as the matrix of our history, either to exalt it or to reject it, in accordance with its hopes and dreams. We have always felt at home in it as a result of the works of those who through the generations have written about it. It is now necessary for us to resume its study using the means afforded by our times, such as our computers, but also with the light thrown on it by the wars and revolutions of the second half of the twentieth century. If it is true that the past determines the present, the other side of the coin is that our reflections on history are enlightened by our present experiences and can, in turn, influence action. The movement of history reveals little-by-little to each generation of historians more and more numerous factors and more and more complex interaction. The very point of view which the historian holds of his time and of his class and of the conflict in which it is involved, if he knows enough not to hide himself away in his ivory tower, can make him aware of some completely new aspects of past reality which up until now have been hidden in darkness. Who does not recognize that some of the problems which arise today in the revolutionary movement already have existed in other forms, at the heart of the complex and frightful social and political by-play of the Year II? Problems such as the duality of power, the necessary establishment of cadres within the governing apparatus, as well as the problems of revolutionary bureaucracy and of a new conformism. . . . And at a more general level, the problem of transition from an old society to a new one: should it be by the way of revolution or the way of compromise? Should it involve the total destruction of the old economic and social system, or should one hold on to the old mode of production within the new society? We know how between 1789–1794 the French Revolution resolved these issues.

Certain persons may perhaps at this point accuse the historian of hiding a subjective viewpoint under the mask of erudition. Or perhaps he may be accused of relativism, of substituting for a definite and inflexible historicity a moving and fluid historicism with the historian proceeding by projecting a conception of himself and his times into the past and interpreting it accordingly. And still others may ask whether the totality of history can be realized except through a multiplicity of approaches arising out of different interpretive systems and independent accounts? . . . No, undoubtedly dialectical materialism provides the requisite diverse lines of investigation with the unity of a theory.

The French Revolution was a total phenomenon arising from a process which encompassed all aspects of historical development. In the stream of historical writing, which itself reflects the movement of history, the different aspects of this totality are revealed in turn to successive historians and thus are brought to light some aspects formerly concealed by the very multiplicity of phenomena. Moreover, the French Revolution having made possible a certain number of lines of development (we have in mind the problem of equality of rights from the Declaration of 1789 to Babeuf and the Conspiracy of Equals), each time a development such as this takes place it projects new light on the revolutionary past which can bring greater understanding to both the historian and the politician, if he has eyes to see at all. The same thing applies to reflections on the problem of the modes of transition to socialism as compared to the revolutionary transition from feudalism to modern capitalist society.

The French Revolution is situated at the very heart of the history of the contemporary world, at the intersection of the different social and political currents which have divided nations—and still divide them. The classic bourgeois revolution, by its uncompromising abolition of feudalism and the seigniorial regime, marks the beginning of capitalist society and the representative system in the history of France: the system of bourgeois liberalism which was affirmed with such *éclat* in the nineteenth century and which as a result of its socially conservative compromises has lost nothing of its political validity. But having been a peasant as well as a popular revolution, the French Revolution tended on the other hand on two occasions to move beyond its bourgeois limits. First, there was the attempt in the Year II (1793–1794) which in spite of its inevitable failure maintained for a long time its value as an example. The egalitarian Republic of 1793–1794 remained in spite of its real anomalies a Utopian goal— an Icaria continually sought but never reached. The second instance was the Conspiracy of Equals, that episode which was to prove to be the fruitful origin of contemporary revolutionary thought and action, because Babeuf gave the first sketch of a revolutionary idealogy for the new society which would arise out of the bourgeois revolution itself.

These episodes undoubtedly explain the vain efforts to deny to the French Revolution, as a dangerous precedent, its historic reality or its specific social or national significance. But they also explain the tremors which the world has experienced and the impact of the French Revolution on the conscience of men of our century. The memory of it is in itself revolutionary. It still exalts us.

The history of the French Revolution will never be finished nor ever totally written. From generation to generation as the history which it has made possible unfolds, it will never cease to stimulate men's thoughts, and also their enthusiasm.

Claude Mazauric

THE FRENCH REVOLUTION—A BOURGEOIS REVOLUTION

Claude Mazauric, a member of the Faculty of Letters and Human Sciences of the University of Rouen has devoted his principal research and publishing efforts to the activities of Gracchus Babeuf and his followers during the Revolution. He has also published materials on the Revolution in Rouen. He is an avowed adherent of the Marxist interpretation of history. Professor Soboul's approval of M. Mazauric's effort is evident from Professor Soboul's remarks (the second part of the preceding article), which originally appeared as Foreword to the book from which the following excerpts are taken. In the first excerpt Mazauric discusses the significance of the Marxist interpretation for today and indicates why he feels its critics must be attacked. In the second he presents evidence that traditionally even the non-Marxist and reactionary historians have seen the Revolution as a bourgeois revolution. In the third section, he presents in technical detail the Marxist theory of the causes of the outbreak of the Revolution. The final section, a critique from the Marxist viewpoint of a history of the Revolution published by F. Furet and D. Richet in 1966, was published originally in the Annales Historiques

From Claude Mazauric, *Sur la Révolution française, Contributions à l'histoire de la Révolution bourgeoise* (Paris, Editions Sociale, 1970), pp. 11–12, 15–17, 21–27, 51–56, 58–61, 65–69, 71–79. Reproduced with permission of the author and the publisher. Editor's translation.

de la Révolution française, *the periodical of revolutionary history edited by Professor Soboul.*

The Significance of the Marxist Interpretation for the Modern World

The history of the Revolution still provides an appropriate ground for polemics and ideological confrontations, since this is the means by which it progresses. Whether one wishes to or not, one must take a stand. Moreover, the history of the Revolution—it must be admitted and from our point of view deplored—no longer enjoys among French historians the same prestige as formerly. At a time when the field of historical research has broadened immeasurably, the French Revolution attracts proportionally much less attention from professional historians, but without a corresponding gain in other sectors of historical knowledge of equivalent significance. But as much from the point of view of its importance in the national history of Frenchmen as from its more purely theoretical significance for the history of contemporary revolutions and mass movements, the French Revolution deserves to maintain a privileged position as a field of historical investigation. One might have thought that the bicentennial of Napoleon's birth (1969) would have focused attention on the origins of contemporary France, but the political and ideological situation now prevailing has led to the exaltation of Napoleonic grandeur, the power of the Consular and Imperial state—which certainly was very real—but except for a few instances involving specialists in the field, did not arouse the interest of the country in the "why" and the "how" of the French Revolution of which, it should not be forgotten, the Napoleonic system was at the same time both the heir and the perversion. The final word has not been spoken, however, and nothing is definitively established with respect to the history of the Revolution! Anyone attracted to its study knows that at each step new questions arise, even in the area of political history where one might think that everything is known. Furthermore, as with all historical knowledge, the present, and in this respect especially our own time because of the spread of socialist revolutions, can shed new light on the revolutions of the past. It appears to me as if research into the lines of development of socialist revolutions ought to stimulate interest on the part of historians to become acquainted with the paths followed by bourgeois revolutions. This might arise either from a desire to try to comprehend the extreme diversity of the forms that even predetermined historical events can take, or from a rigorously Marxist viewpoint to pursue research into the processes affecting the structural relations by which the capitalist mode of production was freed from the feudal mode of production. The fact that the French Revolution was the most spectacular movement and most advanced example of a bourgeois and democratic revolution ought to be enough in itself to stimulate the interest of a large number of historians.

But there is even more to be said. An old current of hostility to its popular and democratic content still persists, as it certainly always has, but is today reinforced by the utilization of modern means of developing and diffusing information. At the lowest level innumerable articles on Marie-Antoinette periodically invade the screen, the book trade and the magazines, all directed especially toward women and children (youth). In contrast to the admirable teleplay of Stellio Lorenzi, "The Terror and Virtue," how many bad films and plays do we not have to suffer through? For the "Death of Danton," which presents an equivocal but powerful version of the Great Revolution, how many "Poor Bitos"? At another level there is no one who does not recall the frightful commentaries which accompany tourist tours of the Palace of Versailles, of national museums and of various churches or chateaux in the provinces. Reactionary ideology, whatever concrete objective it may be pursuing, is still full of calumny for the revolutionaries of 1789 and 1793, and even in some instances of Bonaparte! The scientific world is also subjected to the influence of these interpretations, all coming straight, whether they know it or not, from the most reactionary conservative tradition. Here, however, this hostility is based clearly today on certain recent cooperative efforts—ordinarily fruitful—between the human and social sciences. It is that which in the eyes of those who are open about it endows these old opinions with a certain modernity. It should be said in passing that one has ample proof, as a result of this simple fact, that the principal cause of the relative decline in historical study of the Revolution stems not so much from the proliferation of the areas of concern of historians, which is the excuse with which some console themselves, but rather from the "scorn" in which the dominant ideology wishes to hold the Revolution not only because it was a popular revolution, but also because it has provided the most fertile field of study for progressive historians since the nineteenth century. . . .

But that very fact [referring to a contemporary historian who has played down the importance of the Revolution] reveals a state of mind which would appear to be more serious when it is manifested among historians whose profession, whose interests, or whose publishing commitments require them to study the French Revolution. Under the pretext of not neglecting new methods of history or the new influences of particular sciences, certain recent historians have contributed theoretically to the minimizing of the importance of the Revolution. They do this by retrospectively putting on trial the classical historians of the Revolution and in particular those in the progressive or Marxist tradition, such as Jaurès, Mathiez, Lefebvre, and their disciples. We should be allowed to judge such an interpretation of history in an objective way even if those who practice it refuse to accept either the nature of the judgment or the responsibility which it imposes on them against their will. In our eyes this *a priori* revisionism of Revolutionary historical study, whether one knows it or not, facilitates assimilation with those ideologies of our time which consider it to be pure and simple scandal, not just the persistence of positivist or idealistic theories in the interpretations of history, but, on the contrary, the penetration in force of historical materialism into the methodological field of the so-called human and social sciences. This is because it was first in France in its great Revolution, as described in the *Histoire socialiste* of Jaurès that Marxism was recognized as being more than just a guide to social and political action for the working class, and was recognized as an extraordinary instrument for achieving a more profound historical understanding in the employment of which even Jaurès confessed to a certain intoxication.

When it comes to the ideological struggle between the different forms of idealism and historical materialism, anything bearing on our knowledge of the French Revolution is for the protagonists, of either side, of decisive theoretical importance. There are three reasons for this. In the first place, it is because of the familiarity of Marx with the history of revolutionary France. It had, as everyone knows, a major influence in shaping the fundamental notion of the Marxist theory of history as a history of the class struggle, and accordingly any questioning of the bourgeois nature of the French Revolution has the effect of putting the basic tenets of Marx and the Marxists on trial. In the second place, because the struggles of the masses from 1789 to 1795, from the Estates General at Versailles to the Babeuf Conspiracy, have brought to subsequent revolutionary practice a style and modes of action—such as utilizing the district, the club, the petition, etc.—as well as a source of inspiration and a whole arsenal of slogans and watch words that, taken altogether, constitute a living cultural heritage which, as a result of the subsequent events of 1848, 1871 and 1936, continues to influence the political action of the French masses, not only on the Left *but also* on the Right. There is no question, however, but that the working class has been the recipient of the most vital element of this tradition. Thus the history of the French Revolution is still more or less an introduction to a knowledge of the political sagacity of the French people. This is why it remains a matter of national interest to maintain historical research on the revolutionary period at the highest level, and in all cases an essential political task for a Marxist historian.

Finally the sharpness of the ideological struggles in our daily life, even when played out through or under the guise of scientific or polemical debates between specialists, requires that those in the historical profession in France today who would oppose investing in a better knowledge of this particular episode in the national heritage, designated "in block" as the French Revolution, give significant evidence of their incompetence as historians to be guides for the nation.

These then are the reasons that convinced me to make of these essays, in all true sincerity, more than just a polemical discourse, to include among them an appreciation of some recent points of view, as well as presenting a defense and illustration of classic materialist theses relating to the French Revolution. The tone will be sharp, as it traditionally is in this area, because from the beginning, and especially since the polemics that characterized the debate between Aulard and Mathiez about the person of Robespierre and the question of "Robespierrism," it is recognized that historians of the Revolution have a pugnacious temperament. It is because what is at stake is so important. Who today can ignore the scientific contribution of Mathiez as well as that of Aulard? The polemical vigor of a historian is not a guarantee that he speaks truly, but it also happens that great vigor may be necessary to defend even modest truths. . . .

The Role of the Bourgeoisie in the Coming of the French Revolution—Traditional and Marxist Views

The revival of questioning about the proper interpretation to be given to the French Revolution also means a reopening of the debate on the character of the society of the Old Regime. . . .

Most of the historians of the nineteenth century and the first part of the twentieth century ignored Marx even though he was, nevertheless, an outstanding connoisseur of the history of the French Revolution. One would be astonished at the widespread ignorance of Marx's views in France before the political success of the workers' parties, the October Revolution, and systematic education of the masses in Marxist theory by the Communist party caused an increasing number of historians to take Marxism seriously, particularly in the Faculty of Letters. In spite of the great importance of *L'Histoire socialiste de la Révolution française* (1900–1904) [by Jean Jaurès], reedited by Mathiez (1922–1924) and again reprinted in 1939 for the one hundred and fifteenth anniversary of the Revolution, until recently the contribution of the Marxists to the history of the Revolution has been systematically underestimated. A similar situation prevailed with respect to the official or scholarly histories with their mass of documents on social and economic history collected by the researchers—who for the most part were not Marxists—of the *Commission d'histoire économique de la Révolution* which was established by the government in 1903 at the suggestion of Juarès. It was only with Albert Mathiez—and then not really directly—but finally with E. Labrousse, Georges Lefebvre and their French and foreign pupils, that a history of authentic Marxist orientation or inspiration was established in France. It has played the role of guide in the opening of new sectors of research and simultaneously has provided new means of extending our knowledge of the Revolution as a bourgeois, antifeudal and mass revolution—as understood by Marx. At the same time in the Soviet Union, a large school of Marxist historians has contributed greatly to our knowledge of the French Revolution as a decisive stage in the transitions from "feudalism to capitalism."

One can thus see that this acceptance of a Marxist approach is a matter of recent history, paralleling the establishment in our country of a predominantly Marxist and Leninist workers' movement and contemporary with socialist revolutions in the different nations of the world. *But there is also a recently developed historical approach, parallel to the preceding which is questioning the social, bourgeois and antifeudal character of the French Revolution.*

But even Tocqueville—generally considered by Georges Lefebvre to be the most perceptive of the historians of the nineteenth century —saw the French Revolution as a social revolution. Just as it was earlier for Buonarotti, Thiers, Guizot, and finally for Louis Blanc—not to mention Michelet who saw it as the culmination of the struggle of the bourgeoisie guiding the people! Tocqueville looked at the Revolution primarily as a peasant revolt directed against the seigneurial regime and secondly as a popular *democratic* movement, but guided by what was generally thought of as the "middle class." For Taine, the urban bourgeoisie and the peasant proprietors triumphed in the Revolution by taking over the lands and property of the former nobles and the former privileged clergy. While it is obviously not entirely factually accurate, the critical approach and the fruitfulness of this kind of analysis is what interests us here. Whether they were neo-Jacobins, or republicans, radicals, neo-Babeuvists or socialists, moderates or conservatives, nostalgic for the Old Regime or confessed reactionaries, the historians of the nineteenth century recognized the fact and never denied that in the end the Revolution placed the bourgeoisie in power as the dominant class with the positive support of a vast number of the peasant proprietors who had been liberated from "feudalism." Differences of opinion appeared with respect to the question of the *legitimacy* or the "how" of the Revolution, or more generally over specific revolutionary events (July 14, the death of the king, Ninth Thermidor, Eighteenth Brumaire, for or against the "Hebertists," on the significance of the popular movement, etc. . . .). But no one thought of invalidating the prophetic conclusion of Jean-Paul Marat, the Friend of the People, who feared that "the aristocracy of wealth" would merely succeed to "the aristocracy of birth," with the well-provided merely filling the former place of the well-born. It was in this following important line that Philippe Sagnac in his thesis on feudal rights and the civil legislation of the Revolution (1898), Alphonse Aulard, and, in 1921–

1924, Paul Caron and Philippe Sagnac engaged in research (later interrupted) on feudal rights and the abolition of "feudalism" as a social and economic factor rather than a juridical one.

We will conclude by citing J. Carcopino who notes in a passage relating to "officials" that "those of the old monarchy who *had their origin in that bourgeois class which was to overturn it,* have been for the most part enlightened and conscientious workers" [Mazauric's emphasis]. Thus when the historical viewpoint of earlier periods is questioned with respect to the nature of the French Revolution, even though obviously it carries within it all sorts of judgments of a moral kind, and is permeated with all kinds of irrational views, it nonetheless affirms strongly the objective fact of its being an anti-feudal revolution and one favorable to the bourgeoisie, but it does this empirically and seemingly spontaneously since this was not the main point they were trying to demonstrate.

Liberal historians, both democratic and moderately democratic, look upon the Revolution as the culmination of a long evolution leading to the emancipation of *Man;* for them the Revolution in proclaiming the Rights of Man realized a kind of achievement for all humanity. They accepted the fact that it was a bourgeois revolution, but for that very reason it seemed to them that the Revolution needed to assume the garb of a humanist justification in order that it not be theoretically and primarily known as the revolution of the bourgeoisie. At the same time, while it tried to demonstrate that the coming to power of the bourgeoisie had liberated the whole of society—which is an authentic historic truth—it presented this liberation as absolute and final, and so this line of historical writing nourished a fundamental ideological pretension. It tried to escape from the relative character of the historic need for the development of the bourgeoisie as a class, which was precisely the point to which the clear assertion of the French Revolution as a revolution of the bourgeoisie must lead. The interplay of contradictions between the requirements of true scientific knowledge and the presuppositions of bourgeois ideology has always existed, and has not yet ceased to obscure our knowledge of the history of the French Revolution.

For certain historians, whether advanced democrats or incipient socialists and even to some extent with Jaurès who owed so much to them, the French Revolution was most important as a revolutionary precedent—even if one criticized it—and one which provided the justification, *a priori,* of political, moral and even juridical legitimacy by establishing the "right of revolution" for the revolution to come. The Revolution in all its different phases, with its different clubs and leaders, became the archetype of the revolutionary process. In this way, through the essential link of the experience of 1848, was formed the revolutionary and democratic tradition of the French masses. But since Lenin and the October Revolution of 1917, and paradoxically even more clearly in certain circles since the experience of 1968, it can be seen that the mechanical theory of how to achieve a successful revolution, leaving aside the impossibilities encountered in practice, is not different in theory from the empirical and bourgeois conception which formerly was used to explain the *why* and the *how* of the French Revolution. . . .

The Marxist Approach to the Question of the Origins of the Revolution

For Marxists the French Revolution provided the means for the transformation of the society that was emerging from "feudal society" into a capitalist society. Accordingly this bourgeois revolution cannot be understood without reference to the overall theory of historical materialism. This theory is not only capable of being further perfected, as shown by the historical debates on modes of production and earlier feudal and Asiatic societies as well as the political discussions on the means of transition to socialism, but it is always perpetually under reconstruction. But historical materialism, which is simply another way of saying history as both a theoretical science and a practical science of politics, reveals the bourgeois revolution as the means by which the superstructure or the social, political and ideological institutions are transformed in the inevitable change from the feudal mode of production (feudalism) to the capitalist mode of production. Accordingly it is the bourgeois revolution which accomplishes the required changes in the social structure supporting production to make it adequate to the needs of growth of the productive forces. This revolution was the culmination of a long succession of peasant and popular uprisings which accompanied the infusion of capitalism into feudal society—which preindustrial capitalism had tried to destroy even before the Revolution itself—and of the long ascent, not always in a straight line, of the bourgeoisie as a revolutionary class.

It is, then, this interpretation which guides Marxist research on the problems of the society of the Old Regime and the French Revolution, and which is also the view elaborated by Marx and Engels after 1845 and set forth unequivocally and in such an exemplary way in 1847–1848 in the *Communist Manifesto,* which revisionism and anti-Marxism primarily try to combat. . . .

There are some good authors who pretend not to understand the Marxist approach and confuse the Marxist use of the word "bourgeois" with the juridical meaning it carried during the Old Regime in order to deny both the concept of the bourgeoisie and the idea of a bourgeois revolution! Often they also do not understand Marxism, or they understand it badly for lack of effort in studying its theories with attention. This is a vast problem, apparently outside the general line of the debate, but one which justifies a brief digression for a clarification of method.

Many historians seem to believe that historical materialism is to be entirely found in the splendid pages written by Marx in 1859 in the Preface to his *Contribution à la critique de l'économie politique [A Contribution to the Critique of Political Economy].* To aid them there is the codification which Stalin introduced into the body of Marxist writings with the pamphlet drawn from the *History of the Communist Party* entitled "Dialectical Materialism and Historical Materialism," which is a sort of simplified commentary. Very many also seek to compare it to the "General Introduction" of 1857 which Marx did not publish and which, if it is to be considered an important text, raises some problems other than those brought up in the Preface [mentioned above]. M. Rubel, for example, who presents himself as the "scientific" editor of the works of Marx in the *Pléiade* collection believes that he does not even have to raise any question about that Preface to the *Contribution* and ignores it. Also D. Richet, at the end of a very critical study of the ruling elite during the Old Regime, concluded that there was in 1789 no bourgeois revolution, in spite, he says, "of the model magnificently presented by Marx in his Preface . . ."—as if Marx had said there all that there is to say about the materialist theory of history. This explanation sounds more like an alibi than a justification, for there is no justification for describing this text, however celebrated, as a "model."

Marx wished to indicate "briefly" in his Preface "the general conclusion" to which his works and his leading role in the workers'
struggles of his time had led him. Thus he summarized in pedagogical manner—what an admirable presentation!—the theses on
which were based his particular researches in political economy, to
which in addition he had given the first important expression in his
Contribution. This is the reason why Marx suppressed the "General
Introduction" which he had previously written; it appeared to anticipate the same direction as the demonstration contained in the body
of the work. The Preface of 1859 is therefore a presentation of the
theoretical aspect of the subject, necessarily general, and purposely
concise so as not to divert the reader from the primary subject of
the book, political economy. So to use the term "model" to describe
this formulation designed for teaching purposes—while at the same
time questioning it and paying tribute to its formal beauty—is too
much like those embraces that stifle.

The Preface of 1859 can raise some difficulties of interpretation if
one is not careful to weigh the value of each formula. Marx intended
there only to sketch out in "broad outline" the dialectical progres-
sion of historical periods with the understanding that they might be
changed as a result of further analysis and the results of the additional research which he was carrying on at the same time. Most importantly he demonstrated that the "bourgeois" mode of production
ended the long preceding period qualified as the "prehistory of humanity." Marx maintained, in effect, that capitalism involved the
expansion on a worldwide scale of a dominant mode of production
based on the mobilization of a significant mass of resources, all progressively concentrated toward the goal of producing the surplus
value extorted from the workers by the capitalists. The generalization
and uniformization of the exploitation of growing masses of human
beings was what distinguished capitalism radically from all other historical eras, either earlier or to come, that have been based on
the appropriation by the ruling classes of the products of the surplus
labor of the exploited masses. In addition, by making productive
forces more and more social in character, capitalism created the
necessity for their socialization, and thus by giving birth to the modern proletariat it prepared its own historic destruction.

A half-century later, Lenin drew on a comparable affirmation of
the generalized expansion of imperialism over the entire world, to

propose the thesis of the possibility of a direct passage from a pre-capitalist society to a proletarian revolution. The existence in the twentieth century of a worldwide socialist system has made possible the realization of this Leninist proposition.

There is, then, properly speaking, only a single revolution prior to the socialist revolution, insofar as that moment sees the establishment of a society without class antagonisms, and that is the bourgeois revolution! That had already been said by Marx in the *Manifesto* he wrote with Engels in 1847 for the Communists of the League of the Just and the workers of Europe; he repeated it in the Preface —more philosophical in appearance—which he wrote in 1859 for the German socialists. . . .

Historical materialism, however, is not a "developmental model" —as if the marriage of these terms were possible—but an approach which brings to light the reciprocal interaction between the economic base, which in the last analysis is the determining element, and the social history of the masses. Basically it provides us with precise knowledge of the relations between modes of production, the situation and level of development of productive forces and an understanding of the structure of social relationships arising from these forces of production. The task of the historian of the bourgeois revolution is first of all, then, to reveal the necessity for an increase in productive forces and the obstacles standing in the way as a result of the state of the social organization of production—with both the obstacles and need for an increase arising precisely from the very same movement of social history. This knowledge of the hierarchical system by means of which a social structure functions allows one to define the specific duration of an historical period: even if one adapts the chronology of years, centuries, or multiples of centuries to express the technically defined reference. A good example is the fact that the historical period of feudalism fundamentally is defined by reference to the duration of its particular mode of production. . . .

If one compares the system coming out of the French Revolution with the contradictions of the feudal mode of production, based on the appropriation by the landholding aristocracy of the increasing surplus labor of the peasant masses, one can demonstrate how that appropriation, carried out by constraint, principally of the juridical kind, led to a result unfavorable to the progress of a bourgeois-type economy, even though at the same time it was able to satisfy to some degree the social and economic ambitions of the bourgeoisie. And one can relate in the same way the social, political and ideological structure of the absolutist Old Regime to the crisis in the mode of production. Nothing mysterious about it, even if not without difficulty, but the range of *possible and actual principles* which orient historical research as though on another level; these provide the basis for a practical science of politics.

Historical materialism does not lead then to the production of ready-made history by means of deduction; nor is it a "historical construct," but it simply provides a means for constructing the concepts necessary to a better scientific exploration of the field of history.

In an academic debate, a denial that the Revolution which began in 1789 was an inevitable revolution of the bourgeois class might seem to arise from a specifically historical judgment, and such an affirmation might truly represent the subjectively based opinion of the historian. In a debate concerning theory, which supposes explicit references to the complex of expressions of contemporary knowledge and political practice, to deny that the French Revolution was a bourgeois revolution is in fact one of the best evidences of bourgeois ideology's acceptance of the Marxian concept of historical necessity. Just by chance, denial of the necessity of a bourgeois revolution also seems to validate a refusal to admit the inevitability of socialism—just another example of the fact that historical discussions cannot be understood in all their ramifications if taken out of the context of the ideological and political determinisms of our time, which is particularly characterized by the struggle between socialism and imperialism.

However, when it comes to France and the French Revolution, such an effort encounters some difficulties. The weight of materialist historical writing—as for example the decisive support of Georges Lefebvre and the vigor of the tradition issuing from the nineteenth century, which saw the French Revolution as hostile to the "seigneurs" and therefore antifeudal, and favorable to "mobile wealth" and therefore bourgeois—provide examples of the solidity of the positions established by progressive historiography. Accordingly it has become difficult in France to deny the bourgeois character of the French Revolution except by playing with words, or by affirming its fortuitous character, making it in some way a matter of chance; in doing this, however, one reverts to the kind of spontaneous empiricism of historians of earlier times which it was thought had been repudiated as the price for adopting a viewpoint which appears to be "modern" and which sees Marx as the theoretician of the historicism, evolutionism and sociology of the nineteenth century, amiable to be sure, but now "outmoded," as he ought to be.

The simplest and most common attitude outside of France consists primarily in saying nothing about, or refusing to make any reference to, the class struggle, and thus to base the study of pre-Revolutionary French society on a neo-positivist theory of circumstance. And so the history of the French Revolution steers its way between the "political" and the "ideological" while it is in fact at the heart of the political and ideological determinants in our contemporary world. . . .

Today the debate on the meaning and the nature of the French Revolution becomes more and more a debate on the character and contradictions of the society of the Old Regime and of its economic base. With respect to university courses the history of the Revolution, although taking place at the very beginning of the appearance of a society corresponding to a capitalist mode of production in France, ought for these reasons accordingly to be considered "modern" history, which is to say as covering synchronistically the centuries which have seen the process of implantation—advances, retreats, changes—of capitalism and bourgeois society in the breast of feudal France of the Old Regime.

It is not, then, in the name of a teleological conception of history, as one sometimes accuses it of being by which one would be able to know the meaning of history by a reading of words from on high, but as a result of one's proper historical understanding of the objectives of his research as a historian of the French Revolution that ought to justify one's great interest in the study of the contradictions of the Old Regime as the last stage of feudalism in France. In some way he should organize his work by starting with the reflection of Georges Lefebvre that "there was antagonism between the general progress of capitalism and the maintenance of feudal obligations and payments arising from land ownership" (*La Révolution et les paysans,* 1933). In one's study therefore one should not separate the Revolution from those causes which have led to it.

A Critique of Furet and Richet's View of the Origins of the Revolution

The years 1965 and 1966 saw the publication of two volumes . . . on the history of the French Revolution written by two historians of recognized ability, Francois Furet and Denis Richet. The publication of both volumes was followed by a high-pressure publicity campaign in the press and on radio and television, and they were reviewed by prominent critics and discussed by the authors in numerous interviews. This kind of red-carpet treatment which was received, especially by the first volume, would seem to be rather unusual. One is really not accustomed to seeing a serious history of the Revolution enjoy such popular success. The main reason for this success was the explicit intention of the authors to depart from classical interpretations of the Revolution and to propose a new reading of the history of revolutionary events. In fact, F. Furet and D. Richet, as can be seen from both their style and their intentions, did not hesitate to resort to critical polemics in discussing their predecessors. They wished to be thought of as part of a generation of very brilliant historians of vast culture (doubtless of more than one school) who try to go off the beaten paths and hold themselves to be above traditional conflicts of opinion. They oppose what they judge to be the ideological biases against which, according to them, the historians of the Revolution have vainly struggled for many decades. "The Bastille in its symbolism has confined too narrowly the history of the Old Regime. History must first of all be concerned with the everyday realities of gaining a livelihood."

With this affirmation as their starting point they propose to establish a new interpretation of the meaning of the Revolution by evaluating the precise importance of those unexpected incidents it experienced between 1789 and 18 Brumaire (1799). As a result their approach is chronological, except for a few instances in the second volume, and the narrative for the most part consists of a recital of events. . . .

The *Ancien Régime* as described by F. Furet was overturned as a result of a variety of internal contradictions and out of the clash of these was to be born the new society. He first discusses those arising from an agricultural economy and its social counterpart in rural areas, and presents them in terms quite similar to traditional Marxist analysis, but with the addition of the qualification "traditional" as in the statement "the clergy and the nobility lived not only from the cultivation of their own agricultural land but also from the annual collection of a traditional percentage of all agricultural production" (the Marxists have generally held that the percentage was being increased in the second half of the eighteenth century). This kind of exploitation of the surplus value produced by the peasant, our authors, following the precedent of Jaurès and E. Labrousse, see as happening in a prosperous and expanding French economy. "The events of 1789 were not the culmination of a century of poverty but on the contrary came at the end of a prosperous century in a rich country." It is not made clear, however, that this increase, arising as a result of the interaction between prices and income, greatly accentuated social extremes. In fact their study of the movement of rents compared to the income of the people or wages does not see them as related in a structural sense as two aspects of the same economic reality. But still this can be readily corrected by the forewarned reader, or at least one could suppose so. The analysis of the Old Regime is extended by a lengthy reflection on the role of ideas and on the influence of the Enlightenment. Following the same approach as the course at the Sorbonne of A. Dupront, the Enlightenment is seen as having resulted in a devaluation of the values of the Old Regime. According to this point of view the Revolution took place first in people's minds. All that remained was to realize its effects in the material and public realm. Can one speak of the dominant philosophy of the century appropriately as a bourgeois ideology? That question is not posed directly, but the explicit response to that implicit question is certainly negative. The men of 1789 did not choose between "masters," they were won over to a general spirit of reform whether it was aristocratic liberalism or bourgeois ideology. Nevertheless, when it came to using ideas as practical weapons of revolution it is clearly indicated that beyond a tactical alliance against absolutism, aristocratic and bourgeoisie society remained fundamentally opposed. It can thus be understood how a temporary alliance between ruling social groups could have come about in the prerevolutionary period and what was the role of aristocratic liberalism; namely, to be the sorcerer's apprentice of the bourgeois revolution. This affirmation that 1789 was a bourgeois revolution incontestably places F. Furet and D. Richet in the mainstream of historical interpretation on this side of the Channel and the Atlantic. What follows, however, leads one to question whether this appearance is really to be taken seriously. What we see, in fact, is that in treating the movement known as the Enlightenment—and particularly the role played by aristocratic influences in the philosophy of the eighteenth century—we are quite far from any analysis such as that of L. Althusser of Montesquieu and very close to the traditional classical and idealist line of Ernest Cassirer. In particular there seems to be no clear perception of the sociology of ideas about which a number of recent works have been published by historians of literature or philosophy.

What was the extent of the push for reform, of this desire for change in 1789? "The plaintiffs were quite ready to grant a reprieve. They were seeking reforms, not revolution. Reforms! There was the heart of the matter, for it was just at this time that the reforming tradition of royal absolutism was dying out." And further on the authors say, "Was the revolution inevitable? Theoretically it still depended on the capability of the king of France to act as an arbiter and reformer." But alas, "the king was losing his effectiveness as a balance wheel." We accept this interpretation, but wouldn't contemporary historians be in a position to demonstrate more clearly than Aulard, whose principal idea this was, the true possibility for arbitration with a political power as narrow in its interests and as harassed as the one with which we are concerned here? For the decisive question here as Georges Lefebvre correctly discerned was not so much the immediate one of the intentions of the monarchy, but rather the nature of the monarcho-aristocratic state at the end of the eighteenth century.

As a result, if one asks, as Furet and Richet do at the end of the first part of their study, what were the origins of the French Revolution, it appears that two series of facts made it possible. First there was a desire for change, which is to say to put into effect a revolution that was already accomplished in people's minds (for according to the authors "Enlightenment" had already won the day by 1789), and secondly there was the inability of the monarchy to reform itself. In spite of their use of psychological analysis of the mental hang-ups of rulers—"a clumsy, self-conscious and inhibited king" and a queen who experiences a "transfer" of her frustrated femininity to the political realm—and their analysis of the material bases of social conflict—they remain essentially faithful to traditional history. In fact, except in a kind of cursory way the nature, not of the government of Louis XVI but of the monarchical state at the end of the reign, is not treated directly. As a result it is difficult to understand why the policy of the court had to favor one particular side. In addition one reads that "the royal weakness was not only psychological, it was the result also in the last years of the Old Regime of the firm hold on power by a united aristocratic order." But such a view undoubtedly requires an in-depth analysis of the nature of the state as well as of the concept of an order, and a more precise definition of what they mean by "aristocratic." The aristocracy did not constitute an order in a legal sense but a social force, of which the nobility and the clergy of noble origin constituted the essential elements. Approaching the matter from this viewpoint one can only regret that the reforms of St. Germain and Segur, as well as the mode of recruitment of the upper clergy, all of which *eloquently* attest to the reality of this aristocratic force, are treated in other places in the book.

As for the "alliance" between the well-to-do bourgeoisie of the eighteenth century and the people of the countryside and the towns, the authors describe it as "unexpected." To explain it only by the rise in rents and the chance conjuncture of rising prices and falling wages without referring it in any fundamental way to the basic structure of the Old Regime is truly, in this instance, to twist the work of Ernest Labrousse in an acrobatic way, and especially to ignore the reservations which he himself formulated with respect to his primary concept of "how revolutions happen." It is indeed the ready acceptance of the idea of the fortuitous character of this joining together of the bourgeoisie and the masses that provides the basis for the most fruitful new hypothesis of the authors, the notion of the "three revolutions of 1789." This concept is essential to an understanding of the certainly more spectacular hypothesis that follows, that of the Revolution being "blown off course" between 1792 and the Ninth Thermidor (1794).

How did the unfolding of these three revolutions come about in 1789? The "aristocratic revolt" accomplished by means of "one of the most typical institutions of the Old Regime," the Parlements, gave initial impetus to "setting public opinion in motion," by which is meant the ideas of the Enlightenment which had already permeated everywhere. The bourgeoisie, in the name of this new set of values which the privileged classes and the members of the Parlement had generally accepted before, ultimately revolting against their egalitarian thrust and "seeking refuge in the past," took advantage of this aristocratic revolt to lay down its own terms. The king gave in—not trying "to take advantage of the divisions implicit in the movement." But in such a version what is the role in this conflict of the massive popular pressure, the agitation for food and higher wages and the generally vast popular aspirations of 1789 about which Georges Lefebvre wrote in such ringing terms? It is not made clear that this great collective mobilization provided the basis for, or even was the cause of, the conversion of the aristocratic revolt into a national revolution under bourgeois direction.

In any case, in this movement of opinion thus set underway Richet and Furet discern three revolutions. One is that accomplished by the Constituent Assembly which represents the victory of eighteenth-century ideology as mediated through the *cahiers*. Another is that of the Parisians who "do not become involved in order to safeguard the National Assembly and its conquests—that was only an indirect result of their wish to save themselves." The third finally is the one which takes place in the countryside, "the peasants are aroused ... they knock loudly at the door of the bourgeois revolution which is opened to them very hesitantly." As for the October days, they appear to be only a kind of reverberation set off by the food shortage which afflicted the housewives, "but still undoubtedly in the mind of the people they unconsciously hoped to evoke the king's pity by showing him the situation of those most vulnerable to poverty and to humiliate the queen by calling attention to her situation as compared with that of others of her sex."

The idea of three revolutions has one obvious great advantage in that it points up the absence of any common and previously agreed-upon revolutionary program between the masses and the bourgeoisie who were seeking political power, and thus contradicts the idea of a specific agreement between the forces which contributed to the upheaval of that summer. But who today would argue for such an idea without qualifications? But can one, however, deny that there was a common basis for all that ultimately successful agitation? Because the popular revolt arose from the crisis brought on by the high price of bread and was supported by traditional antiseigneurial or antitaxation sentiment, are these reasons for disassociating it, understood in these terms, from the revolution of the bourgeois elite? The authors certainly argue that "the traditional working-class riots did not put them at odds with the revolutionary bourgeoisie . . . all factors conspired to lead the urban working classes into the political camp of the bourgeoisie." Nevertheless the striking concept of "three revolutions" suggests the idea that the concatenation of the diverse social forces which destroyed the Old Regime was primarily a matter of mere chance. This obviously is a proper matter for debate since it places in question the viewpoints of Albert Mathiez, Georges Lefebvre and in spite of appearances to the contrary, of E. Labrousse as well. . . . It should be noted besides that it is regrettable that they do not mention in this connection the famous three-way interaction described by Georges Lefebvre between the *pacte de famine,* the aristocratic plot, real or imagined, and the defensive reaction of the masses which in turn provoked their wish to punish their oppressors in the summer of 1789. It is regrettable, because this genuine discovery of Georges Lefebvre enables one to understand the objectively necessary character of the participation in the struggle by the masses—a necessity subjectively understood subsequently by the leaders of the people who thought of it as a vital obligation requiring their constant political mobilization.

It is reasonable to try to look at things from the viewpoint of the authors, even if one considers it to be false from the point of view of a more traditional concept of the "profession of historian." The idea of the Revolution being "blown off course" arises in response to a legitimate concern: a refusal to accept a kind of "natural history" of the Revolution—a renunciation of the approach of those historians described as traditional of "perpetually justifying what has happened." F. Furet and D. Richet refuse accordingly to read things back into the past. It is certainly obvious that a certain kind of historical determinism leads to the presentation of history as the endless movement of a machine toward previously determined goals. Isn't this what is encouraged by a certain rhetoric about a "three-part scheme," the first part of which is necessarily devoted to the study of "conditions"? The concept of "being blown off course" is used therefore in response to an effort to place oneself at the heart of the revolutionary process in order to try to discern all its possible lines of development. I share, for my part, this concern for innovation, but I hold that such an attempt can be fruitful only on condition that the concepts are meticulously constructed and that an effort is made to disengage the content from the form for which it provides the basis of existence; in this way one can conceive of the forms of development of the process as being innumerable. For example, one might suppose that there might have been no Robespierre or no Lafayette, or the Seine might not have been frozen in the Year III, etc., but that which is subsumed in the general process of which the concept makes possible the discovery ought to be previously defined both in terms of how far it goes and what it includes. Under any other terms, what mirages might we not become victims of? To what neo-positivist usage will the brute facts that the inquiry reveals not be submitted? But what, here, is the basic concept underlying the whole demonstration? It is that the liberal revolution was made necessary by the eighteenth-century Enlightenment. On this point it suits the authors to be rigorous and even from their viewpoint to set forth precisely under what conditions this "necessary" revolution was possible. But this approach naturally requires the elaboration of other concepts; principally some which make the Old Regime in France understandable. For even though the Old Regime is described in detail by the authors and frequently with remarkable talent, it is hard in the end to see why there had to be a revolution, or how it could have been undertaken, or to what degree it was possible. But modern methods of scientific analysis allow these questions to be posed with a certain security. One is required, for example, to reject the chronological event, "diachrony," if one wishes to use the vocabulary of Saussaurien structural analysis—for a structure in which the whole is in movement, or a "synchrony"—previously defined in its components and having been given a conceptual form. At the same time, however, it should be kept in mind that synchrony itself is not a static concept since the synchronistic structure of a society can be considered as being in itself diachronus. From this point of view the Revolution is nothing more than the manifestation of the structural crisis of the Old Regime in its totality and in its excesses. Without such a concept one can attribute only to pure chance the fact that there were so many crises in 1789—that conjunction of "three revolutions" and those other unpredictable chance events which are ultimately responsible for the Revolution being "blown off course." Since chance accounts for nothing, being in the last analysis only a rhetorical figure, the action of social groups, not in their exterior form, but in their deeper aspects, appeals to some minds. In the last analysis the source of all men's actions has its origins in the "myth" which holds them. But even this recourse to myth as the more or less creative force, the new *deus ex machina* of historical explanation, scarcely gets us away from the old psychology of crowds, the old sociology of Durkheim, or perhaps the characterology of Lesenne when individuals are involved. But because history goes on endlessly and myth gives us no basis for understanding itself—all modern ethnology demonstrates it—it is necessary to search in the irrational depths of the soul and even in a typology of souls and character, for the cause of the creative action of men. But why then affirm in accordance with tradition that the French Revolution is a bourgeois revolution? Such an affirmation under these conditions becomes absolutely gratuitous. It would be better in this case for the authors to renounce it and remain consistent in both premises and conclusions to the exact implications of what they have written.

In reality, it seems as though while under the apparently legitimate pretext of refusing to accept the idea of historical necessity and accepting its implications, the authors actually come to look once again toward psychology and prior random but determining events as providing the reasons for the present and the future. The effect is to rediscover in new form the old historical positivism condemned to the scaffold by very many scholars today and denied by the authors themselves. It amounts to reconstructing a history made up of separate events developing autonomously.

Thus the notion of "being blown off course" is intelligible only on the condition of admitting that the popular Revolutions of 1789 (the "second" and the "third") were only useless incidents in the achievement of bourgeois aims. That in turn is admissible only on the condition of supposing that the scheme of that bourgeois revolution was clear and coherent and that the bourgeoisie was absolute mistress of its destiny. On this last point, a very disputable comparison is proposed to us: "Lenin and the Bolsheviks have admirably foreseen the form, the alliances and the rhythms of the great Russian Revolution, but their vision of the society of the future is full of Utopian ideas: Stalin accepted responsibility for a return to reality.

On the other hand the French bourgeoisie of 1789 knew very much better than the Marxists of 1917 where it wished to go, where it was going. Basically it understood better the history it was making. But it refused to speculate about the accidental. It had no idea of the bloody and difficult places through which its path would pass." We leave to others the responsibility for determining the respective roles of Utopia and reality in the practice of the Bolsheviks, but in that part which concerns revolutionary practice in the period 1789–1795, it appears that on the contrary the bourgeoisie was brought to revolution not only by accident but even more fundamentally by the fact of the "repeated failure to achieve reforms" or to have a part in any great "reform of the state" throughout the whole century. The permanent objective of these enlightened bourgeois become revolutionaries, from Mounier and Bailly to the Feuillants and the Girondists, was to find propitious grounds for a political and social compromise with the aristocracy. This was the situation even before August 1789, but more precisely during the debate on the decision as to which feudal and seigneurial rights were to be declared redeemable and those to be considered as property. It was the case again in the course of the debate on the constitution of 1790–1791, and finally at the time of the trial of the king, as A. Soboul reminds us in a recent book. It follows that potentially the counter-revolution, although timid at first and most extreme later on, was situated at the very heart of the Revolution, in compromise itself. That is shown in a little-noted study of the refusal of the right-wing in the Constituent Assembly to declare the king guilty after Varennes, by the maintenance of the suspensive veto, and by the refusal during the ministry of Roland, after the tenth of August, to pursue the royalist journalists in the provinces. It follows that the episode of Châtillon-sur-Sèvre, the camp of Jalès and their results are no longer insignificant little stories if one places them in this framework.

Besides, this permanent search for a compromise with the institutions and the norms of the Old Regime was not in itself a novelty. Wasn't that what Turgot was seeking as early as 1775? Wasn't that similarly the theme of the "legal despotism" of the Physiocrats or the "enlightened despotism" of the Encyclopedists? In fact a compromise of this sort would have satisfied the essential aspirations of the "middle class." It is known from other sources that too many bonds united large segments of the bourgeoisie to the seigneurial and aristocratic world, to the royal administration, to its colonial policy, including colonial and slave trade and to the policy of owning *rentes,* for such a compromise not to have been a high-priority objective. The whole drama arose precisely from the fact that this basic compromise became possible only with the help of a popular revolt, which was itself fundamentally determined by conditions under the Old Regime. It is no exaggeration to suggest that the bourgeoisie only became really aware of its revolutionary vocation when it first accepted, and then sought, the popular support which it had ignored in 1775 and refused as long as possible in 1789. It was Jaurès who said that it was the people who stepped in to save the bourgeois revolution of the Enlightenment. It was this fact which led the middle class to undertake, sometimes even against its immediate interest, the systematic destruction of all those who might favor any possible counter-movement by conservative forces.

Looking at things from this perspective, one will find not three revolutions in 1789, but only a single one, liberal and bourgeois in character but with the support of the people and especially the peasantry. One will not see any "blowing off course" of the Revolution in 1792, but an essential effort on the part of the bourgeoisie to maintain the cohesion of the Third Estate, which is to say, of the nation, in order not to isolate themselves from the masses without whose support the gains of 1789 would have been compromised. Seen thus the Year II was not a "time of distress" but primarily a moment of intense radicalization of the bourgeois revolution. It follows as a simple corollary that from this viewpoint Robespierre will no longer appear as the parliamentary manipulator suggested to us, but as the man of " '89" who accepts the popular revolution because of his faithfulness to the equalitarian and humanistic message of the Enlightenment. It is a simple problem of definition, if there were no such thing as being "blown off course," one can still think of a rising phase of the Revolution, the end of which was signalled by the Ninth Thermidor and confirmed by the events of Prairial of the Year III when the *sans-culottes* were disarmed by the troops, and a stabilization phase which includes the period of the Directory and which is confirmed during the Consulate by the regime described by Albert Soboul as the "reconciled nation of property owners."

This reconciliation between "Frenchmen"—which means between the ruling classes—that was celebrated again by M. Georges Pompidou at Ajaccio on August 15, 1969 on the occasion of the two hundredth anniversary of the birth of Napoleon Bonaparte in order by analogy to validate the attractions of a Gaullist-centralistic government, this reconciliation was possible only once the resistance of the nobility had been broken and the counter-revolutionary assault repulsed.

A last question leads us finally to the fundamental problem of the origins of the Revolution. Why did the monarchy and aristocracy not accept unreservedly the compromises of the first years? According to Aulard, F. Furet and D. Richet a final answer can only be given by resorting to such factors as the psychology of the king and the stupidity of a large part of the nobility.

In reality it appears that the monarchical state, in conformity with its aristocratic character, could not abandon the maintenance of a juridically constituted society of orders and privileges; in other words an inequality of rights, in spite of a seeming acceptance of a completely aristocratic kind of liberty. But the political conflicts with respect to institutions only reflected social conflicts, and the assault against absolutism was leading in reality to the establishment in fact and in law of a new social hierarchy. It follows that the compromise of the years 1789–1791, bad by definition from the aristocratic viewpoint but immediately favorable to the interests of the bourgeoisie, led in the end to the liquidation of the nobility as a legally dominant social force. Above the diversity of the successive waves of resistance to the revolutionary movement, the refusal to accept the process of complete dismantlement of the Old Regime provided the common ground on which all the forces successively won over to the counter-revolutionary movement have taken their stand. Also, in the beginning the counter-revolution was not effective in fighting the Revolution from the outside, and it kept alive some chance of being effective only by situating itself within the new political structure and trying to prevent the formation of a state of the kind demanded by the bourgeoisie. It was the flight of the king which blew the cover on this strategy.

And thus were revealed the political-ideological means by which aristocratic resistance checked or modified the direction of the process by which "feudal" social relations necessarily disappeared and were replaced by "bourgeois" social relations....

The wish to provide historians with a new approach by making a conscious attempt to avoid the real or supposed prejudices of their predecessors—such, on the basis of a careful reading, appears to have been the ambition of F. Furet and D. Richet. The idea of proposing a new and fruitful account of the history of the Revolution was legitimate, and the recognized talent of the authors put them in a better position than most to accomplish it. If they have failed in their attempt they owe it only to their own prejudices and feelings.

Their allusions, both explicit and more frequently implicit, to the Bolsheviks and to the contemporary history of the USSR, as well as to Communist parties and the contributions of Marxist and socialist historiography, are sufficiently numerous so that no one can be accused of unjustifiably attributing guilt to them in suggesting that their hostile prejudice has put them in the position where they falsely accuse others of standing. But the case which they have brought before the bar for judgment they have lost primarily and for the most part on the grounds of insufficient knowledge. Their prejudices simply conform to the anti-Marxist and anti-Communist line which was current in France when the two volumes on the French Revolution appeared.

To put it simply, this consists in the first place of an anti-Marxist prejudice which looks upon historical materialism as a nineteenth-century ideology that has been outmoded by twentieth-century science, and upon the class struggle, and even the existence of classes arising from certain modes of production, as a kind of simplistic historicism arising out of the evolution-oriented thought of the last century. It is well known that such a view was very much in vogue in France between 1962 and 1968 as a result of the defeat of the popular forces in 1958, and was especially strong during the period of the rising intensity of the class struggle as a result of the activity of the French working class between 1965 and 1968. It is this same idea of breaking with the past which inspires the revisionist position of F. Furet and D. Richet. Actually a double revisionism; first on the theoretical level of refusing to accept the historical dialectic of Marx..., and secondly on the level of the specific history of the French Revolution by scorning more or less all the fruitful hypotheses and findings of Jaurès, Mathiez, Lefebvre and A. Soboul on the aristocratic revolt of 1789, and on the nature of the popular movement between 1792 and Ninth Thermidor (1794). This double-barreled attack on historical materialism will not astonish anyone. From the beginning, which is to say, literally, since Marx, bourgeois ideology has attempted to keep the Marxists, in the name of historical truth, from raising questions about the bourgeois revolution as the social phase of the transition from feudalism to capitalism, and accordingly the creator of the conditions for the emancipation of the proletariat. Thus in certain respects, it is a matter of a traditional position being taken up again.

In the second place there is an anti-Communist prejudice (moreover subtle) which manifests itself in putting socialism on trial as a sort of "Utopia" engrafted on the pragmatism of Lenin and his companions and which is revealed in the new policies turned to in the Soviet Union after the death of Lenin. From this actually arises the allusions "to Stalin who was responsible for the return to reality." A "reality" which one sees patently transferred with a double meaning to refer to the popular phase of the French Revolution. With a double meaning because this history speaks a double language—a concrete and explicit one which will be understood by those who are only interested in reading "a good history book," and another, allusive and implicit which will be understood by all those who have had, have yet, or will have need to exorcise any anti-Communist demon which they may have in them. But the use of this kind of crude double entendre in writing history ought surely to be ridiculed.

This is the kind of antipopular prejudice which ends up in producing a fantasy about a coherent and orderly revolution being suddenly blackened by the appearance on the scene of the masses —those country bumpkins and workmen of the slums whose appearance was not expected. For if this picture were a true picture, it would seem to demonstrate the principle that elites can without violence or adverse effects lead a good and true revolution, an "honorable revolution," but only on the condition of not being divided within—by hereditary privilege, for example—of being able to recognize beyond immediate circumstances their more fundamental common ties of wealth and culture, and, to put it in a single word, their enlightenment.

But can they be serious about attempting to revolutionize the scientific study and knowledge of the French Revolution with this pious view, this fantasy of a frightened intellectual?

Finally, out of this prejudice as just described—I say what I think —there seems to arise a sort of morbid feeling of guilt that a past such as this belongs to the French people. And this in turn gives rise to a kind of antinational prejudice which in turn leads to a real attempt to place the patriotic period, by which we mean the Jacobin period, of the French Revolution on trial. As a result the description which is proposed to us of the patriotism of Frenchmen of 1793 and the Year II bears the stamp of a real misreading of history. The patriotism of that period is in effect adorned with the same tinsel of nationalism and colonialism as the French bourgeois has used to try to decorate, in order to legitimize—not without success one must admit—the military and colonial ventures of the nineteenth and twentieth centuries. To allow that to be believed would be almost as bad an error as to pretend that the flag of Valmy and Fleurus was soiled in advance by the crime of Versailles in 1871. But doing this is also in its way "leftist"—from the point of view of anti-Communism.

This being the case and because a Marxist historian cannot ignore the ideological and political implications of a historical discourse, in spite of the constant affirmations in so many discourses that they are above ideology and politics, and precisely because in this instance as a French Marxist he has everything to gain by the circumstances of the rise of the bourgeoisie being well known, there is no legitimate reason why he should not admit the validity of a revisionist position when it is obvious, even if it displeases him. It is all the more true when, as in this case, the political roots of a scientific misunderstanding take refuge behind the claim of presenting an absolutely new interpretation, of destroying tabus and putting an end to dogma when actually only the newest materialist analyses are in fact attacked. If the critical argument were presented first in accordance with the *scientific method* and not as a deduction from the principles of a theory it would be a shame to refuse even to the slightest degree to apply the Leninist critique— the very one which Lenin gives an example of in his *Materialism and Empiriocriticism* in a very much more difficult area. This is why, in our eyes, it is the same for this new interpretation of the French

Revolution as it is for any intrusion of idealism into the domain of what are called the "human" sciences. One must refute it and re-affirm that no amount of talent or money can deprive Marxism of its distinction of having given its full dimension to our understanding of history.

II A FRENCH CRITIC OF THE ORTHODOX VIEWPOINT

François Furet

THE CATECHISM OF THE FRENCH REVOLUTION

François Furet (b. 1927) is director of historical research for the prestigious Sixth Section (Sciences économique et sociale) of the Ecole Pratique des Hautes Etudes *in Paris. Almost his entire scholarly career has been devoted to the investigation of the social and intellectual history of eighteenth-century France. His initial work was a complex detailed study of a particular district of Paris in the eighteenth century. More recently he has been examining books and the book trade in the same period in an effort to discover more about the movement of ideas. In his position he has been able to support the research and publication of many excellent detailed social analyses of the various regions of France, both before and after the Revolution. Because of his intimate knowledge of the most recent research he was ideally equipped to write, in collaboration with his colleague D. Richet, a general history of the French Revolution, which was published in 1966. When this work was violently attacked as much on ideological as scholarly grounds by M. Mazauric, M. Furet felt compelled to respond. The article below is M. Furet's reply, and it constitutes a major assault on the orthodox Marxist interpretation of the origins of the Revolution by a leading French scholar with impeccable credentials as a social and economic historian.*

> The tragedy of the French, not to mention that of the workers, lies in their memories of the great days of the past. It is necessary that events put an end once and for all to this reactionary worship of the past.—(Trans.) Marx, "Letter to César de Paepe," September 14, 1870.

Have we then returned to the battles of the good old days? Does the specter of the counter-revolution threaten the work of our noble ancestors? Despite the rather gloomy calm of our public life, one might get that impression from reading a small book recently published by Claude Mazauric, with a preface by Albert Soboul. The author solemnly denounces a history of the Revolution intended for the general public which Denis Richet and I published five years ago. Our book is suspected of contradicting the Marxist interpretations of the Revolution of Soboul and his disciples, and thus by im-

From François Furet, "Le catéchisme révolutionnaire," *Annales, E.S.C. XXVI* (March–April 1971), pp. 255–284, 288–289. Reproduced with permission of the author and the editors of the *Annales.* Translation by Vincent Ventrone, University of Pittsburgh. Footnotes omitted.

plication the works of their great predecessors, from Jaurès to Georges Lefebvre, which they monopolize to their own profit with the piety of true believers. As a result—for the reasoning has its Manichean logic—Richet and I stand accused of playing the game of "bourgeois ideology," whose adherents supposedly promoted our book through a "powerful publicity campaign in the press, on the radio, and on television." Summoning his courage, Mazauric twists the rules of rigorous scholarship to his own advantage by a number of pioneering innovations. He makes what amounts to an appeal to the patriotism of his readers in order to better stigmatize what he calls the "antinational prejudice" of his adversaries, who are suspected of being lukewarm in their support of Jacobin expansionism. "I say what I think," he states with respect to this proposition, in a self-revelatory change of position provoked by this attack of rabid nationalism. Finally, at the end of a long exposition, this intrepid investigator reveals the secret of his shrewdness: "The method of the historian is, in its theoretical aspect, identical to that of the Leninist Workers Party." Thus is arrayed against a book suspect of heresy the bases for a double indictment: the prosecuting attorney drapes himself simultaneously with the mantles of our national honor and of Leninist theory. One might expect the verdict to be severe. But the accused had surely brought it on themselves.

The reader should understand that this debate, in its politicotheatrical aspect, is in reality a farce—a war of shadows. On the political level, nothing nor anyone in present-day France threatens the work of the French Revolution. Since the defeat of fascism, the Right has ceased to maintain a position against the Revolution of 1789–1794 and the Republic. In university circles Marxist historiography (which I prefer to call Jacobin) of the Revolution is today more than ever the dominant position: it has its ancestors, traditions, canon, scripture, and one can hardly say that it cultivates a taste for impertinence or nonconformity. In brief, the French Revolution is firmly entrenched in our society and its institutions, and above all in the universities. Thus all the historical debate about its principles has no connection with any real political issues.

If, in spite of this, the historian continues to believe that there is a genuine threat, it is because he needs to believe so. Imaginary participation in the struggles of the world comforts the man in the

Ivory Tower, all the more because it is an illusion: it provides a maximum of psychological satisfaction with a minimum of real disruption. But if in turn this illusion is perceived as a reality it is because through the history of the French Revolution the historian shares in or exalts a set of values still very much alive. For though the latter constitute the very foundations of our political life, they have lost none of their power of exaltation; even though no longer at issue in real struggles they have not yet faded from people's memories. This is so not only because this national memory, the object of so much pedagogical concern, lags behind the events of social life, but because it is of almost infinite elasticity. Every revolution since the French Revolution—and especially the French Revolution—has a distinct tendency to be regarded as an absolute beginning, as a zero-point in history pregnant with all its future achievements implicitly contained within the universality of its principles. Such is the explanation for the special difficulty which societies claiming a revolutionary "foundation" have in writing their contemporary history—especially if their revolution is of rather recent vintage. All history of this kind then becomes a simple commemoration of origins, much like the mystique of national holidays, and thus precludes any critical discussion of the heritage itself.

In this sense it is perhaps inevitable that all history of the French Revolution will be, to a certain extent, a commemoration. For the Royalist it is a commemoration at which one weeps for the misfortunes of the king and the nation's subsequent loss of legitimacy. For the "bourgeois" it is an occasion to celebrate the establishment of a new national contract, while the revolutionary is inspired by the dynamism of the founding episode and its promises for the future. From this point of view all historical writing on the Revolution may legitimately be related to the evolution of the conjunctions of political and social events in the nineteenth and twentieth centuries: thus is obtained a strange product, a sort of residual history in which each stage of the French Revolution is defined by that part of the present which seems to bear some relation to it. This exercise is undoubtedly useful, and even salutary, to the degree that it is done with a conscious recognition of the ambiguous conditions in which history and actuality are rooted and intermingled. But unless we are willing to accept a history completely relativistic and strictly subordinated to social demands, one which produces only an illusory anchorage in the uncontrollable drift of contemporary affairs, the historian cannot limit himself simply to setting forth those aspects of the total history of the Revolution deemed significant for the present. Instead, it must be carried on with a refined expertise, with as precise an understanding as possible of the intellectual and psychological constraints of *our* present.

The Revolution: Past or Future?

To begin with, it is clear that these constraints are far from being equally fruitful, or equally sterile. A counter-revolutionary bias, for example, even if it forms the background for some histories of the Revolution of considerable interest (such as that of Taine), seems to me to preclude an understanding of the phenomenon itself. Such a bias always has the tendency to minimize the Revolution, or even to deny it, and leads almost inevitably to certain moral explanations —Providence, conspiracy, etc.—which are scarcely suited to provide an understanding of periods and events characterized by exceptional popular activity. In order to understand the Revolution it is still necessary to accept it, at least to some extent, though it all depends upon the way in which this is done. The outstanding historians of the first half of the nineteenth century were still hypnotized by the event in 1789 which had dominated their lives, though none of them, neither Guizot nor Michelet, nor even Toqueville, permitted himself for that reason to regard it as familiar, "normal," or easy to comprehend. On the contrary, it was their astonishment when confronted with the strangeness of the phenomenon which is responsible for the existential determination which characterizes their work. All of them divided the immense episode into various periods and aspects, which they then reconstituted in a long developmental chain in order to grasp the significance of each. All truly historical analyses of the Revolution begin, at least implicitly, by criticizing the consciousness of the revolutionaries themselves: their profound belief that they were making a complete break with the past, that they were standing on the threshold of a new and radically different era; for them, the New Era would be separated from the Old Regime by a yawning gulf. In this respect it was Toqueville who went intellectually furthest in overturning the conception which the revolutionaries had of themselves and their actions by demonstrating that, far from having been the agents of a radical break, they had in fact merely finished the establishment of the centralized bureaucratic state which was begun by the kings of France. As for Guizot, his political conservatism liberated him from the mythology of the founding event: to him the French Revolution was an ending rather than a beginning. Of the three, Michelet was the one most profoundly affected by revolutionary ideology, yet he deals with the Revolution only after having traveled through the entire history of France. His passion for studying the past for its own sake combined with the extraordinary diversity of his analysis of revolutionary history delivers him from the teleological pitfall: in order for the Revolution to be both the harbinger of the future and its foundation, it must be—as was said during the Third Republic—viewed as a "bloc," as an indivisible unit.

The struggles at the beginning of the Third Republic (1871) not only reinforced the spontaneous ideology of the "Mother Revolution," but also, and even more importantly, the development of the socialist movement. For the latter is the principal bearer of a second revolution dialectically destined to deny the order of things established by the first, to finally realize its promises. Thus was born that bizarre configuration, that naive ideology, that linear design according to which the "Mother Revolution" is again, in the twentieth century, held to have the same fundamental and innovative significance that it had for its own participants. Yet the resurrection is also a transformation, for it has been achieved through a narrowly selective process: the French Revolution no longer represents that radical overturning of values, that reshuffling of the social structure and ruling elite which produced the contemporary French state and society. This revolution, which is now called "bourgeois," stopped on the Ninth Thermidor at the precise moment when the non-"bourgeois" phase of its progress ended. Henceforth, its heart dwelt in the Jacobin period at the moment when moral and utopian ideologies most effectively mask the real processes of history, the interplay between society and state. The historian's emotional commitments to these values and ideologies transport him back into the grand illusion of the participants in the events of the Year II, and thus allow him to see the French Revolution as the bearer of benefits not merely national, but universal in their effects. When Albert Soboul speaks of "the mother of us all," I fear that this classic refrain adds nothing to the clarity of the debate; but at least it reveals, like a cry from the heart, the depth of his passion.

Since 1917, the French Revolution has no longer been that matrix of future events out of which there could and must spring another definitively liberating revolution. There no longer exists that vast seedbed of future developments discovered and described by Jaurès. Instead, it has become the mother of a real event in October 1917: the Russian Revolution. In a pamphlet published in 1920 Mathiez pointed out the kinship between the government of the Mountain (June 1793–July 1794) and the Bolshevik dictatorship in the years of the civil war: "Jacobinism and Bolshevism were dictatorships of essentially the same kind, both born of civil and foreign war, both dictatorships of class, both operating by means of terror, requisition and taxes, and proposing as their ultimate aim a similar goal: the transformation of society. The transformation not just of French or Russian, but of universal society." In addition, as pointed out by Mathiez, the Russian Bolsheviks were profoundly conscious of the example of the French Revolution, particularly of its Jacobin period. In 1903, at the time of the split of the Russian Social-Democratic party into its Bolshevik and Menshevik factions, Lenin pointed to the Jacobin model: "The Jacobin was indissolubly committed to the *organization* of a proletariat *conscious* of its class interests, precisely the same as the *Social-Democratic revolutionary*." This reference fed a long polemical exchange with Trotsky, who at the time leaned toward the Menshevik position. In a too little-known book, recently republished, Trotsky underlined the anachronistic character of Lenin's analysis: "either the Jacobin . . . is bound to the 'organization of a proletariat conscious of its class interests' and thereby ceases to be a Jacobin," or else he remains a Jacobin, which is to say necessarily radically different from a revolutionary Social Democrat. At the end of a long historical analysis of the deadlocks and ideological follies of the Jacobin terrorism he concludes that "they represent two worlds, two doctrines, two tactics, two minds, separated by an abyss." But this recall to the intellectual realm, with its irreproachable Marxism, naturally failed to prevent the permanent telescoping of the two revolutions in the minds of the Russian revolutionaries. It is known, for example, that after the death of Lenin, when the specter of "Thermidor" loomed, Stalin made his tactical alliance with Zinoviev and Kamenev on the basis of their common fear of a new Bonaparte—who was none other than Trotsky, the former chief of the Red Army.

As well as the participants in events of the twentieth century, historians of the French Revolution are guilty of indiscriminately mixing past and present, especially since most of the histories of the French Revolution have, in France at least, been the work of the Left. Yet the "displacement" of the French Revolution by the Russian Revolution, with a corresponding shift of emphasis and research away from the period of 1789–1793, has had some positive effects in the field of scholarship. For one, it has provided a powerful incentive for a much more intensive study of the role of the urban masses in the revolutionary process. Some important works such as *La vie chère* of Mathiez, the *Bras nus* of Daniel Guérin, and *Les sans-culottes* of Albert Soboul probably owe their existence to this development. It is clear—and there are legions of examples, from Tocqueville to Max Weber—that the investigation of contemporary problems can aid in the interpretation of the past.

But, obviously, this holds only if this investigation is based on new hypotheses, and is not simply a passionately mechanical projection of the present onto the past. The interpretation of the French Revolution, for example, has gained neither richness nor depth by the constant, implicit attendance of the history of the Russian Revolution: Preoccupation with the future has proliferated like a cancer within the vitals of historical analysis to the point of obliterating all complexity, and even all significance. I see at least three effects of this situation. First, the search in the history of the French Revolution for justifying precedents for the revolutionary and post-revolutionary history of Russia. An excellent example are the purges of those within the directing group of the Revolution, a characteristic common to both events. Stalin, like Robespierre before him, liquidated his former companions in the name of the struggle against counter-revolution. These two "spontaneous" interpretations of purging, with the French example supporting the Russian, have reinforced the idea that counter-revolution inevitably exists within any revolution and must therefore always be rooted out. A genuine, and potentially fruitful, comparison of the two phenomena would have consisted of examining them—and they are naturally quite different —to discover how the identical process of division and liquidation within the original leadership actually functioned. Instead, the mechanism of justifying the present by the record of the past is invoked—a characteristic of teleological history.

The second result is the substitution of an extraordinarily simplified and over-simplifying Marxism for the few, sometimes contradictory, analyses of the French Revolution, which Marx and Engels have left us. What is substituted is a simple linear pattern of history in which the revolutionary bourgeoisie, with the support of the peasantry and the urban masses, permits the passage from a feudal to a capitalist mode of production. The dictatorship of the Mountain is praised as the phase involving the greatest amount of popular participation, and as a direct result is deemed to have had the greatest significance as a progressive force in bringing to a successful conclusion, by means of war and terror, the tasks originally assumed by the bourgeois revolution. At the same time the whole episode foreshadows future liberations, most notably and specifically the Revolution of October 1917. The Revolution thus finds its true chronology more and more distorted, being shifted from 1789 toward 1793, and then suddenly interrupted in July 1794 at the moment when it was setting all Europe ablaze while finally being established in France. Distorted in this way, the concept of a "bourgeois revolution" has the effect of squeezing a long-term process into an absurdly narrow time span.

If this evident contradiction does not embarrass the "Marxist" historian (in the sense defined above), it is because he is less Marxist than neo-Jacobin. He superimposes a Marxist pattern, established by the Soviet Revolution, on a powerful politico-emotional attitude which in effect interprets the French Revolution as simultaneously the cornerstone of national greatness and the liberator of universal society—a point of view much more "Jacobin" than "Constituent." What the neo-Jacobin finds attractive in the Soviet Revolution is that which Mathiez—who was not a Marxist—perceived as early as 1920: the superimposition of two liberating images which together provide the sinews of contemporary society's faith in the religion of progress, with the Soviet Union playing in the second instance the role assumed by France in the first. It seems to matter very little that the history of recent decades has provided some fundamental challenges to this interpretation which it has not been able to meet: it is precisely the function of ideology to mask reality, and thus to survive it. The neo-Jacobin historian, intoxicated by the idea of a nation invested with the divine purpose of enlightening humanity, refuses to leave this rarefied atmosphere. On the contrary, he speaks once again through the lips of A. Soboul in repeating the "lessons" of a history which teaches a faith in progress, in speaking of events from 1793 to the present as follows: "Who would not recognize that many of the problems which arise in the revolutionary movement today were already, in other forms, at the heart of the complex and terrible interaction of society and politics in the Year II?"

Thus is established, at the level of interpretation of the French Revolution, a sort of Leninist-Populist Holy Writ of which the *Précis d'histoire de la Révolution française* of Soboul is undoubtedly the best example. In this particular work the canons seem to be all the more strongly established since they preempt for support all of the historical writing "of the Left" on the Revolution, from Jaurès to Georges Lefebvre. Woe to the one who strays from the straight and narrow for he will, by this single act, betray Danton and Jaurès, Robespierre and Mathiez, Jacques Roux and Soboul. In this extraordinary amalgam, which is only slightly exaggerated, one recognizes the Manichean spirit: the sectarian conservator of a tradition of historical writing which substitutes value judgments for ideas, final ends for causes, and arguments from authority for open discussion. Thus, they are the bearers of an inheritance for both the present and the future, of a simple alternative—revolution/counter-revolution —which they are obliged to bequeath to posterity as a record of these events which is at once religion and pedagogy. Any other history of the Revolution is therefore necessarily counter-revolutionary, or even antinational. The "logic" of the reasoning is impeccable, except that it is not a question of reasoning but of a repeated ritual —and henceforth a rigidly fixed one of commemoration alone. It is the tomb of the unknown soldier: not one from the battle of the Marne, but of Fleurus.

The most recent book by Soboul is a perfect example of this type of history, though its importance is not as slight as its organization and format might suggest. For in the very simplicity of its structure lurks an historical consciousness which is at once commemorative and teleological. His title is a promising one, borrowed from the theme of the series: *Civilization and the French Revolution.* Such an alluring theme should have carried us around the world in search of an immense cultural heritage. Instead, what Soboul offers us is a classical "crisis of the Old Regime" survey of the eighteenth century. From the very first pages it is clear that the entire century is one of crisis, with the whole panorama of events, at all levels of analysis, careening toward 1789 as if sucked in by that inevitable culmination upon which they are founded *a posteriori:* "Philosophy, closely related to the general line of historical development, and in synchronization with the movement of the economy and of society, has contributed to this slow maturation which suddenly flowers into the Revolution to crown the century of Enlightenment."

The reader, a bit surprised by this exordium, which coldly strikes him with so many metaphysical propositions, quickly turns to the table of contents wishing to know if he should continue! There, another surprise awaits him: the organization. The work is divided into four parts: the peasantry, the aristocracy, the bourgeoisie, and the "fourth estate" (i.e., the urban masses). Of course any organization is arbitrary and imposes, by definition, certain logical constraints upon the author. But this one obliges the historian of the eighteenth century to perform some acrobatics with his material. Into the above social categories he must divide demography, economics, politics, and culture, as they are supposedly "related" to each social group. Thus, Soboul deals with some of the Enlightenment figures in the section on "aristocracy," while other *Philosophes* are lumped in with the "bourgeoisie." And the crucial subject of absolutism is introduced only in the section on aristocracy, and then almost in passing, as simply an aspect of the relationship between the monarchy and the nobility. Without hesitation Albert Soboul embraces this brand of neo-Aristotelian surgery, in which social classes function as metaphysical categories.

Having assumed the risks of such an artificial division, one would like to believe that it was not simply the result of M. Soboul's reluctance to reorganize a body of material which he has already presented under a different—and more exact—title: *French Society in the Second Half of the Eighteenth Century.* Rather the reason is that, in his eyes, whatever may be the formal title one uses, all history of eighteenth-century France implicitly involves two fundamental propositions: (1) that the eighteenth century was chiefly characterized by a general crisis of the Old Regime, as proven by the similarity of developments at all levels of historical reality; and (2) that this "crisis" was essentially "social," and must therefore be analyzed in terms of "class struggle." Of these two propositions the first is either tautological, or teleological—or both. In any event, it escapes all rational judgment by its very imprecision. The second is simply an historical hypothesis, and it is interesting that it is exactly the interpretation which the revolutionaries themselves gave to their role in the Revolution at the moment it broke out. The eighteenth century of Soboul is that of Sieyès and his pamphlet "What Is the Third Estate?" according to which a whole century's history was determined by the contradiction to which its evolution gave rise: the conflict between the Third Estate and the aristocracy. Never has the tyranny exercised over the history of the eighteenth century by the Revolution been more naively placed in evidence. After 180 years of research and interpretation, after countless detailed analyses and syntheses, one might indeed wonder if it is a great intellectual triumph for historians to simply arrive at the same image of the past held by the revolutionaries themselves. And is it not a rather paradoxical performance for an allegedly Marxist historian to align himself with the contemporary ideological view of the event which he is supposedly seeking to explain? For Soboul, as for Sieyès, the Revolution of 1789 was not just one of several possible outcomes for the development of French society in the eighteenth century; it was the *only* possible result—its culmination, its purpose, its very meaning. Just as the melon of Bernardin de Saint-Pierre is made to be eaten by the whole family, so the eighteenth century of Soboul is cut up to be eaten in 1789. But what is left of it?

The author must have felt a certain awkwardness, for he has appended to the end of his sociological breakdown a concluding chapter whose title simply summarizes that of the book: "The Crisis of the Old Regime." Yet this is not a new conclusion, but simply a new amalgam of the classical explanations of the immediate origins of the Revolution: the interacting regressive economic cycles of Prof. Labrousse, the social crisis, the exhaustion of the intellectual forces of the Enlightenment, the impotence of the state, the aristocratic revolt. From this point of view where was the "crisis" of the Old Regime truly located? In the decade of the eighties which Soboul describes in conclusion? Or in the increasing number of social contradictions which appeared during the course of the century? All of this is never very clear to the reader, but it seems that the answer, implicitly at least, is: here and there. The materials for the bonfire were accumulated during the entire century, and the decade of the eighties provided the spark. By this approach the ultimate intrusion of chronology into the analysis of social stratification modifies neither the conceptual framework, nor the philosophy of underlying final causes. On the contrary, it intervenes only to confirm them. It is the new Providence of the new theologian.

In this Procrustean bed, what has become of the poor eighteenth century? It is a vast field of latent social contradictions, the bearers of the future to which they have been assigned, the forerunners of the great class struggles of 1789–1793. The teams have already squared off: on one side, the vigorous bourgeoisie and its popular allies, the peasants and the urban masses; on the other, the foredoomed aristocracy.

The Problem of Seignorial Rights and the "Feudal Reaction"

In Soboul's analysis the peasants receive the lion's share of his attention, nearly half of the book. In these 200 pages—in my opinion easily the best part of the text—he neatly synthesizes a number of detailed works on the various facets of rural life under the Old Regime: social structure, technology, demography, daily labor, culture and beliefs, etc. From these pages emanates a genuine feeling for the world of the countryside and an understanding of the life of the humble, which gives them an undeniable savor. Yet, on the level of basic interpretation the analysis raises a very great problem which it solves a little too quickly: that of seignorial rights and the weight of the feudal system in the eighteenth-century French countryside.

The position of Soboul is fixed: on the conceptual plane, although he is evidently aware of the distinction between "feudal" and "seignorial," just as jurists of the French Revolution were aware of it, he constantly confuses the two concepts, just as revolutionary ideology had always confused them. This confusion allows him to speak of a "complex," of a "feudal regime," as defining the essential elements of the economic and social structure in the countryside. Such a confusion of the terms "feudal," "seignorial," and "aristocratic" forces the historian to align himself with the contemporary understanding of the Revolution. Again he becomes the prisoner of the division which the ideology of 1789 had made between "old" and "new," with the "old" being defined simply as "feudal." Thus, he is compelled to blame the "feudal system" for all the negative, and ultimately explosive, features of rural society: the exploitation of the peasant and his resulting misery, the impediments to agricultural productivity, the slowness of capitalist development. Since this "feudal regime" had in fact been the victim of radical assaults in France for four or five centuries prior to 1789, the old idea of an eighteenth-century "feudal reaction" is rushed in to shore up the threatened concept. For a fleeting moment one might imagine himself seated in the assembly on the famous night of August fourth.

As everyone knows, statistical analysis on the national level of the relative weight of seignorial rights in land rents—and in the income of peasant and noble—is not available, and is not likely to be in the near future. These rights are incredibly diverse and the documentary sources are sparse, and the data in the *terriers* cannot easily be grouped into statistical series. Soboul writes on page forty-four: "Land rents, *feudal in their fundamental character,* dominated agricultural life. . . ." The underlined portion of this statement is obviously false for eighteenth-century France, when incomes from tenant farming, sharecropping and direct production for the market were incontestably more important than that from the old seignorial rights. It is surprising to find such an affirmation being made by a specialist, but the question which must be asked is what is the degree of its error? The numerous monographs which are available confront us with a wide divergence in this matter: the peasants of Prof. Le Roy Ladurie, in the south of France which had been relatively little "feudalized," seem to have liquidated the seignorial dues very early —from the beginning of the sixteenth century. In the region of the Sarthe, described by P. Bois, the weight of seignorial payments seems to have been very light, perhaps even the least element in the total amount of farm rents. And the revision of the *terriers* in the seventeenth century does not reveal the addition of any supplementary seignorial rights. "One can say," concludes P. Bois with scarcely any exaggeration, "that the question of seignorial dues did not concern the peasant." The same refrain is found in the Auvergne of A. Poitrineau, where the percentage of seignorial rights in proportion to net product seems not to have exceeded 10 percent, though in this case it is necessary to add that there was a tendency for it to increase during the course of the century. On the other hand, in the Brittany described by J. Meyer, as in the Burgundy of Saint-Jacob recently restudied by R. Robin, the seignorial assessment on the net products of the land remained important, particularly with respect to levies in kind. The *champart* in Burgundy, and the rights attached to the lord's domain in Brittany, seem to have been the only economically burdensome seignorial obligations.

Given the present state of our knowledge, it is not possible to speak of a "feudal reaction" as an objective process affecting the internal economy and agrarian society of the eighteenth century. It is not even certain that real seignorial rights on property, which weighed most heavily on the proprietor (since, like the *dîme,* they were generally deducted from the value of the lease), had significantly affected the standard of living of the poorest of peasants—the small farmer. But even if the opposite were true, even if an increase in the seignorial share were the cause of peasant pauperization at the end of the eighteenth century, it would not follow that the movement had to have been aristocratic and "feudal" in nature (in Soboul's sense, i.e., at the same time noble and anticapitalist). In the last decade A. Poitrineau published a very interesting graph which showed the growing commercialization of *seigneuries* in Auvergne, of their developing organization for production for the market in the second half of the century. As for Burgundy in the middle of the eighteenth century, P. de Saint-Jacob (who uses the term "seignorial reaction" with caution) has demonstrated how the *seigneurie,* through the mediation of the farmer of seignorial rights, was integrated into what he calls the "physiocratic revolution"—that is, the development of capitalism in the countryside. Thus, rather than an "aristocratic reaction" would it not be more correct to speak, as suggested by Alfred Cobban, of the commercialization of the *seigneurie?* From this point of view peasant resistance to the *seigneurie* may have been neither antiaristocratic nor antifeudal, but rather antibourgeois and anticapitalist. And the zest displayed on the night of August 4 may then be viewed as the mask which hid a basic disagreement, or at least a radical misunderstanding, rather than as a result of an antifeudal alliance of classes. Besides, it is only too evident in the history of French rural society that the abolition of seignorial rights did not end resistance to the development of capitalism. As the book of P. Bois suggests, the hostility of the peasant to the *seigneurie* may have been simply an archaic form of his opposition to economic change.

In this respect a recent German article suggests an interesting hypothesis resulting from a comparison between Bavaria and France. The author shows that in the Germany west of the Elbe the clergy and the nobility, while retaining their rights of eminent domain, had abandoned all of their former domain land to peasant holders who, as a result, possessed from 80 to 90 percent of the arable. In France, on the contrary, the primary phenomenon in the evolution of the *seigneurie* from the sixteenth to the eighteenth century was the renting of the domain to the detriment of the receiver of the *cens.* This trend was heartily disliked by the nobility due to the resulting decline in the value of the *cens.* At the end of the eighteenth century in France peasant holders possessed scarcely more than one-third of the land, which, contrary to widespread opinion, was not a great deal. This comparative analysis of the evolution of the *seigneurie* in France and western Germany helps to explain the pauperization of rural France on the eve of the Revolution, as well as the presence of a vast peasant proletariat for which there is no equivalent on the other side of the Rhine, where 90 percent of the land was held by farming proprietors. At the same time it underlines the fact that the development of rural capitalism in France was achieved by the renting of the seignorial domain. Far from having been an obstacle, the *seigneurie,* with its bailiffs and bourgeois intermediaries, has been the means. There is a good chance that P. Bois is right, and that in protesting some of the residual and secondary feudal obligations— resented all the more because they were a marginal drain on a marginal productive process—the French peasantry at the end of the eighteenth century was actually objecting to the extension of capitalism onto the land.

If, nevertheless, the confused concept of an aristocratic reaction characterized by an extension of seignorial obligations has been accepted by historians for such a long time, it is only because it fits in so neatly with a simplistic view of class struggle and the arrangement of class alliances; or because it allows Albert Soboul to rediscover schoolboy Marxism in writing that "the capitalist transformation of agriculture requires the abolition of privilege and the feudal structure." The idea is all the more firmly entrenched as it receives support from a series of "literary" accounts of the eighteenth century, and above all from the *cahiers* of the Estates-General. Discussion on the value of the *cahiers* as documents—and Lord knows this discussion has been extensive since the beginning of the century—has until now concerned itself primarily with determining if, and to what extent, the compilers were faithful to the genuine desires of their communities. If one supposes that the answer to this question were positive, which it most often is, there remains a second—and probably more fundamental—question which must be answered before using the *cahiers:* are these texts to be read as records of the actual state of affairs, or as reflections of the political and ideological state of mind of French society in 1789? I lean, along with R. Robin who has set the example, toward the second interpretation, for it appears to me at the very least preferable to the first. However, before making any comparisons with the social reality from which they have issued, it is necessary to first describe the contents of the *cahiers* at each sociological level.

It is true that the peasant *cahiers* are often packed with grievances against seignorial obligations. Less, however, than against the *dîme* and the *taille,* the two running sores of rural communities. And with respect to seignorial rights the peasant *cahiers* are often much more vigorous in their attacks on personal obligations, such as the *banalités* and the lord's hunting rights, than on those of property. Indeed, hints of an aggravation of such property rights in the recent past are also to be found, notably in the form of hostility to the commissioners employed to revise the *terriers.* But even supposing that the peasant *cahiers* were unanimous in their complaints of a recent increase in seignorial burdens—which is far from true —what would that prove? Practically nothing.

I imagine that if a poll similar to that of 1789 were conducted in present-day rural France the result would be much the same: unanimous cries against taxes. And this despite the fact that the French peasantry, as a group, has been notoriously undertaxed for over 150 years. It is in the nature of a political text, and of a political consciousness, to impute evil to men and not to things—what Ernest Labrousse, who remains the outstanding Marxist historian of the origins of the French Revolution, very correctly calls "putting the blame on the political situation." Poverty at the end of the eighteenth century, of which there is so much unmistakable evidence, may well have been the product of demographic growth; and those five or six million additional subjects of the French king certainly had to find a little place in the sun for themselves. Misery's career is also traced in the admirable curves of E. Labrousse, in which the prices of leases—that is, of the ground rent in its most "bourgeois" form— climb so much more quickly than wages, and, indeed, even than prices in general. Yet how could the peasants, or even the local notary, for that matter, have known this? Inevitably they would vent their anger, almost spontaneously, against the local image of power: the chateau and its inhabitants. As R. Robin has mentioned, with respect to the *cahier* of Auxois, the grievances of the rural community arose not from historical or economic analysis, but from the concrete facts of daily life: royal taxes, ecclesiastical taxes, hunting rights—in short, whatever deprived them of *things*. Moreover, the *cahiers* were drawn up in the spring of 1789, in the midst of a short-term depression. In such a situation it should not surprise us that the great mass of impoverished peasants looked to the very recent past, with its increasing levies on their labor, for the causes of their current difficulties.

No one has demonstrated better than P. Bois, in the chapter of his book devoted to the *cahiers,* how the seignor—or in the case of the *dîme,* the clergy—probably filled the role of scapegoat, though the example is limited to the region of the Sarthe. In fact, it appears that there is no direct relationship between the intensity of the peasants' grievances against the abuses of the privileged orders (i.e., the objective reality of seignorial and ecclesiastical levies), and the political behavior of their communities. On the contrary, it is in the western half of the *département* that expressions of bitterness in the *cahiers* against the privileged orders, especially against the clergy, are sharpest, yet without corresponding justification in the extent of ecclesiastical property or the rate of the *dîme;* and it is this area which will witness the emergence of proroyalist peasant uprisings. On the other hand, the southeast, whose *cahiers* are particularly moderate with regard to privilege, will become a redoubt of Republican fidelity. In other words, one should not look to some *post-factum* arrangement of an imaginary anti-"feudal" class interest, consolidated by an "aristocratic reaction" in the countryside, in order to unearth the secrets of peasant consciousness and political behavior.

Whence came then that diffuse, but very basic and very real sense of frustration with the nobility and privileged orders in French society at the end of the eighteenth century? It seems to me that the "aristocratic reaction" was much more a political, social and psychological reality than a fact of economic life. The eighteenth century witnessed the growth of a widespread irritation with the snobbery of the nobility, and by a ricochet effect throughout the social pyramid, an exasperation with the world of class differences as such. In one of the notes of his thesis, J. Meyer cites a very amusing and relevant text. Taken from an anonymous pamphlet directed against the *présidents à mortier* of the *Parlement* of Brittany, it is part of a parody of the manual of proper conduct for a *président:* "Since we are few in number, we can't always be together. Thus, it is essential to know how to be alone, and to be bored with dignity; it is our continual study. Molded by habit, I prefer at present the honor of boring myself in solitude, or with some other *président,* to the pleasure that I might enjoy in the company of other counselors or noblemen. One attains this degree of perfection only through the long habit of being a *président.*"

Robe, finance, sword—these distinctions within the noble order retained less and less significance as the century progressed. Seemingly, they weakened in order to reinforce that other, greater social barrier—that which separated noble and commoner, for there undoubtedly was a growing sense of frustration with noble "racism." But this stiffening of the nobility with respect to protocol and the trappings of power was not necessarily related to an increase in its economic drain on the peasantry. On the contrary, noble exaggeration, to the point of caricature, of the symbols of its domination and the rites of its separation may be a sign that it had suffered a loss of power under absolutism—or believed itself to have been so deprived, which amounts to the same thing. Following their example, the whole society played out the psychodrama of domination and servitude: nobles versus nonnobles, great nobles against small, rich against poor, Parisians against provincials, townsmen against farmers. The whole is less a problem of economic ownership than of social domination. As Tocqueville had quite properly perceived, French society in the eighteenth century was a world disintegrating under the dual onslaughts of monarchical centralization and the philosophy of individualism. Thus, the Revolution may possibly be considered as an immense process of socio-cultural integration through the antifeudal patriotism of 1789 and, later, Jacobin ideology. Egalitarianism is the opposite of social humiliation, the "republican" communion of men the reverse of "monarchical" separatism. Naturally, the nobility—the very model of social distinction—must pay the heavy price of this national integration.

The Dominant Classes of the Eighteenth Century

This long digression brings me back to the book of Albert Soboul, to his analyses of the nobility and of the bourgeoisie—the central part of the work, and also the most distressing. Is it because he suddenly loses the attentive sympathy which he carried to the rural world, or simply because he departs from his habitual field of investigation? In any event, the tone drops a notch, the description becomes dry, and the interpretation grows increasingly schematic. And, unfortunately, he continues to wreak havoc in the reality of history. The clergy, for example, is treated along with the nobility to the extent that it is socially "high," and with the bourgeoisie to the extent that it is not. As a result, a socio-cultural institution so characteristic of the Old Regime disappears with a single stroke of the sociological surgeon's blade. As long as the church continued to collect the *dîme,* and thus draw upon itself general hostility and jealousy—and not just among the peasantry, for it occupied a prominent place in the debates which followed August 4—it participated actively in the cultural dislocation of the Old Regime. None of this appears in the analysis of Soboul, unless it happens to be the great wealth of the lower clergy. In this populist reading of history, where are the preachers of Groethuysen, the sprinklers of the "bourgeois spirit"? Where are the Jesuits of P. de Dainville, the educators of Enlightenment France? Where are the Jansenists, or, more importantly, Jansenism itself: without a doubt the fundamentally decisive crisis of Catholic France? *De minimis non curat praetor.*

Another problem: the world of "finance" is broached, at the end of the chapters devoted to the bourgeoisie, through the "bourgeoisie of enterprise." This is a double misinterpretation. "Finance" has nothing to do with enterprise, nor with the bank, from which it was increasingly distinct, and moreover the rival. Even so he manages to confuse the two activities. This closed and privileged capitalism, which concerned itself with the administration of the finances of an agrarian kingdom, is the opposite of the Schumpeterian brand of enterprise capitalism. And the shift of official "finance" to the private "bank" in the attempt to rescue royal finances—a shift of which the ministerial promotion of Necker is the symbol—is an important sign of the crisis in the governmental structures of the Old Regime. On the other hand, finance was hardly of a monolithic nature, a "bourgeois" world: on the contrary, the eighteenth century was the time *par excellence* of passage along the faithful line from commons to nobility. The elite of finance—the general tax-farmers, the treasurers general, the receivers general—bought royal secretarial offices, made their sons into *parlementaires,* and married their daughters to dukes. If Soboul were not locked into his scheme of a "feudal" aristocracy—which even contradicts the types of aristocratic income which he cites—he would have cast a glance at the structures of the fortunes of the great officers of finance, which the works of G. Chaussinard suggest were dominated in crushing fashion by investments in offices and a wide variety of state *rentes.* The purchase of a *seigneurie* was a simple act of snobbery, the private stable of the race of the epoch—the symbol of status and domination, not the reality of wealth.

As a matter of fact, the really sensitive point of the society of the Old Regime was this zone of passage—or of nonpassage, according to particular instances and periods—between what might be called the high bourgeoisie and the high nobility. In this society of "orders" it was more difficult to pass from the small to the great nobility than to leave the commons for the ruling aristocracy through the formation of a grand fortune in trade and access to high office in the state. Soboul's rigid and strictly vertical sociology—recalling at once a number of reactionary and revolutionary ideologues such as Boulainvilliers and Sieyès—masks and ignores this capital fact, which appears to me to be at the root of the crisis of the ruling classes in the eighteenth century. In order to take proper account of this phenomenon, it would be necessary to examine the role of the monarchical state in society, and in the crisis of that society. Yet, in this weighty tome of nearly 500 pages, the tyranny of sociologism is such that not a single chapter is devoted to the functioning of absolutism. Moreover, on one page Soboul slips us the key to this stupefying silence: in his eyes, the monarchical state since Louis XIV is simply an appendage of the "aristocracy" (which in his uniformly imprecise vocabulary is another word for "nobility"). The proof is in the events of 1789, the hoped-for counter-revolution and in the underhandedly organized defeatist war—in short, nothing but the old tautological proof of "final causes."

It is amusing to observe that, in doing this, Soboul abandons one of the principal ideas of Marx concerning the Old Regime, and the history of France in general: that of the relative independence of the state, during the Old Regime, in relation to the nobility and the bourgeoisie. The idea is also one of the fundamental concepts of Tocqueville; but it is so incontestably a part of the thought of Marx and Engels that its inheritor *par excellence,* the Kautsky of 1889, devoted the first chapter of his analysis of the origins of the French Revolution to them. And this chapter is prefaced by a stern warning against the "sociological" simplifications of Marxism, which to me applies perfectly to the case of Albert Soboul: "One is only too easily disposed, when one reduces historical development to simple class struggle, to perceive in society only two causes, two classes in combat, two compact and homogeneous masses: the revolutionary mass and the reactionary one, the one on the bottom and the other on top. In that case, nothing is easier than to write history. But, in reality, social relations are not nearly so simple."

For three centuries the French monarchy played an active role in the dislocation of the society of orders—in the eighteenth century more than ever. Tied to the development of commercial production, hostile to local powers, bearer of the national achievement, it had been the decisive element in the process of social mobility—even more so than its famous partner in the enterprise, money. On both the social and the cultural levels it had progressively undermined, eroded, and ultimately destroyed the vertical solidarity of the social orders, above all that of the nobility: on the social plane by grafting, primarily through offices, a second nobility onto that of the feudal epoch, a new species which came to dominate the Second Estate in the eighteenth century. On the cultural level the monarchy proposed to the ruling groups, henceforth gathered under its wing, an alternative set of values to replace that of personal honor: those of the nation and the state. In short, in becoming the great money-magnet in its role as the distributor of social promotions the monarchical state, while conserving the heritage of a society of orders, had created a parallel social structure contradictory to the first: an elite, a ruling class. The king of France had always been the first of the seigniors of the realm, but he was above all the great patron of the bureaus of Versailles.

Clearly, in the eighteenth century there was no political solidarity within the nobility *as an order*. Only its misfortunes in the Revolution infused it with a belated sense of unity, the image of which has been transmitted to the historian. On the contrary, the era was brimming with conflicts within the noble estate: the edict of 1781 was rooted in the resentment of the lesser nobles toward the great much more than in a common noble scorn for the Third Estate. The hostility toward money, the newly ennobled, and social mobility felt by the minor nobility of the sword was, in sum, hostility to the ruling class which clustered about the eighteenth-century throne. In this respect, the book of Chevalier d'Arc is one of the most interesting witnesses of the epoch.

Neither is there, in the eighteenth century, any solidarity within the ruling nobility, the "aristocracy" in the proper sense of the word. Due to the conditions of its formation and of its function in society, the latter incorporated some very disparate elements: ancient "feudal" families who were the historic and fashionable point of reference for the social hierarchy; the high military nobility, eager to reconquer ground lost under Louis XIV; courtier bishops; rebellious magistrates, as well as those who had passed into the service of the king; newly arrived financiers allied with the greatest families; *intendants* and members of the upper reaches of the bureaucracy at Versailles. In short, all those who might be grouped under the label "court nobility," a group which provoked the gross hostility of the rest of the noble order, but which was in reality shattered, chopped up into cliques and coteries which could hardly be defined in terms of material interests. In the same vein were the great nobles of the robe who, when they were not called to high office at Versailles, dwelt outside the court and dominated fashionable civilization: passing their lives in parlementary opposition, struggling against the people of Versailles and their local representative, the *intendant*. Yet the *intendant,* nine times out of ten, was of parlementary origin.

It is necessary to recognize that the political and cultural attitudes of the eighteenth-century French aristocracy, whose incomes are predominantly landed (which does not mean "feudal"), do not correspond to any sort of social or economic homogeneity, since members of the group may be already capitalist, or still feudal or simply proprietary. What permits one to analyze this politico-social elite is its attitude, or its ambition, in relation to authority and, inseparably, in relation to the mechanism of social mobility established by authority. Through offices, ennoblement, and monarchical centralization the whole of civil society was co-opted by the state, which distributed the coveted titles in return for weighty sacks of bourgeois gold. With jealous care Louis XIV had organized this system of "competing elites," to borrow a term from Louis Bergeron; but his death was the signal for a battle all the more vicious as the stakes were at once political, social, and economic. If the state siphoned off the wealth of the kingdom, it also redistributed the loot.

In this aspect, and in relation to authority, the eighteenth century incontestably appears as a period of "aristocratic reaction"—provided that the term "aristocratic" is used in its true sense, that of a ruling elite. We possess abundant literary evidence of it in the memoirs, correspondence, and administrative documents of the epoch. But the phenomenon may reflect a very great variety of circumstances.

Is it a question of the closing of noble ranks to the upper layers of the Third Estate, and of a monopolization of the state and its great offices by the nobility, which would then become again what it had ceased to be under Louis XIV, an aristocracy? This is the traditional hypothesis, which has the advantage of accounting for the frustration and ambitions of the bourgeoisie at the end of the century. But, insofar as one may judge at present, the hypothesis lacks statistical support; the sale of the offices of secretaries to the king, which had much declined from the death of Louis XIV into the 1750s, attained a wider distribution in the second half of the century than ever before, in step with the mounting financial needs of the state. As for the membership of the *parlements,* neither the works of F. Bluche, nor those of J. Égret, suggest any great changes in its recruitment compared with the seventeenth century. According to J. Égret, of 757 members of the thirteen *parlements* and the two sovereign councils during the last two decades of the Old Regime, 426 were of new social origins: of this total, nearly 100 were from the Third Estate, while many others were of the newly ennobled. These figures, in order to be absolutely demonstrative, must be comparable to others over a long period of time; but they indicate, at least, that there is no proof of a social hardening in parlementary recruitment. Likewise for the *intendants:* the data recently provided by V. Gruder amply testify to a noble exclusivism in their selection (with considerable variation in the number of generations of nobility required for the post), but this exclusivism diminished in the eighteenth century while, at the same time, the number of *intendants* born of "finance" (that is, of the newly ennobled) increased. Episcopal recruitment? At least 90 percent were noble for the period 1774–1790 but the proportion was 84 percent in the period 1682–1700. The same situation prevailed in the ministerial body: all, or almost all, of the ministers of Louis XV and of Louis XVI were noble, but nearly all of those of Louis XIV were as well—notwithstanding the accusations of Saint-Simon, whom Soboul candidly calls to the witness stand. Finally, the army, that guarded preserve of noble exclusivism: but it had never been, prior to the Revolution and the Empire, a channel of bourgeois promotion; of the generals of Louis XIV counted by A. Corvisier, very few were of common origin. Meanwhile, according to E. C. Leonard, the invasion of the upper ranks by the sons of financiers expanded as early as the end of the reign of Louis XIV, at the moment of the interminable war with Europe and the financial collapse. This development continued in the eighteenth century, facilitated by the high purchase price of rank and, above all, the personal maintenance costs of a regiment, provoked the hostility of the "ancient" nobility against the "colonels of the bank," but also against the nobility of the court who were not necessarily of ancient lineage; rather than the Third Estate, it was money, wealth, and its accomplice the state which were attacked. Pestered by this intranoble conflict, the monarchy reacted with the measures of 1718 and 1727, which reaffirmed the noble monopoly of military ranks, and added the edict of 1750, which decreed ennoblement on records of service at once personal and familial: the Napoleonic Legion of Honor anticipated by more than a half-century.

Thus there is no proof, as yet, of a social contraction of the nobility itself. The monarchy, increasingly pressured by its financial needs, continued the lucrative practice of ennobling secretaries of the king, members of the *parlements,* and military commoners purified in the saddle, while the old nobility married its sons to the daughters of finance. A number of objective processes, such as the acceleration in the sale of *seigneuries,* testify to a continuous integration of the upper strata of the Third Estate into the nobility. It is possible, and even probable—though difficult to demonstrate—that this integration was not rapid enough to suit the rhythm of growth in bourgeois fortunes and ambitions. Such is the impression left by the study of J. Meyer, which contrasts the economic dynamism of the bourgeois elites of Brittany to the relatively limited number of ennoblements in the course of the eighteenth century. Even if that were the case on the national level, it is simply an additional reason for not cutting the sociological study of the ruling classes of the Old Regime from the analysis of the zone of contact between noble and commoner, since there may have been passage from one order to the other, or a blocking of one by the other. What is probable is that in the eighteenth century this magic line of promotion had become too rigid to satisfy a growing demand, but also too supple and too venal to remain worthy of being defended.

What is certain in any case is that ennoblement by money and the king provoked, throughout the eighteenth century, a long protest from the "old" nobility, their anguished cries liberated by the death of Louis XIV. The phenomenon which historians have dubbed the "aristocratic reaction" should properly be interpreted as a bitter struggle within the elites of the Old Regime, between nobles and the newly ennobled; likewise, the resistance of the relatively old nobility—often impoverished—should be viewed as opposition to the attempt to establish a ruling class through money and the state. As D. Bien has noted, the famous edict of 1781 was directed not against the commons, but against those nobles who lacked four generations of nobility. It is in the nature of societies of orders to spawn a cult of "difference"; the question which dominated the elites of the eighteenth century was not merely "bourgeois or noble?" but "noble or newly ennobled?" and still further "how recently ennobled?" The powerful bourgeois pressure on a social access gate that was becoming more congested and so, perhaps, increasingly selective, and the struggle once the line was crossed between the various groups of nobles—these two phenomena were not contradictory, but complementary. They both express the increasing maladjustment of the relatively narrow mechanism of social mobility created by absolutism within the framework of the society of orders. It was a quantitative maladjustment considering the prosperity of the century, but also a qualitative maladjustment in that the sole status offered to common fortunes was integration into the state: its court, bureaucracy, army, and magistrature. It is hardly surprising that all of the dominant groups gave primacy to the struggle for power, that intranoble conflicts over control of the state—above all between the *parlements* and the royal administration—dictated the tone of political life and provided a long dress-rehearsal of the gigantic crisis at the end of the century. The absolutist state had created the artisans of its ruin.

Thus, the key to the politico-social crisis of the eighteenth century is neither a hypothetical closing of the nobility, nor its gross hostility to the bourgeoisie in the name of an imaginary "feudal system." On the contrary, it is the opening of the noble estate: too broad to maintain the cohesion of the order, and too narrow for the prosperity of the century. The two great heritages of the history of France, a society of orders and absolutism, entered into a conflict without issue. Louis XIV had been able to control the processes of promotion and the competition of elites within the society of orders and used this as his principle of state-building. But Louis XV could do so no longer, and Louis XVI still less. Perpetually tossed about between fidelity to the old seigniorial tradition and the requirements of the new social and bureaucratic rationality, prisoners of two contradictory modes of hierarchy and social mobility, they spent their time in surrendering to first one group, then to another—in short, falling into line on the multiple conflicts which wracked the ruling elite, first supporting Machault, then Choiseul, then Maupeou, and finally Turgot. They persisted in trying all kinds of policies, without ever carrying them through to their conclusions: each time, the action of the state provoked the lively hostility of a great part of the ruling elites, which never united on a single side—neither for enlightened despotism, nor for liberal reformism. Inseparably, the elites of the eighteenth century were both governing and revolting. In reality, they settled their internal conflicts on the sagging back of absolutism, which Loménie de Brienne finally buried in 1788. Even the crisis of 1789 did not mend their differences, save in the imaginations of the ideologues of the Third Estate; neither the launching of the Revolution with the so-called "aristocratic revolt," nor the behavior of many noble deputies in the Constituent Assembly of 1791, nor the actual work of the Assembly are intelligible without reference to the crisis of power and of the elites of the eighteenth century. If the French Revolution—like all revolutions—met, at least at the outset, with dispersed and badly coordinated resistance, it was because the Old Regime was dead before it was destroyed. The primary characteristic of revolutions is the weakness and isolation of the collapsing regime. But also by the epic reinvention of their history; whence the revolutionary reconstruction of the aristocratic hydra, which constitutes *a contrario* a redefinition of social values, a profound message inseparably liberating and re-mystifying which one would be mistaken to take for an historical analysis.

In this crisis of elites it remains to examine the role played by cultural differentiation—or unification. It is an immense problem, still inadequately explored, as is the entire domain of the sociological history of culture. What is clear, at least, is that the nobility at Versailles and in the cities read the same books as the cultivated bourgeoisie, discussed Descartes and Newton, wept over the misfortunes of Manon Lescaut, and celebrated the *Lettres philosophiques* or *La Nouvelle Héloïse.* The political alternatives of the century took form not at the social frontiers of the orders, but in the bosom of cultivated society. In the face of the parlementary and liberal political claim, the inspired common sense of a Voltaire sketched a monarchical reformism which contested less the authority of the king than civil society, the inequalities of birth, the clergy, and revealed religion. Meanwhile, the Physiocrats were busy theorizing a society of proprietors which would support an enlightened despotism. None of these cultural and political alternatives corresponded to social cleavages; on the contrary, fashionable life, the academies, the Masonic lodges, the cafés and theaters—in short, the city, after the court, had gradually woven an enlightened society predominantly aristocratic, but open to talent and bourgeois gold: A society of elites which excluded not only the popular classes, but also the bulk of the nobility of the kingdom. An unstable and seductive mixture of intelligence and rank, of wit and snobbery, this world was capable of criticizing everything, including and above all itself. Unwittingly, it presided over a profound reshuffling of elites and values. As if by chance the newly ennobled, robe and especially finance, enjoyed a primordial role: they formed a bridge between the world they had left and the one to which they had just arrived. They were an additional witness to the strategic importance of this hinge-zone of French society who gropingly sought, with the slightly masochistic irony which accompanied the double sensation of their strangeness and their success, the road to a "bourgeois" sociability.

To this horizontal solidarity of the Enlightenment Albert Soboul devotes eighteen lines—a brief twinge of conscience over the long expositions devoted to "aristocratic ideology" or bourgeois "philosophy." For him, the cultural world must also take its principles of classification from the aristocratic/bourgeois conflict! Thus, we fall into some extraordinary simplifications where the ignorance of texts and works contends with the platitude of the analysis. Montesquieu is uniformly the champion of the "parlementary and reactionary," as if it were a question of the same thing. Soboul utilizes the work of Althusser, but only in amputating it of its analysis of the modernity of Montesquieu—just as he plagiarizes an article by D. Richet, but reverses its meaning. He simply does not conceive that there was a dialectical link in the evolution of French society between privilege and liberty. The ideological categories of 1789–1793 implicitly serve as a universal standard of comparison for history. In the face of this aristocratic thought, it is left to him to invent a "bourgeois" counter-current: all told, simply "philosophy and the *philosophes*." In the passage we learn that "the industrial bourgeoisie was not yet sufficiently developed so that its accession was expressed on the literary plane: it was necessary to await the nineteenth century." Yet for the nonindustrial bourgeoisie, what incomparable exponents! Voltaire, d'Alembert, Rousseau (over whom, to be sure, the future *sans-culottes* differed with the bourgeoisie), Condorcet; in short, the stars of the "Enlightenment," thus saved from all aristocratic contamination and restored to their preeminent dignity as the heralds of the bourgeois and popular revolution. Such an absurd blend of half-truths and commonplaces discourages all critical commentary. To quote the final reconciliation, which would have delighted Flaubert: "The audience of the Enlightenment was multifarious, just as the *philosophes* were diverse. But philosophy is one and it lives."

Thus, through the belated but faithful voice of Albert Soboul, the French Revolution has just described the dying or prenatal lives of the great personages of history which will ultimately enthrone: the "feudal" aristocracy, the ever-climbing bourgeoisie, the antifeudal

peasantry, and the future *sans-culottes*. The curtain will be able to rise on the grand celebration; perhaps Albert Soboul should entitle his second volume *Memories of a Revolutionary*.

With Claude Mazauric we step into a less spontaneous world: the style is dry; the preaching and the criticism become militant. Fully a third of his slender volume consists of an article which previously appeared in the *Annales historiques de la Révolution française,* and which was devoted to the book *The French Revolution,* published five years ago by Denis Richet and me. And the additions made to the initial article are almost exclusively political or ideological: whence a few problems.

In the first place, it is unusual for an author to respond directly to his critics: once written and published, a book stands or falls on its own merits. The issue is for the readers alone to decide. To publish a book is to submit oneself to criticism. Thus, when Mazauric's review appeared it seemed to me hardly suitable to respond; but now, in writing a book about ours, he has forced the issue. Not that this chance to get even pleases me: at bottom, it is pleasant neither to criticize a critic, nor to surrender to the conceit of authorship regarding an aging book which, for my part at least, I would not rewrite in the same fashion today. Since I would be inclined to strengthen my case vis-à-vis my proxy, to be increasingly "revisionist," perhaps it is more useful to discuss a few problems involved in Mazauric's text, rather than our book.

But first, one last preliminary: how to approach his melancholy prose—semiscientific, semipolitical? How, and even why, does one respond to an author who accuses a history of the French Revolution of being anti-Communist, anti-Soviet, and even antinational? If Mazauric is implying that all history of the Revolution must testify to that other revolution, and that demonstration of this implicit end result is the touchstone of patriotism, then we are precisely in the midst of a moralizing teleology which may salve the conscience of the historian but which is hardly worth a minute of discussion in this rudimentary form. If it simply indicates that every historian of the French Revolution has made, vis-à-vis his object of study (whose conflicts we have all internalized to a certain extent), some assumptions of an existential and political order, then we are confronted with a fact too obvious for debate. Clearly, Mazauric and I do not hold the same view of the contemporary world—and that fact can hardly be without consequence for our subjective evaluations of the past. History which is written is, to be sure, still history. But to avoid falling into complete relativism—which would simply make the present the arbiter of the various readings of the past—it is essential to try to understand the intellectual intermediaries through which the historian's experiences and prejudices weave their way into his work: his hypotheses and assumptions, the preliminaries of scientific proof. To me, those of Mazauric are the same as Soboul's, in truth the most sterile of all for the reasons given above. They consist, through a degraded Marxism, of an internalization of the revolutionary ideology of 1789–1794, according to an implicit scale of values in which the degree of popular participation in the event serves as the point of reference for the commemorative communion and the future hopes of the historian. My point of reference is evidently the reverse, employing the hypothesis that the revolutionary events were, by their very nature, carrying a heavy ideological load, and in which the masklike role played by ideology in the course of the "real" revolutionary process was at a maximum. Every revolution represents an upsetting break in one's patterns of thought; but also a fundamental reconsideration of the past. The historian's first duty is to dissipate the founding and permanent illusion which binds this immense event to its actors and heirs. Naturally, we could discuss to the point of exhaustion whether Mazauric's assumptions are revolutionary, and mine conservative. A better course is to consider those sections of Mazauric's text which permit historical analysis, and thus reduce the disagreements to some precise questions.

A Metaphysical Personage: The "Bourgeois Revolution"

Let us begin with the concept of the "bourgeois revolution." To the interpretation of events in France it offers an almost heaven-sent point of anchorage, for it provides a general conceptualization which allows one to include not only the swelling multiplicity of empirical data, but also the various levels of reality: at once, it reflects economics, society, politics, and ideology. At the economic level, the events which took place in France between 1789 and 1799 are assumed to have liberated the nation's productive forces, and to have given a painful birth to capitalism. At the social level, they supposedly express the victory of the bourgeoisie over the former "privileged" classes of the Old Regime. Finally, in political and ideological terms, they represent the accession of a bourgeois authority and the triumph of the "Enlightenment" over the values and beliefs of the preceding age. Thus lodged within these three historical "trends," the Revolution is thought of not only as the fundamental rupture between "before" and "after," but also as the decisive consequence and founding element of these trends. And the union of the three levels of interpretation is subsumed under a single concept: the "bourgeois revolution," as if the very heart of the event, its fundamental nature, were social in *kind*. It is by this kind of subtle extension of theory that a permanent and insidious movement in French historiography has been consummated: from a Marxism founded on the concept of the "means of production" to one reduced to a simplified concept of class struggle. Such an interpretation only distorts the explanation of the revolutionaries themselves, by returning to that historical tradition which, from Sieyès to Barnave, has elaborated the concept of class struggle— before Marx, and using precisely the example of the French Revolution. It is through this diminution of Marx—who thus becomes simply a kind of relay station in a return to the original interpretation and so responsible for a tautology and an identification—that Soboul and Mazauric return to their supporting ideology, which, far from being theoretical, is rather primarily emotional and secondarily political. It is nothing less than the exaltation of the egalitarian dialectic and thus of its permanent finality, nestled in the bosom of our present, and hereafter living as a double and inseparable legacy.

In fact, neither the Marxist conceptualization through the "means of production," nor a "class struggle" interpretation, is compatible with the short time-span allotted to the French Revolution: usually 1789–1799, often—with greater justification—1789–1794.

If one insists on the substitution of a "capitalist mode of production" for a "feudal mode of production," clearly the changeover cannot be limited to an event lasting only a few years. Within the limits of this article, I cannot enter into the vast debate on the nature of the Old Regime. But whatever may be the meaning attributed to the concept of a "feudal regime," or "feudalism" itself, this lengthy discussion does support the validity of the idea of a transition: one which combines a socioeconomic character and long chronology. Consequently, it is a very arbitrary act to cut the Revolution off from its "headwaters," and to hold at the level of an objective social process, to the meaning given to it by its participants: that of a radical rupture with the past. True, the conceptual model of a "feudal mode of production" is not incompatible with the idea that, in eighteenth-century France, the conditions for its liquidation were created. But it would then be necessary to show to what extent the hypothesis implicit in the model is confirmed. In other words, to demonstrate by specific example just how feudal rights interfered with the development of capitalism in the countryside, or exactly how the structure of a society of orders and the existence of a nobility restrained the attempt to establish an industrial economy of profit and free enterprise. Such a demonstration is scarcely simple or obvious, since capitalism seeped into the pores of seigniorial society, in the countryside, very largely through the mediation of the nobility active in industrial enterprises. Moreover, far from being fettered, the eighteenth-century French economy was prosperous, and experienced rhythms of growth comparable to those occurring in England. The crisis at the end of the century was simply the result of an unfortunate conjunction of developments in a general trend of prosperity. In short, if the French Revolution is indeed subject to interpretation in terms of a shift from one mode of production to another, the same difficulties await us downstream: it was a lengthy process to set this savage capitalism in motion, whose forces the Revolution supposedly liberated. In the countryside it was curbed, to a greater extent than before 1789, by the post-revolutionary consolidation of small properties. In the city, it does not seem that the Revolution insured it a rapid development after having, evidently, either provoked or accelerated the economic crisis of the last years of the eighteenth century. And if it is true that, at the level of ideas and social mechanisms, 1789 advanced a certain number of judicial principles which insured the promotion of the talented and a market type of economy, the vast military escapade of the French peasantry through Europe from 1792 to 1815 hardly appears to have been dictated by a bourgeois calculation of economic rationality. If one insists on a conceptualization in terms of the "means of production," then he must take as his object of study a period infinitely broader than the years of the French Revolution; if not, then the theoretical hypothesis bears little relation to the data of history.

Such is the reason, no doubt, that the Marxist scheme is so easily reduced to the concept of the "bourgeois revolution," to a socio-political analysis which sees the power of the bourgeoisie replacing, through the Revolution, that of the nobility, and bourgeois society succeeding a society of orders. But here again the Marxist framework has its limits. R. Robin, who may be commended for taking Marxism seriously, has recently suggested that we recognize the social group heretofore dubbed the "bourgeoisie" as a body intimately bound to the structure of the Old Regime, and as "basically landed, official and nonnoble." As a result, the term "bourgeoisie" ought to be restricted to its narrow Marxist meaning: that class which received its income through the *direct* exploitation of a wage-earning work force. From a Marxist viewpoint it is a useful classification. But the historical problem remains: on the one hand, the Revolution was created and directed, for the most part at least, precisely by the bourgeoisie of the Old Regime; on the other hand, if one analyzes the revolutionary process at the level of its objective results rather than of its participants, it becomes obvious that the character of the bourgeoisie under the Empire was not fundamentally different from that prior to 1789: trade, the land, and service to the state (though officeholding had been replaced by the army). Again, the conceptual model gains in rigor what it has lost in operative value for so short a time period.

But at least the definitions of Robin have the merit of being logically consistent; in posing problems which cannot be resolved they simply reveal the blind alleys implicit in a strictly structural analysis of an event such as the French Revolution, understood in its narrow chronological sense. With Mazauric, who clings all the more to an ontology whose elements he fails to define, we tumble into the teleology of Saint Thomas Aquinas: "The Revolution is nothing but the ultimate expression of the crisis of the structure of the Old Regime in its entirety, and its resolution." Thus, at all costs, he must maintain that concept which is both passively and actively intertwined in this resolution, the cause and meaning of the event: the bourgeois revolution. And he insists that it is an indivisible whole, in spite of the chaotic appearance of the period 1789–1794, because this "ascendant period" was marked by a growing "radicalization" of the phenomenon and a concurrently growing intervention of the masses.

Here then the supernatural solution: not just a social class, since "bourgeois revolution" does not mean a revolutionary bourgeoisie. Not just the confused unfolding of a crisis which reveals the contradictions of all orders of civil society, but a process inseparably both subjective and objective: an actor and a meaning, a role and a message—united and reconciled against the winds and tides, for they are, in reality, the shape of the future of which they are the chosen heralds. In this sense of always proceeding backwards from results to causes, Mazauric copies the theatre, since he at least retains from Marx an elementary suspicion: the lives of men are never what they believe them to be. Expelled from the individual minds, thought takes refuge in the collective consciousness, but the suspicion rejoins it there: the bourgeoisie pursue objectives which are not necessarily those which it imagines. However, this wholesome suspicion grinds to a halt before this forger of "concepts," who alone remains untouched by ideology. By what right does he see himself as the bearer of *the* Explanation? Quite simply, in the light of the outcome of history he "elaborates" the concept of the bourgeois revolution: the bourgeoisie "won" the Revolution, therefore it must have been their work from the very beginning. And the reader must content himself with this guarantee.

In truth, the reader is not permitted to question the providential, infinite elasticity of this concept. Like the Cartesian God who, discovering existence in the number of his attributes cannot by this very act fail to exist, the Mazaurician bourgeoisie is, from the moment of its birth, a superbly endowed essence. Literally everything dwells there, at least "potentially." Popular support and a peasant alliance are already included, so that in accepting them, the bourgeoisie is only developing according to its "nature," and has never been so much in harmony with itself. But one must pay for this shameful Spinozism with a history frozen solid by logic; we can well understand the advantages which this concept provides to the cautious debater: at one stroke he can wipe out the profusion of chance collisions, the ceaseless improvisations of the Revolution. Included and absorbed from the very beginning in the totality of the essence —and like the counter-revolution and the war, both absorbed in the Revolution—these dangling ends are treated as minor elements in a single grand scheme. Everlastingly they spiral back into the seamless unity of the concept. The "bourgeois revolution" is a metaphysical monster which spawns a succession of tentacles with which it strangles historical reality, in order to make it, for time everlasting, the basis of an established order and an Annunciation.

Actually, the concept of a "bourgeois revolution" is useful to the historian—for, personally, I believe that it is—only if its employment is strictly controlled and limited. At the simplest level, analysis of the "bourgeois revolution" implies studying not only the revolutionary participation of various bourgeois groups, their projects and activities, but also their reactions to such a generalized social disruption. In line with this view, it seems probable, as Cobban has never ceased to emphasize, that those bourgeois groups most involved in the Revolution were, generally, not closely tied to the capitalist mode of production. Furthermore, from 1789 on there were several revolutions within the Revolution and notably right at the beginning just after the drafting of the *Cahiers de doleances,* a peasant revolution which was largely independent of the bourgeois plans. To me, the outstanding merit of G. Lefebvre, and probably one of his capital contributions to revolutionary history, was his initial demonstration of that fact. Since then a number of works of great importance, such as those of P. Bois and C. Tilly, have enlarged upon this theme—following a somewhat different approach—and by analyzing town-country relationships. Even if their conclusions are different and, on certain points, contradictory, they are on common ground in their enhancement of the significance of the broad political autonomy of the peasant world. The nexus of that world was a profound distrust of townsmen, whether they were seigniors, former seigniors, old bourgeois or new bourgeois. As we have seen, according to P. Bois the antiseigniorial grievances of 1789 intersect and, to a certain extent, prefigure the antibourgeois distrust of 1790–1791, as well as the subsequent antirepublican royalist uprising. Thus, the peasants of Haut-Maine did not *become* hostile to the bourgeois revolution because they had been deceived because so little had been done for them—which is how Mazauric, securely locked into his scheme of things, imagines it. Simply put, they were, if not actually hostile, at least indifferent, and distrustful of the townsmen after 1789. And it is precisely the same frustration which was felt against seigniorial rights and against the rural capitalism symbolized by the bourgeois, the townsman. If the bourgeois revolution laid the foundation for a network of capitalist social relationships, the peasant revolution worked for its own set of goals. And the familiar image of "antifeudal" agreement between the two, masks a very different set of images of desirable changes, whether at the conscious level or at that of an objective process.

There is a widely held, though false, idea that revolutions are necessarily born of a conscious desire on the part of certain social classes or groups to hasten a social change which is evolving too slowly to suit their taste. But revolution can also spring from the resistance of a section of society—one directly involved in the overthrow of the traditional order—to a change considered to be too rapid. The revolutionary front is not formed like the neat battle lines depicted in old military handbooks where on one side you have all the classes spurring on the "movement," seeking and proclaiming a common view of the future; and on the other, all those resisting quickly lining up behind a common image of the past. On the contrary: by its very nature a revolution fluctuates, being subject to political circumstances which evolve very quickly. And it is above all a heterogeneous movement made up of factions whose objectives may be divergent, and even contradictory.

When the French Revolution burst onto the scene the kingdom of France was hardly characterized by an absence of change—quite the contrary. For over half a century it had had to weather a series of extremely rapid economic and social changes to which the state had found it difficult to adjust. In fact, nothing is more difficult, nor indeed more dangerous, for an absolutist system than to modify certain of its fundamental elements, and, even more difficult, to liberalize itself. And the same is true for social classes. Not only for the nobility, but for the more populous classes as well, which are particularly vulnerable in a rupture of the traditional equilibrium, and who are politically less conscious of the stakes and aims of the struggle for power. So much so that things are far from being as simple as Mazauric imagines them when he describes on each side of the royal road of Revolution occupied by the bourgeois-with-popular-support, the two groups left to shift for themselves in the great adventure, excluded from the national union. These two groups are the *mouvement sectionnaire* of Paris on the left, the peasant *Vendée* on the right. Actually, while the revolutionary torrent, from 1789 to 1794, may have been diked and channeled by the groups which succeeded to power—after having perhaps surrendered at first—it had never really been controlled, simply because it included contradictory interests and visions. This undoubtedly explains the fundamental, compensating role of a powerfully integrative ideology such as Jacobinism. But should the historian take it at its face value?

III OTHER CRITICS OF ORTHODOXY AND SOME RESPONDENTS

Alfred Cobban

THE SOCIAL INTERPRETATION OF THE FRENCH REVOLUTION

Alfred Cobban (1901–1968) was certainly the foremost English historian of eighteenth-century France and especially its political ideology, but it was only in his later years that Professor Cobban turned his attention specifically to the French Revolution and particularly to its social aspects. Longtime professor of French history at the University of London, editor of History *from 1957 to 1967, and a frequent visitor at American universities, he is clearly far better-known in the English-speaking world than in France. The Wiles Lectures of 1961–1962, from which the following excerpt is taken, further elaborated a theme he had presented originally in 1955—that the view of the French Revolution as primarily a social and economic revolution was an erroneous one. As he saw it the people who emerged with money, status and property at the end of the revolutionary turmoil were, for the most part, those who had possessed it in 1789. In one of his final essays Professor Cobban seemed to be pleading for a return to an emphasis on political history, but a highly sophisticated political history which would be informed by the most sophisticated social and economic data available, though not conceived as necessarily primarily determined by that data.*

History and Sociology

The established theory of the French Revolution, put forward in a broad sense at the time by the actors in the revolutionary drama, expanded into a general historical theory by the historians of the French Restoration, and taken for granted in most of the work that has since been done on the history of the Revolution, is put in clear and concise language by one of the greatest of French historians of this century. "The Revolution," writes Georges Lefebvre, "is only the crown of a long economic and social evolution which has made the bourgeoisie the mistress of the world." M. Albert Soboul, in an excellent précis of the history of the Revolution, repeats Lefebvre's formula in almost the same words. He makes it more explicit, however, when he adds that though this idea was first proclaimed clearly by the bourgeois historians of the Restoration, they failed to see the

Reprinted with permission of the Cambridge University Press and Mrs. Cobban from *The Social Interpretation of the French Revolution* (Cambridge, 1964), pp. 8–24, 36–67.

essential fact. This was "that the Revolution is explained in the last analysis by a contradiction between the relations of production and the character of the productive forces." With such views we seem to be at the opposite extreme from that represented by those historians who tried, if unavailingly, to take the meaning out of history. Lefebvre and M. Soboul seem to be putting almost too much meaning back into it, when they reduce the greatest happening in modern history to the deterministic operation of an historical law.

Being an historical law, though it was first detected by historians of the French Revolution, it had to be capable of application to the interpretation of other revolutions. Thus, the Russian historian, Porchnev, among others, has seen the troubles in seventeenth-century France in terms of a feudal society under attack from the people; while the English civil war also has been widely interpreted as a bourgeois revolt against feudalism. After a period when such views had the authority of almost unchallengeable orthodoxy, they have come recently under serious criticism as an attempt to force historical evidence within the strait-jacket of a preconceived theory. "Porchnev," writes Professor Mousnier, "was determined at all costs to bring correct facts, justly observed and appreciated relationships, within the limits of a Marxist theory that the material itself exploded." In the historiography of the English civil war the explosion has already occurred, and it has blown up the supposed bourgeois revolution, leaving aristocracy and gentry, royal officials, lawyers, merchants, people, rising and falling classes, feudal and bourgeois society, landowners and peasants, scattered in fragments about monographs and textbooks.

Some eight or nine years ago I suggested that the same process of disintegration was likely to take place in the history of the French Revolution, and that the interpretation of the Revolution in terms of the overthrow of feudalism by the bourgeoisie, always rather meaningless, was becoming increasingly incompatible with the results of modern research. This suggestion, although it was based in part on the results of Lefebvre's own researches, met with his criticism. The suggestion that the theory of the Revolution as the overthrow of feudalism by the bourgeoisie was a myth, he took to be equivalent to a denial of the whole actuality of the Revolution. At the same time, he agreed that, in a different and Sorelian sense, it was indeed a myth. "The convocation of the *États généraux*," he wrote, "was a 'bonne nouvelle': it proclaimed the birth of a new society in conformity with justice, in which life would be better." A Dutch historian has subsequently observed, not I feel unjustly, that in this defense of the traditional view of the Revolution the great French historian went some way towards justifying a different criticism, that of Professor Talmon, by identifying the Revolution with the kind of political Messianism for which Talmon condemned it.

Indeed, it is difficult to avoid the conclusion that the orthodox theory of the Revolution has now assumed some of the characteristics of a religious belief. M. Guérin gave his reply to the critics of his *Bourgeois et "bras-nus"* the title *"Bataille autour de notre mère,"* invoking with filial devotion "the great Revolution, mother of the revolutions of the present and the future." The East German historian, W. Markov, sketching the last days of the left-wing agitator, Roux, could say, "Jacques Roux had already found, while he was writing these lines, at Bicêtre, *le terme de sa passion.*" And so on. This tendency of the Marxist theory of the Revolution to culminate in a sort of semireligious exaltation is far from being an accident. Marxism is a philosophy of history: its strength is that, like all philosophies of history, it embodies a view of the nature and ends of human existence. In other words, it is a sort of secular religion.

However, the Marxist theory of the Revolution would not have had the same general appeal if it had not also been something else. If one source of the strength of Marxism is the satisfaction it can give to the human desire for a purpose to justify and provide an end for the life of the human animal, another is its appearance of providing a scientific statement of the laws of social development. As well as a philosophy of history, it offers a theory of sociology. Particularly in the latter capacity it evidently appealed to Georges Lefebvre, who seems to have come to believe, in his later years, that Marxism could provide both a theoretical basis for his researches and a conclusion he could draw from them.

The relations of history and social theory need not be discussed, however, simply in terms of Marxism, though this is the sociological theory that has so far had the greatest influence on historical studies. There is now a strong, and possibly a growing tendency, for non-Marxist historians also to look for explanations to what in a general sense may be called sociology. This tendency has recently been put in forceful language by Dr. E. H. Carr. "The more sociological history becomes, and the more historical sociology becomes," he writes, "the better for both." The present trend towards faith in the powers of sociology is perhaps the nemesis of a period when it was believed that history could be written in the form of a simple collection of unique events related to one another only by successiveness in time. On the other hand, it may be that the absence of sociological theory is the explanation of what now seems inadequate, or superficial, in what is sometimes called naive history. The possible contribution of sociology, even apart from Marxist sociology, to historical study needs to be considered seriously.

In the first place, however, there is the difficulty that any general theory of sociology must also be, like Marxism, a philosophy of history. Marxism, it has been said, is not a theory of classes but a theory of the evolution of classes, just as Toynbee has given us a theory of the history of civilizations, not a theory of civilization. Now the inherent assumption in any philosophy of history is that the evolution of humanity is a single process; but if this is allowed, then there cannot be a scientific law about it, because as Professor Popper has pointed out, a scientific law cannot be deduced from a single example. Even if it could be, the relation between history and any general theory of sociology is one which essentially prohibits scientific verification. The sociological historian uses his theory as the criterion for the selection of the relevant historical facts, and then on the basis of those selected facts he illustrates and confirms the theory by which they have been selected. Part of the fascination of general sociological theories is that success is built in. There is also another way in which sociological laws are self-confirming: by taking one factor in history as basic, all the others can be reduced to conditions in which it operates. Thus if different responses occur in economically identical circumstances, the primacy of the economic factor is maintained by making the factors which produce the aberration into conditions, on which the economic factor acts as a prime cause. Again, a general system of sociology differs in one fundamental respect from every recognized science. The natural sciences depend on the possibility of abstracting and isolating their data from the total world of experience; sociology professes to apply to society as a whole, that is, to a universe, incapable of isolation, from which nothing can be excluded.

In practice, general social laws turn out to be one of three things.

If they are not dogmatic assertions about the course of history, they are either platitudes, or else, to be made to fit the facts, they have to be subjected to more and more qualifications until in the end they are applicable only to a single case. General sociology is thus no answer to the need for some theoretical element, other than inherited stereotypes, in our history.

The Problems of Social History

It might seem that we are now thrown back on what may be called naive history—on the belief that the facts will speak for themselves, and presumably even select themselves, that all historical events are unique, and that generalization is the crime against history. Of course, this belief is nonsense. All coherent thought requires general ideas: classificatory terms are necessary for rational discourse. A unique event could only be a miracle. Historical research begins with the discovery of "facts" it is true, but, to be understood, these require to be given some meaning, just as do the facts that impinge on us, or that we observe, in everyday life. The task of reacting to common experience provides us with a set of rough concepts for dealing with these, and naive history gets little farther.

A more sophisticated kind of history calls for a more sophisticated analysis. This is not to say that it needs a general theory, but it does need a language. In some respects it already has this. Thus, most of the history that has been written is political history, and since a long series of political scientists, from the time of Aristotle to the present day, have analyzed political structures and events, there is no lack of a coherent and comprehensible political vocabulary, though even this requires to be continually redefined and brought into relation with new usages and changing political conditions. The language of economics was a much later invention. It did not exist when Hobbes, wanting to describe what we would call consumption and production, had to entitle his chapter "Of the Nutrition and Procreation of a Commonwealth." Now, however, economic history has a precise and carefully analyzed set of terms, and this I suggest, is one reason for the high standard it has achieved.

With these considerations we approach the crux of this discussion and begin to envisage the possibility of stating in more specific terms the problem of the relation of sociology and history. In the first place, the desire for a general sociological theory, applicable to the whole course of human existence, must, I have suggested, be dismissed as incompatible with critical history. What is needed, at least in the first place, is a set of concepts. It may be asked why the political and economic terms which we already have are not sufficient for this purpose. The answer is that there is now a desire for something more than political or economic history. If we are still far from clear what is meant by social history, this may not be unconnected with the fact that we still lack not only a workable vocabulary, but even the principles on which to build one. So far the tendency has been to rely on the terms provided by general sociological theory. This has led to an increasing tension between the theoretical pattern assumed in the language and the actual evidence discovered by historical research: alternatively, history written under the influence of sociological theory becomes a work of supererogation, since the theory has predetermined what the history will be. On the other hand, naive, untheoretical history is reduced to attempting to employ for historical purposes the common language of the present day, regardless of fundamental changes in ideas and institutions: this is equally unsatisfactory.

If there is a way of escape from this dilemma it must be by abandoning both positions and trying to find some other solution. Here, I think, it is relevant to suggest that the historian does not normally solve his problems by abstract argument but does so in the process of dealing with actual difficulties presented by specific periods or subjects. The problem of social history appears, I believe, in one of its most crucial aspects in the history of the French Revolution, and a great deal, perhaps most, of the history of the French Revolution that is being written, or has been written for some time past, may be called social history in one sense or another. It therefore provides a valuable field for examining the problems of writing social history. One of the chief of these, the difficulty of terminology, can be illustrated by a brief essay in semantics, which may also serve as an explanation why the ordinary terms of contemporary society cannot provide the historian's social vocabulary.

Since society changes, while words remain, the relevance of terms of social description can alter radically. Thus, in eighteenth-century France a *manufacturier* was one who manufactured products with his hands, a *laboureur* was a fairly substantial peasant proprietor, and a *fermier* primarily anyone who paid a rent for property or position. None of these terms would convey the same meaning today. Not only at different times, but also in different countries the same word can have very different meanings, as for example the French *fermier* and the English farmer. Again, the French *paysan* is one who lives in and earns his living out of the country as opposed to the town, whatever his economic status; he is not necessarily, as in the English idea of the peasant, one of the poorer cultivators or a small-holder. A more important, indeed a major, source of confusion, is the fact that the social structures of two countries such as England and France have been for centuries so different that the terms employed in one, although often carried over to the other, are usually inapplicable. The English aristocracy did not correspond to the French noblesse, nor the English peer to the French *pair*. The bourgeoisie was not the same as the middle class. The French *officier* had no English equivalent, and the French *ordre* or estate no real parallel in England. The English class structure in the eighteenth century had more differences from than similarities with the social pattern of France; just as the European idea of class is now something of an alien term in present-day American social vocabulary.

The idea of class introduces another difficulty: there is a strong subjective element in all social descriptions. Who is, and who is not, middle-class today? Not everyone in eighteenth-century France who is down on the lists as a lawyer—*avocat*—had anything in practice to do with the law. During the Revolution many a well-to-do employer appeared on official lists as a worker—*ouvrier,* and a landowner as a *cultivateur.* On the other hand, the secret agent, Noël Prigent, who described himself to the English as *négociant,* was said by his contemptuous fellow-Malouins to have earned his living selling fruit in the streets of St. Malo. A *négociant* usually meant someone engaged in substantial commerce, whereas *marchand* was the most indeterminate of descriptions. The small country towns or villages of France produced innumerable *marchands,* who represented merely the higher level of the rural artisanate.

The same word could have a variety of meanings at the same time. As I have said, the eighteenth-century *fermier* was one who paid rent. Excluding the use of the term in the realm of finance, as the *fermiers généraux,* and confining ourselves to its use in the countryside, a *fermier* might be a steward or agent, who paid a fixed sum for the right of collecting rents or dues and made what he could out of them, or he might be one of the tenant farmers who rented land. Since the latter often worked fairly large farms, they could be equated with the better-off peasant proprietor—the *laboureur,* who might himself sometimes be a tenant, or *fermier,* for part of the land he cultivated. Hence, when a man is described as a *fermier* or a *laboureur,* it really tells us nothing except that he has an area of land above a certain size to cultivate. He might also be described as a *paysan,* which would tell us even less.

A word such as *métayer,* like the large social group which it described, has no English equivalent. This does not mean that it presents no problems. Indeed, I suspect that it reveals yet another source of confusion—that the same term may have very different meanings at the same time in different parts of the same country. The generally accepted picture of the *métayer,* as we find him, for example, in Arthur Young, who was an acute and reliable observer, is of a poverty-stricken tenant of a small-holding, with a short three-, six- or nine-year lease, hiring the equipment and stock as well as the land, and paying for it partly, if not wholly, in kind. Western France in particular, according to Sée and Lefebvre, was dominated by this type of land tenure. A more recent historian has suggested that, at least in one district, this whole picture is based on a misunderstanding of the word *métairie.* In the Maine, and in the West generally, says M. Paul Bois, it refers not to the system of letting but to the size of the holding. In Maine and Anjou there were two main types of tenure, the *métairie* and the *bordage* (or *closerie*). The former, unexpectedly, proves to be the larger farm, sometimes of even 50 hectares, and the *métayer* is therefore equivalent to a *laboureur* or *fermier,* while the *bordage* was a small-holding of 3 to 10 hectares, cultivated by hand and not by the plow, except when one could be borrowed or hired.

Many more examples of the difficulties of terminology might be given, but these should be enough to illustrate the scope of the problem. If this has generally not been adequately appreciated, it is, I believe, partly because the complexity of French society of the *ancien régime,* which is revealed by a detailed social analysis, has been concealed by the use of broad omnibus terms, such as bourgeois, *paysan,* noblesse. By and large, the legal division into orders—clergy, noblesse and third estate—has in the past provided the pattern for social historians, although in practice this legal classification had long before 1789 ceased to bear any close relation to social realities. To appreciate a man's real position in French society it would have been necessary to know, as well as his legal status, also his actual economic functions, the sources and extent of his wealth, his mode of life, his profession or office, his family, and during the Revolution even his political affiliations. His rank on one scale might be very different from that on another. To add a final complication. the man who fell only into a single category was by no means the rule, and might even have been the exception. The peasant proprietor could also be a tenant farmer for part of his land, a merchant when he bought and sold produce, or a wage-earner when he worked on someone else's land. A lawyer might also be an estate manager and a merchant; he might also be a landowner, for most persons of any social standing probably owned at least some land in town or country. In rural areas the smallholders and the rural artisanate might be quite distinct or might overlap. A noble could be a local official or a judge, an army officer, an ecclesiastic, a great landed proprietor or a working smallholder.

Amid the shifting sands of an uncertain and uncritical social terminology, the historian of eighteenth-century France has too often been content with broad generalizations possessing even at the time only a very rough relation to social realities, and now distorted by all the overtones of nineteenth-century sociological thought and present-day social conditions. The first necessity for writing the social history of the Revolution is therefore to abandon the existing terminology. This is far from being a mere negative requirement. It is indeed a revolutionary step, for this terminology, with all its defects, embodies, as will be seen, a specific theory of the Revolution, and to abandon the language is to abandon the theory.

Adequately to deal with the social history of the Revolution, an empirical examination of social facts is needed, such as a contemporary sociologist would make of his own society. An estimate of social position must not be based on a single criterion, legal, political or economic, as it often has been in the past, but on a plurality of tests—actual wealth and its nature, sources of income, social status and prestige, origin and direction of social movement of the individual and his family, legal order, political orientation, contem-

porary esteem, economic function, personal aspirations and grievances, and so on.

Not only the social classification but also the nature and direction
of social movement in history needs to be considered afresh. The
whole conception of rising and falling classes, which is closely involved with the idea of revolution, is in need of revision. The movement of individuals from one class to another, if on a sufficiently
large scale, has been equated with the rise or fall of a class. This is
clearly unsound. However many sons of peasants, say, move into the
town and become lawyers or merchants, this cannot be called the
rise of the peasantry. A class has been compared to a hotel, which
remains the same though a continually changing clientele passes
through it. A class rises, properly speaking, when it acquires political
power and increased economic well-being and yet remains the same
class. Put in this way, the "rise of the bourgeoisie" in the French
Revolution ceases to be a platitude and becomes a problem.

The essential thing is that we shall cease to take theories for facts.
The distinguished French historian, M. Albert Soboul, almost in the
same breath tells us that the triumph of the bourgeoisie is the essential fact of the Revolution, and that we have no history of the bourgeoisie during the Revolution. In other words, what he calls the
essential fact is no more than an act of faith. We will have to choose
whether we will believe M. Soboul when, as a theorist, he tells us
that he knows for certain what the Revolution was, or when, as an
historian, he admits that only after many local and regional social
studies have been made will works of synthesis on the different
classes and social categories be possible. Of course, even while
assuming that he knew in advance essentially what will be discovered, it was a step forward to recognize that the research which
should demonstrate it has not yet been done. I believe that we can go
a little farther than this, and that quite a lot in fact has been done.
If it has only very partially been used by historians, this is because
much of it does not fit conveniently into the accepted theory. In this
study, therefore, I do not propose to begin with any kind of theoretical discussion. The weakness of much social thought, it seems
to me, is that it is so largely concerned with packing its bag (or even
with working out a general theory about the way in which a bag
should be packed) for a journey which is never taken. I shall try to
avoid this danger by treating the problem of the social interpretation

of the French Revolution as a series of specific historical problems, and ask such questions as: what are the facts of the so-called bourgeois revolution, and in particular who were the bourgeois? What was the feudalism which they are supposed to have overthrown? How was the bourgeois revolution related to the revolt of the peasantry? This raises the problem of the relationship of town and country. Again, what part was played in the revolutionary situation by the lower social elements? This broadly raises the problem of the relation of rich and poor. Above all, my aim will be to try to get away from the traditional sociological clichés and to break down the large omnibus classes which are calculated to accept practically any passenger who can pay a minimum set fare, regardless of where he gets on or gets off or what may be his real station in life, and to substitute for them social distinctions and classifications based on historical actualities.

The Attack on Seigniorial Rights

Contemporary references can be found in the eighteenth century for the view that seigniorial rights and dues were largely obsolete in practice. In 1735 d'Argenson wrote, "There only remains the shadow of the *seigneurie,*" and rather later Letrône, "There is nothing real in feudalism except the expenses, that is to say there is no profit except for the agents and the compilers of *terriers.*" But they cancel this out themselves when Letrône goes on to call it "a social evil," and d'Argenson adds, "all the same it is annoying and harmful." Seigniorial rights certainly survived, even if not as universally as has sometimes been supposed, and they were an object of widespread attack; but is this attack correctly described as the struggle of the bourgeois against feudalism? I have already suggested that the equation of the system of seigniorial rights with feudalism is historically unjustifiable, but this can be disregarded for the moment, as a matter of terminology, though it is rather more than that: M. Méthivier, following other French historians, has rightly protested against the confusion of feudal and seigniorial. There is a problem involved, however, which is a matter of historical fact. Is the identification of the bourgeois as the social force responsible for the attack on seigniorial rights a valid one?

This is not a new doubt. Georges Lefebvre pointed out that, up to

14 July 1789, the bourgeois had neither the desire nor the intention to attack the seigniorial rights, and that they had no idea of calling on the peasants to revolt, or of abolishing seigniorial rights without compensation. It was observed long ago that the abolition of seigniorial rights was not among the articles of which the *bailliage cahiers* demanded immediate adoption, or, if they did, only in districts where towns were rare, or had little preponderance, as in Brittany. There is no lack of evidence to support this view. Only a few examples need be given. The *cahier* of Reims ignores the whole subject, as does that of Rouen. The peasants of Neubourg in Normandy complain of the *taille* but not of the seigniorial régime. Normandy may have been an exceptional area, in which seigniorial rights were of only slight importance. Another example is provided by the *bailliage* of Mirecourt in Lorraine. Here the original *cahier* of the town makes no mention of seigniorial rights; on the other hand, the rural *cahiers* are full of protests and demands for their suppression, sometimes with, and sometimes without, compensation. In the final *cahier*, drawn up for the whole *bailliage*, it was evidently impossible to ignore the subject entirely, but the townsmen, whose influence was dominant in the *bailliage cahier*, shuffled out of what seems to have been a difficulty for them by saying that they thought the *États généraux* would probably not be interested in the matter. Where the *cahiers* of the *bailliages* do recognize the need for something to be done about seigniorial dues, they most often moderate the demand by putting the abolition in terms of *rachat*—abolition only in return for a purchase price. As the *cahier* of Autun declared, "In abolishing these servitudes, the *seigneurs* should not be victimized."

A further indication of the attitude of the towns is to be found in the fact that there was one seigniorial right, if it can be called such, which they commonly opposed. But this was franc-fief, and it was a payment not to the *seigneur* but to the crown, due after land that was part of a fief passed from noble into nonnoble possession. The motive for demanding its abolition was frankly expressed by the *tiers état* of Rouen, which said that franc-fief harmed the sale of property. The *cahiers* of Walloon Flanders complained that by hindering *roturiers* from buying fiefs it lowered their value; the nobles of the *bailliage* of Lille called for its abolition on property under 100,000 livres in value.

Apart from franc-fief, the *cahiers* of the towns are conspicuously reluctant to suggest that anything should be done about seigniorial dues. Nevertheless it is true that the National Assembly did take the decisive step towards their abolition. This must be accounted for somehow. There is no difficulty in doing so. It is accepted by practically all recent historians of the Revolution that what forced the National Assembly into the decisions of the night of the fourth of August was the widespread and alarming peasant revolt of the spring and early summer of 1789. The view once held that the fourth of August represented a spontaneous outburst of idealism on the part of an assembly of nobles, clergy and bourgeois, anxious to relieve an oppressed peasantry from its burdens, has not survived a closer examination of what actually happened. A number of the more liberal, but also more realistic, members of the Assembly had come to the conclusion, almost certainly a correct one, that unless concessions were made to the peasantry the whole of rural France would remain in a state of endemic rebellion. The generous gestures of 4 August were contrived in advance, and planned for a night session in the hope that many who might have resisted them would be absent. True, a wave of emotion swept the members present and many more sacrifices than had probably been intended were spontaneously announced, but there were second thoughts during the following seven days, from 4 to 11 August, when the principles proclaimed in the enthusiasm of the first night were given specific form. It was in these discussions, and the consequent legislation, that the intention of abolishing feudalism was particularly emphasized; but it was for the purpose not of extending but of limiting the scope of the changes.

The Assembly based its final legislation on the distinction between feudal and nonfeudal property. In fact this was almost an impossible distinction to make. The confusion of the two had been facilitated by legal fictions. For example, when a *seigneur* in the Nord sold the right of *terrage* (a payment, or *cens,* on the harvest, but attached to the land and not the type of product), without specifying that he was also alienating the *directe,* or seigniorial title, in the hands of the new proprietor it was held to become a simple land rent.

Another illustration of the difficulty of distinguishing between feudal privilege and property rights is provided by the case of seigniorial pews in churches. These would seem as clear a case of mere privilege as one could hope to find; but petitions to the Feudal Committee show that the matter was not always so simple. Thus the directory of the *département* of Finistère explains that in 1741 the church of Saint-Louis at Brest was presented with four marble columns. In 1751 the sons of the donor paid for the columns to be carved, on condition that a pew should remain in their family in perpetuity. The confiscation of this pew, says the directory, is a violation of the right of property. Either it should be restored, or at least the 2,500 livres paid for carving the columns should be given back, since the columns themselves cannot be.

In August 1791 a citizen of Caussade in Lot explains that he formerly possessed the right to a pew in the church, which he had sold in 1776. The purchaser, who had now been summoned to give it up, was demanding a return of the 400 livres purchase price. The petitioner asks for an opinion on this demand. From Carcassonne came the suggestion, in April 1790, that pew rights should be abolished where they were based solely on seigniorial right, but preserved for those who had obtained them by founding chapels, or making considerable repairs or improvements in the church fabric, so long as their contributions constituted a capital sum sufficient to furnish an income equal to the annual rent of a pew.

The attempt to draw a distinction between payments and services which were feudal and those which were nonfeudal and so susceptible of being adjudged strictly as property rights was unrealistic at a time when for centuries they had been subject to sale and purchase. It was used by the Assembly in an attempt to save what could be saved from the wreck of seigniorial fortunes, and a good deal would have been saved if the Assembly had been able to achieve its aim. The Feudal Commission, given the task of putting the legislation of 4–11 August into practice, took the view that was favorable to the owner of seigniorial rights whenever possible. Thus it decided that *mainmorte réelle* could be considered as a payment by the freed serf in return for the concession of land to him, and hence as a contractual property right and not a feudal payment. It adopted the interpretation of *triage* most favorable to the *seigneur*. The Committee, replying to a question on 22 September 1791, ruled that a *ci-devant seigneur* was to be maintained in his rights unless and until it was clearly proved that their possession did not derive from an original grant of land.

The eminent feudal lawyer Merlin de Douai, reporting to the Assembly on behalf of the Committee on 8 February 1790, practically admitted that its aim was to consolidate the former dues under a new name. "In destroying the feudal regime," he told the Assembly, "you did not mean to despoil the legitimate proprietors of fiefs of their possessions, but you changed the nature of these properties. Freed henceforth from the laws of feudalism, they remain subject to those of landed estate; in a word, they have ceased to be fiefs and have become true freeholds (*alleux*). . . . There are no more fiefs; hence all the actual dues (*droits utiles*) with which the formerly feudal property is burdened should no longer be considered as anything but purely property rights."

The aims of the National Assembly, and of its Feudal Committee, are hardly in doubt. How far they were able to achieve them is another matter. What actually happened to the feudal dues in the first years of the Revolution is still in dispute. Did the peasants stop paying their dues at once, whether they had been legally pronounced feudal or not? For those which had been decreed purchasable was compensation paid, and if so for how long? These are questions to which we do not know the answer. Probably there is no answer, or rather there are too many, varying from district to district all over France. These temporary doubts and hesitations, reluctances and oppositions, do not affect the basic fact that in one way or another, quickly or slowly, legally or by usurpation, the seigniorial dues and rights disappeared.

The question that interests us here is not what happened, which by and large is not in dispute, but why it happened in the way in which it did. That the peasantry, once they envisaged the possibility, should have fought for the abolition of seigniorial dues in every way in which they could, is easily to be understood. But if the "abolition of feudalism by the bourgeoisie" means anything, as has been said above, it can only mean the abolition of seigniorial dues; and whatever we understand by the bourgeoisie—a point to which I must revert later—it must include the men who drew up the *cahiers* in the towns and the members of the *tiers état* in the National Assembly. The actual historical fact which needs to be explained, therefore, is not the supposed "abolition of feudalism by the bourgeoisie," but on the contrary their opposition to its abolition—for there can be no doubt of their opposition to the abolition of the system of seigniorial dues and rights which represented what, if anything, was left of feudalism in 1789.

Was this reform—even if the leaders of the *tiers état* in the towns and the National Assembly accepted it under pressure—one which was contrary to their material interests? If this were so it would explain their attitude in 1789. This point deserves investigation. It has been suggested that by 1789 seigniorial rights had often passed out of the hands of nobles into those of *roturiers*. The conquests of the land by nonnobles had already begun in the Middle Ages, and this included the acquisition of fiefs. The process has been described as the decapitation of the commercial classes by the desire to own land. It was facilitated by the inherent tendency of the nobles to accumulate debts and so to be forced to sell their lands of *seigneuries*. By the eighteenth century, says Georges Lefebvre, in Walloon Flanders seigniorial rights were as active a market as land. Of course, some of the purchasers themselves became nobles in their turn; but by 1789 the *tiers état* included many owners of seigniorial rights. Nonnoble *seigneurs* are noted in Guyenne, around Bordeaux, Rouen, Reims, Valenciennes, and doubtless far more examples could be collected.

A single case which is of interest in itself is that of the *seigneurie* of Villeneuve-de-Rivière in the *généralité* of Auch. Jean d'Estrémé, of the same village, bought the *seigneurie* in 1761. He was of peasant origin, but the family had acquired wealth in the wool trade and the trade of mules with Spain, and he is described as *négociant*. His history also illustrates another aspect of the situation. D'Estrémé seems to have been a regular village tyrant, greedy to gain all he could from his seigniorial rights, as well as to assert his rank as "maître et seigneur." He engaged in long lawsuits with the community over the forge and the mill, and took the cases right up to the Conseil du Roi, where the peasant opposition finally won, in 1787, on the eve of a greater victory.

Again, the commune of La Capelle-Cabanac, in Lot, protested in January 1790 about a *seigneurie* sold in 1743 to one Jean-Baptiste Bonnamie Duroc, a *roturier,* who hastened to adopt the title of *"messire,"* began lawsuits against the inhabitants to claim his dues, and forced the local consuls to wear hoods in his livery and take the oath to him bare-headed and on their knees. The petitioners add, as not irrelevant to decisions he obtained in his favor, the fact that his son was a *conseiller* in the *parlement* of Toulouse.

A recent historian of the peasantry of Burgundy has described the investment of urban wealth in the country during the eighteenth century as a veritable "capitalist offensive." It destroyed, he says, the old village community and dealt a death blow to the former *seigneurie*. The peasants complained that the good old *seigneurs* (doubtless greatly idealized in retrospect) had sold their lands and their *seigneuries* to bourgeois who were indifferent to the interests of the rural population. It was even complained that the money of the bourgeois was more dangerous to the villagers than the obligations of *mainmorte.* In 1751, the intendant of Dijon, Joly de Fleury, wrote to Paris that where *mainmorte* survived outsiders could not buy up the lands of the villagers, but elsewhere bourgeois from the towns had become proprietors of all the land and reduced the inhabitants to the status of mere day-laborers. Perhaps this was special pleading, but it sounds not implausible; and in this case the great campaign against *mainmorte* need not have been so purely inspired by humanitarian sentiments as we had supposed.

The rise of capitalist enterprise in the countryside drove the owners of *seigneuries* into a search for enhanced profits. There are many indications that the new owners were determined to obtain the maximum return from their investment, and that their exactions were particularly feared by the peasantry. It is customary, says the *cahier* of Albas in Cahors, for *parvenus* to abuse their authority. It is not difficult to believe that this was true, but more to our purpose is the actual ownership of the rights, whether they were abused or not. To what extent, and subject to what local variations, the seigniorial rights had passed into nonnoble possession, we cannot at present say; but that the movement had been on a considerable scale, and that it affected the attitude of the town middle classes to the question of their abolition, cannot reasonably be doubted.

The Russian historian, Porchnev, has described this process, the existence of which he implicitly admits, as the "feudalization" of part of the bourgeoisie. Lefebvre interprets it in the same way, and argues that it caused the bourgeois landed proprietors to identify their interests with those of the feudal *seigneurs*. Alternatively, it has been described as the "embourgeoisement" of the land, and Lefebvre seems to move a long way towards this latter view when he allows that it was partly by way of the seigniorial right that capitalism entered agriculture. The two views are hardly reconcilable, and the latter, which seems the more realistic, calls for closer examination.

To understand the problem presented by seigniorial rights in the eighteenth century, their real nature must be appreciated. It has been pointed out that a seigniorial fortune was made up of a host of petty dues and claims, some in money and some in kind or services, the effective collection of which called for careful management. Many of the nobles, unable to provide this, had tended to let their petty seigniorial rights fall into disuse. *Seigneuries,* it is said, only prospered in the hands of those with other sources of revenue, who could invest their surplus profits and their business experience in a fief. In this respect, at least, it is possible to describe the so-called "feudal reaction" as less a reversion to the past than the application to old relationships of new business techniques.

Another way of coping with this problem was for the *seigneur,* whether he was noble or not, to save himself the worry of management, and at the same time increase his revenue, by letting out the collection of his seigniorial rights to agents or *fermiers.* This resulted in the rise of a large body of intermediaries—officeholders, seigniorial judges, *procureurs,* notaries, lawyers of various kinds—and a lesser world of clerks, collectors, *feudistes* to draw up *terriers,* and so on, all with a material interest in the system of seigniorial dues. Everywhere in Burgundy, it is said, the *fermier,* either as owner or as agent, was getting control of the *seigneuries.* The *fermier* might be a small business man, buying the farm of the dues, or exploiting seigniorial mills and so on for a fixed sum, and taking his profit out of whatever over and above this sum he could raise. Or he might be a well-to-do peasant, often also controlling small artisan enterprises and acting as a middleman for the sale of crops, hides, wool, or any other products of the land. Or he might be a *procureur,* notary or other kind of lawyer. In his *Tableau de Paris,* Mercier describes the notaries as much more financiers than lawyers, "true Proteuses, go-ahead financiers, speculators." He adds, "The profession has become so prosperous that from the highest to the lowest every bourgeois wants to put his son in the office of a notary."

There were widespread complaints of the excesses of the seigniorial agents or collectors. The *feudistes,* or *commissaires à terrier,* especially when they were paid on a commission basis, had an interest in screwing up the seigniorial dues to the highest pitch. They were bitterly attacked in the *cahiers*. By discovering and exploiting rights of escheat, it was said, they were a menace to heirs. D'Aiguillon, in the National Assembly on the night of 4 August, argued that the *seigneurs* allowed, or by exacting excessive payments from their agents even encouraged them, to exploit the system. The *fermiers* were denounced for the rapacity and bad faith which they exhibited as collectors of ordinary rents as well as of seigniorial dues. The *cahiers* of the Autunois say that its farms were worked by peasants who formerly shared the produce or profits equally with the proprietor. Now the collection is let out to *fermiers,* who overcharge the cultivator and leave him only a quarter of the proceeds. Their word is taken for any advances they claim to have made to the peasant during the course of the lease, although, it was alleged, most of the *fermiers* cannot read or keep books.

The author of a treatise on seigniorial rights compares the *fermier* to "a ravaging wolf let loose on the land, who extracts the last sou out of it, crushes the people with burdens, reduces them to beggary, forces the peasants to desert the land, and renders the master who finds himself compelled to tolerate these exactions odious." When in Auvergne one *fermier* was knocked down and nearly killed, and another fired at, the *sous-délégué* excused the inhabitants because of the conduct of the *fermiers*.

The best preserved, and the most universally hated, of the seigniorial rights, were the *banalités* of mill, wine or olive press, and oven. Of these, the right of the banal mill was the most valuable and most widespread. It was the most widely denounced abuse in the *cahiers*. The millers with rights of *banalité* exercised a stranglehold over the bread trade. Bakers complained that if they got their flour elsewhere than at the mill of the *banalité,* they had to pay a fine to the miller, and that at the banal mill they had to pay excessive prices. Another result of the millers' monopoly is implied by the demand that certified royal weights should be placed in each mill. The peasants of a Breton parish complain that they have neither weights nor weighing machines, and that if they demand that their flour shall be weighed, the millers know how to add water to make it up to the proper weight. Another complaint is that the *banalités* are an inexhaustible cause of lawsuits. If no one were restricted to purchasing from the seigniorial mill, says another Breton *cahier* sarcastically, all the millers would become honest men.

The blame for the abuse of banal rights was not confined to the millers, as the story of one *seigneur* reveals. He abandoned his seigniorial oven in 1770 and the villagers had to build their own ovens, which they did. In 1775 the *seigneur's* steward announced that he intended to restore the seigniorial oven, and that any inhabitant who made use of his own oven, instead of the lord's, would have to pay a fine annually. It was sometimes added in the complaints against the millers that they were forced to rely on fraud because of the excessive rents that were exacted by the *seigneurs* or their agents.

The *banalités,* then, were a patent and flagrant abuse, and one which was generally condemned. Yet even here the attitude of the town *cahiers* is hesitant. The *cahier* of Mirecourt, while it asked for their abolition, stipulated that the same millers should continue to have the monopoly of the mills. A miller in the Meuse, after the legislation of 4–11 August had ended the system of *banalités,* demanded compensation, on the ground that he had purchased the right in good faith. If the *banalités* represented feudalism, the *cahiers* of the towns showed little anxiety to be rid of it. But can they be regarded in any real sense as feudal, whatever may have been their origin in remoter centuries? They seem to me to be much better described, in more modern terms, as a commercial racket.

The whole matter of seigniorial dues takes on a different aspect when we look at what actually happened, instead of seeking for illustrations to support a preconceived theory. There is ample evidence that the peasantry was very conscious of the burden they represented in the years before the French Revolution, and it is probable that the burden was increasing. This is what is commonly called the "feudal reaction." It would be premature to suggest that we know in sufficient detail the situation in different parts of France to be sure of any one particular interpretation; but perhaps we already know enough to feel safe in suggesting that the term "feudal reaction" is a misnomer. Even if the surviving or revived seigniorial rights could be described as feudal, what was taking place was certainly not a reaction to the past. If they were becoming a heavier burden it was, as can be most plainly seen in the case of the *banalités,* because of their increasing commercialization. They had entered the nexus of buying and selling, and those who bought, and also of course many of those who did not sell, were determined to get their money's worth. There is at least some excuse for believing that the Revolution in the French countryside was not against feudalism but against a growing commercialization; and that it was not a "bourgeois" movement but on the contrary was directed partly against the penetration of urban financial interests into the countryside.

There remains one final line of retreat for those who wish to identify the peasant movement against seigniorial dues with a "bourgeois revolt against feudalism." This consists in the discovery of a class called, among many other names, the "rural bourgeoisie," which is supposed to have led and profited by the movement against the seigniorial system. If it did so, this was clearly in opposition to the urban bourgeoisie, which makes the assumption of a single bourgeois class interest difficult to maintain. . . .

There is really no alternative to accepting what every historian who had looked at the evidence would have been bound to have accepted if it had not been for intellectual enslavement to a theory. The abolition of seigniorial dues was the work of the peasantry, unwillingly accepted by the men who drew up the town and *bailliage cahiers,* and forced on the National Assembly through the fear inspired by a peasant revolt. It follows that the "overthrow of feudalism by the bourgeoisie" takes on very much the appearance of the myth I suggested it was in a lecture some eight years ago. So far, however, the discussion has turned mainly on the nature of the so-called feudalism of the eighteenth century. Even if it is agreed that by feudalism can only be meant the survival of a system of seigniorial dues, and that these were abolished as a result of the action of the peasantry, and against the wishes and interests of the urban elements who led the revolution, this is not to deny that in other respects there may have been a "bourgeois" revolution. We have therefore to ask who, in fact, were the revolutionary bourgeois.

Who Were the Revolutionary Bourgeois?

Historians are generally agreed that the Revolution was a bourgeois revolution. "The class," writes Mathiez, "which was going to take control of the Revolution was fully conscious of its strength and its rights." M. Albert Soboul echoes the same judgment: "The commercial and industrial bourgeoisie had a penetrating consciousness of social evolution and of the economic power which it represented. It guided, with a sure awareness of its interests, the Revolution to its objective." All this is so clear and obvious and simple that it tempts one to ask some simple and obvious questions. In the first place, was it a class? Mathiez, I think, would have had no doubts. M. Soboul represents a later generation of historians and cannot escape the influence of a more sophisticated analysis. In contradiction to his earlier verdict, he says, "The bourgeoisie was diverse, it did not form a homogeneous class."

A detailed analysis is provided by Georges Lefebvre, who divides the eighteenth-century French bourgeoisie into five groups—(a) the bourgeois proper "living nobly and on his property;" (b) members of the royal administration, *officiers,* proprietors of venal offices, some of them ennobled; (c) lawyers—notaries, *procureurs, avocats;* (d) members of the liberal professions—doctors, scientists, writers, artists; (e) the world of finance and commerce—shipbuilders, wholesale traders, entrepreneurs, and the upper grades of financiers starting with the Farmers General. Within each of these groups there were widely divergent levels of wealth and status. Their attitude to the Revolution varied greatly, as did the effect of the Revolution on them, though the use of the general term bourgeoisie has concealed these differences. Since French historians themselves invariably use it, I may have to do so in referring to their views, but this must not be taken as implying any acceptance of the existence of a large, uniform, bourgeois class.

There is a general assumption that the eighteenth century witnessed the rise of the middle classes in France as a whole. I have mentioned above the ambiguities involved in the idea of the rise of classes. Leaving this on one side, we may at least ask whether the general assumption is true of all the different elements mentioned above. There is ample evidence for the increasing prosperity in the eighteenth century of the world of finance and business. Finance, above all, was the way of rising in the world: the possession of wealth—in sufficient quantity—was a key that opened nearly every door. References to *hommes nouveaux, nouveaux riches, conquérants financiers,* abound in the literature of the eighteenth century. Marion refers to "the ostentation of a 'new man' who has become the master of great estates by financial dealings." Sénac de Meilhan, writing at the time, draws attention to the way in which diverse social groups were coming together. "The children of financiers," he writes, "were raised to positions in the magistrature, and reached the highest places, even in the government. The wealth of the financiers became the recourse of great families in difficulties, and marriage connections multiplied between the greatest noble houses and rich financiers." "Persons of standing," wrote Duclos in 1750, perhaps with some exaggeration, "have already lost the right of despising finance, since there are few who are not connected with it by marriage."

Secondly, there were the greater merchants, obviously rising in wealth and influence in ports like Bordeaux and Nantes, and also, though less spectacularly, in a more industrial city like Rouen. These formed only a small group, a fact which has been obscured by the use of the term merchant, as has been said above, to include a range extending from the merchant princes of Bordeaux down to the village pedlar. Far from there being any sense of solidarity amongst such "merchants," there was intense enmity: the wealthy *négociants* had only contempt for their lesser fellows.

A regular jungle of terms is included in the idea of the merchant— *négociant, trafiquand, grossier, commerçant, régratteur, détailleur* —and we can never take any of them at its face value, because it was only human nature for a merchant to describe himself by a term which strictly applied to a higher grade. To refer again to an illustration mentioned earlier, the Breton secret agent, who served the English from Jersey, Noël Prigent, said of himself that he was *"né négociant."* When, on one of his missions to the royalists in the Vendée, armed with a letter of credit from the British government as its "ambassador," he was captured, the revolutionary authorities made great fun of the pretensions of "this Prigent," whom, they said, they had known when he was pushing a barrow round the streets of St. Malo selling apples and pears. Even if they exaggerated, this particular *négociant* at least could be described, not implausibly, as a barrow-boy.

Even in the Constituent Assembly there were many described as merchants who came from towns far too small for it to be supposed that they could support a substantial commerce. The intendant of Alençon wrote that trade in his province was *"fort peu de chose"* and that its merchants were *"fort peu aisés."* This does not mean that they were doomed to remain so. A recent study of the area that was to be the department of the Sarthe suggests that the small business men of the little bourgs were profiting by their close connection with the peasants to act as middlemen, selling to and buying from them, exploiting their artisan labor, operating as seigniorial agents, buying small patches of land, gaining by the rise in land rents, building up their property both before and during the Revolution. In spite of the great range of wealth or comparative poverty that was represented in it, at both ends of the scale the trading interest seems on the whole to have been rising—but rising into what?

In this connection little need be said of the industrialists. They were few and uninfluential, and they played little part in the history of the Revolution. As St. Simon wrote, "It was not the industrialists who made the Revolution. It was the bourgeois"—a verdict which incidentally suggests that industrialists were not normally included in the term "bourgeois."

So far, however, I have not mentioned those who in the eighteenth century were the bourgeois proper. These were the *rentiers* and proprietors, living "nobly," that is, without any occupation, mainly on the income or *rentes* from property, and from government or private loans. By their wealth and manner of life they belonged with the moderately prosperous noblesse, and very largely shared its fate— whatever that was—in the Revolution. Whether they were rising or not, they were part of the conservative and not the revolutionary section of society.

There remain from Lefebvre's list the *officiers,* holders of venal posts, lesser officials of the royal administration, lawyers and members of the liberal professions. Among these, the description of lawyer is too general to be of use in a social analysis, or it is about as much use as a classification by the possession of a university degree would be today. Even among those who filled one or another of the various legal functions, the differences were so great as to make any common treatment misleading. Of the largest, clearly identifiable, single group, however, we can make some positive statements. A section of society which was definitely not rising in wealth, and was barely holding its own in social status, was that of the *officiers.* The test of this is the decline in the value of venal offices and the failure to find purchasers for them. The decline seems to have been general, from the *parlements* downwards, though until the end of the eighteenth century it was much less marked in the offices of the *parlements* than in those of the *présidiaux, élections, maréchaussées* and other local courts. One specific example, from the lowest end of the scale, is provided by the *huissiers* and sergeants at Rouen, who complained in 1789 that their offices, worth 3,000 livres each in 1700, were now only worth 300, and that out of 22, 12 were vacant. Similarly, the *bailliage* of Rouen, which had formerly had 29 *officiers,* in 1788 only had 16.

As the commercial and financial classes were rising, so, it seems, the class of venal officers was declining. The inevitable result was a conflict between the rising and declining groups, which particularly took the form of a struggle for control of the towns. While the *bailliage* offices remained in the hereditary possession of the old royal officers, places in the municipal government were bought up by members of the wealthier commercial class. In Rouen, dominated by the greater traders, these controlled the municipality and the consular jurisdiction. The *officiers,* in *chambre des comptes, bureau des finances,* sovereign courts and so on, constituted a conservative faction which opposed the reforms supported by the merchants and some of the lawyers. A similar conflict developed in Bordeaux, where, in the elections to the *États Généraux* in 1789, the lawyers, with public support, overthrew the previously predominant influence of the great merchants. Vire, on the other hand, had been dominated by the *officiers.*

The municipal struggle also took the form of rivalry over the administration of justice, the *bailliage* judges having to face the competition not only of the intendants and their subordinates, but also of the consular jurisdiction of the towns. In an effort to protect the interests of the royal courts, a decree of 7 April 1759, confirmed in January 1764, restricted consular jurisdiction to the limits of the *bailliage* or *sénéchaussée.*

This was only part of a general struggle for precedence and influence in the towns, waged between the business world and the liberal professions. To a certain extent it may be justifiable to describe it as a struggle between a rising and a falling bourgeoisie. In the view of M. Labrousse the former was the dominant element. The eighteenth century, he argues, was a great period of economic expansion, of growth in bourgeois wealth and power, which led up to a "revolution of prosperity." This is on the unproved, and indeed mistaken, assumption that the prosperous merchants, financiers and manufacturers inspired and led the Revolution. The reverse is patently true. That the *officiers* and the men of the liberal professions prepared and directed the Revolution, and that the businessmen were not its prime movers, was the sounder view of Lefebvre. Professor Marcel Reinhard agrees that the men of business played no leading part in the Revolution. An analysis of the membership of the revolutionary assemblies, showing the overwhelming preponderance of *bailliage* officers and members of the liberal professions helps to confirm the same view. This was the revolutionary bourgeoisie.

But if Lefebvre's scrupulous regard for historical evidence forced him to recognize that the leadership of the Revolution was not in the hands of the rising commercial, financial and industrial class, he argued that all the same it represented their interests. The Revolution, writes Lefebvre, "for the first time in Europe proclaimed liberty of enterprise," it opened the way to capitalism. Professor Labrousse similarly sees the social philosophy of the Revolution in the abolition of corporations and trading companies, in free trade and enclosures. This is the bourgeois, capitalist policy that is said to have triumphed in the Revolution, and it will repay a little closer examination if we are to understand the composition and ideas of the revolutionary bourgeoisie.

Undoubtedly the corporations, trading companies, *maîtrises* and *jurandes,* which exercised a stranglehold on French trade and industry, were breaking down in the second half of the eighteenth century. The *métier libre* was already widespread and work in *jurandes* the exception. Efforts were made to encourage the people of the countryside to take up the manufactures which were restricted in towns by *jurandes.* An *arrêt* of 7 November 1762 authorized inhabitants of the country to buy raw materials and tools for the manufacture of all kinds of fabric. For a short period, when Turgot was Controller-General, the *maîtrises* and *jurandes* had been abolished, only for the decree to be reversed on his fall. The corporations were upheld by the *parlements* as a means of controlling the workers, "those beings born to trouble society" as the Parlement of Paris put it in 1776, but by 1789, though in their *cahiers* the corporations naturally opposed their own abolition, many more *cahiers* were in favor of it. The legislation of the Revolution completed the process of their elimination.

There were other respects in which revolutionary legislation on economic matters continued *ancien régime* trends. The *loi le Chapelier,* banning combinations of workers to raise wages, has been described as a new, revolutionary measure of defense by the bourgeois against the workers. This, said Braesch, is to judge it by modern ideas. Henri Sée pointed out that it merely repeated the legislation of the *ancien régime.* Advanced economic thought before the Revolution, as represented by Turgot, had developed something like a theory of the iron law of wages as a justification for keeping these down to the minimum necessary for existence. Necker, on the contrary, held that the workers were exploited, that technical progress had been of no advantage to them, and argued for government intervention. Such a view found practically no support in the revolutionary assemblies. A petition from the workers of Beauvais led the *rapporteur* of the National Assembly to write, on 4 October 1790, warning the municipal officers that "the wages of workers are not within their competence, these can only be fixed by natural laws." For any different views we will have to look below the level of the revolutionary assemblies.

An attempt has been made to discriminate between different sections of the revolutionary leadership in this respect, and to attribute such "bourgeois" views specifically to one section of it, distinguishable by its social composition and political affiliations. This is the so-called *"bourgeoisie girondine, bourgeoisie d'affaires."* The chief evidence given for the belief that there was a socially distinct "Girondin" party is the identification of certain leaders of this supposed party, such as Isnard, Kervélégan, Buzot, Pétion, as men of substance. The whole legend of the Girondin bourgeoisie is a model example of what results from ignoring the most elementary techniques of social science. In the first place, before the existence of a large, coherent and influential social grouping can be postulated, a rather bigger sample than some half a dozen specially selected cases is needed. Secondly, even if we could identify a substantial Girondin party at the center, and make a social analysis of its composition, no satisfactory conclusions could be drawn without knowing how this compared with the composition of the whole group of which it formed part, that is, of the Legislative Assembly and Convention as a whole. As for the "Girondins" of the provinces, hardly any attempt has been made even to identify them.

In his study of the Girondins, Dr. Sydenham has shown that the existence of a large and coherent Girondin party in the Convention, consisting of some 200 members, backed by a great body of opinion in the country, is a myth, created for propaganda purposes by the Mountain. The reality was the existence of a few loosely connected political groups, the Brissotins, Rolandists, Pétainists, as they were sometimes called, and including leading members of the deputation of the Gironde. In all, some twenty or twenty-five loosely associated deputies can be identified. They exhibited little in the way of a common policy and no political coherence, and were in any case too few to be statistically significant. Further, the belief that this supposed Girondin party represented the wealthier middle class, as contrasted with their poorer Jacobin opponents in the Convention, is a pure supposition with little factual basis. M. Soboul indeed writes of *"la bourgeoisie montagnarde, haute bourgeoisie souvent"* and agrees that doubtless most of the Mountain was equally of bourgeois origin. Yet he still believes that the struggle between the Mountain and their opponents in the Convention, who were later labeled Girondins, took on the form of a class conflict.

The failure of the attempt to distinguish the social composition of the "Girondin" group from that of the huge majority of the Convention has led some historians to fall back on a supposed difference in their economic and social principles or policies. Unfortunately, it is hardly in dispute that practically the whole Convention, with at most only a handful of exceptions, was devoted to the new economic orthodoxy of *laissez faire* and individualism. The argument, however, is that while one party, the Girondin, clung to its bourgeois principles at all costs, the Mountain, in the interests of national defense, willingly adopted (or alternatively, had forced on it, because both views are expressed) a policy which for a time protected the economic interests of the masses. Even if this view of the economic policy of the Mountain is correct, it should not affect our general verdict on the social policy of the revolutionaries, in which the economic measures of the Mountain have to be seen as a temporary aberration.

What, then, was this social and economic policy? The accepted view cannot be better given than in the words of M. Soboul. "Thus," he writes, "was the traditional economic order overthrown. Doubtless the bourgeoisie was before 1789 the master of production and exchange. But *laisser faire, laisser passer* freed its commercial and industrial activities from the fetters of privilege and monopoly. Capitalist production had been born and had begun to develop in the framework of a still feudal property system: the framework was now broken. The bourgeoisie of the Constituent Assembly accelerated the evolution by liberating the economy."

This seems an extremely plausible theory: difficulties only begin to arise when we look at the facts. In the first place, of course, we need not confine the judgment to the Constituent Assembly; nor—apart from the interlude represented by the rule of the Committee of Public Safety—do I think that M. Soboul intends to do so. Whether the organization of industry in France was capitalist before the Revolution has been a subject of some debate. Jaurès, Levasseur, Germain Martin, des Cilleuls, Picard, Ardachev, said that it was; Kovalesky, Tarlé, Petrov, Loutchitsky argued that France remained a *pays agricole*. This is mainly a matter of terminology. The essential point is to decide if the Revolution does in fact represent an important stage in the economic history of France, and whether the direction in which its influence operated was in fact that which is suggested.

The questions that need to be asked can be put in specific terms. Did the Revolution promote a policy of freedom of trade and industry? Did it liberate, or in any way change, the role of finance? What was its influence on the commerce and the industry of France? These should not be regarded as superfluous questions, and in seeking for answers the fact that the revolutionary bourgeoisie was primarily the declining class of *officiers* and the lawyers and other professional men, and not the businessmen of commerce and industry, should warn us against any preconceived conclusions.

Jacques Godechot
AN ORTHODOX CRITIQUE OF COBBAN'S
SOCIAL INTERPRETATION

Jacques Godechot (b. 1907), dean of the University of Toulouse, is one of France's most renowned historians of the French Revolution. He has published extensively on both the internal and external history of the Revolution. He is perhaps best known to American students for his book examining the relationship between the French Revolution and other revolutions in the Atlantic region. His study of the institutions of the Revolution and the Empire made him a logical persons to review Cobban's Interpretation, *since it involves an examination of the transformation of social groups and institutions during the Revolution. Although Dean Godechot is not specifically committed to a Marxist interpretation, his review does indicate his loyalty to the so-called "orthodox" viewpoint.*

One of the conditions of progress in the historical sciences is the continual questioning of previous findings. Therefore, works supported by valid arguments which challenge particular conclusions advanced by even the most respected or celebrated historians ought to merit our attention. Such is the case of the current book by Alfred Cobban which raises the question of whether the present social interpretation of the Revolution ought not to be reconsidered. This little volume is of great interest, and it has the particular merit of causing one to reflect. Certain of the criticisms directed by Alfred Cobban at the social history of the Revolution appear to be justified, some others on the other hand seem less well founded, while others finally call for more than reservations.

The work is divided into thirteen short chapters, followed by a conclusion. After having posed the problem, the author raises the obviously fundamental question of the relationship between history and sociology. Alfred Cobban reproaches historians of the Revolution for not keeping up to date with contemporary sociology and for limiting themselves to the sociological theory of Karl Marx, which is already more than one hundred years old. His criticism bears

From the *Revue Historique* 235, 1 (1966): 205–208. Reproduced with the permission of Dean Godechot, the editors of the *Revue* and the Presses Universitaires. Editor's translation.

somewhat on the work of Georges Lefebvre and very much more on that of Albert Soboul. His is not the first. It follows the criticisms formulated by Roland Mousnier in several books and articles, and most notably in a recent study entitled "Problems of Method" and published in the *Festgabe für Max Braubach*. Similar criticisms have been enunciated by R. Palmer in the review article in which he analyzed the thesis of Soboul for *French Historical Studies* (1960) No. 4, and in a more brutal and controversial manner by R. Ciampini in the *Bulletino italiano di studi napoleonici* of October 1964. These criticisms are certainly not without foundation. It is certain that, because of the poor organization of upper-level history teaching, the social sciences and especially sociology either are not taught at all or are not adequately taught to apprentice historians in France. It is also certain that social history is a young science in the process of formation and is still establishing its methodology. The use of large quantities of materials that can be handled by computers makes it possible to give it a new orientation. On the other hand, Alfred Cobban reproaches those working with the social history of the Revolution for wishing, at all costs, to force the facts to make them fit into theories developed by Marx. Can such a reproach really be addressed to Soboul, whose thesis showed precisely that, contrary to what Marx has written, one cannot speak of a class struggle in the Year II because Parisian *sans-culottes* did not constitute a class but only a rather heterogeneous group made up of some true proletarians, but also including at the same time some proprietors or heads of independent enterprises? It is to be feared that the criticism directed against the social history of the Revolution is more the result of prejudice (*parti pris*) than of any real effort to advance that history. For what do the authors of these criticisms propose? The use of the "methods of sociology" without saying what they consist of.

In Chapter 3 of his little book, Alfred Cobban insists on the necessity of defining precisely the meaning of words used in France at the end of the eighteenth century. We are so well aware of that need that the Commission for Social and Economic History of the Revolution has decided to undertake the establishment of a dictionary for the revolutionary epoch. Nevertheless it must be noted that the words cited as examples by Alfred Cobban, *manufacturier, laboureur, fermier, pair, officier, ordre, ouvrier, cultivateur, métayer,* etc., had at the time of the Revolution particular meanings which ought to be perfectly well-known to all candidates for a degree with any pretensions of obtaining it. In fact, Alfred Cobban is breaking down open doors.

After these preliminaries, Alfred Cobban declares that he wishes to examine the four following questions:

1. What is the truth about the so-called "bourgeois revolution," and in particular, who was a bourgeois?
2. What was the feudalism which is supposed to have been abolished?
3. What was the relationship between the "bourgeois revolution" and the revolt of the peasantry?
4. To what degree have relations between town and country influenced the Revolution?

Alfred Cobban answers the second question first. We are in complete agreement with him when he affirms that the "feudal regime" in France at the end of the eighteenth century bears scarcely any relationship to that of the thirteenth century. But is that a reason for concluding that it had disappeared? In the eyes of contemporaries it was very much alive and they wished to destroy it. A great number of *cahiers* demanded its destruction, and as a result of the decrees of 4–11 August, the National Assembly declared "the feudal regime entirely destroyed." The committee charged with applying the decrees was called the Committee on Feudal Rights. The nobility, with its rights, its privileges, its wealth—was it just a fantasy? Alfred Cobban tries to show that by 1789 seigneurial rights constituted only an insignificant expense for the peasants. Perhaps, and yet *champarts,* one of the obligations levied in kind rather than money, was sometimes heavy. But they were bothersome. In any case, rightly or wrongly, the men of eighty-nine also included among the feudal obligations the ecclesiastical tax of one-tenth, which was very heavy and was abolished also, as we know, by the decrees of 4–11 August. It is true that there is little justification for identifying the seigneurial rights and *dîmes* with classical feudalism. But that makes little difference since contemporaries judged them to be so identified. The most specific characteristics of the so-called "Atlantic Revolution" was its destruction of "feudalism" not only in France but in most of

Western Europe as well as the United States, where the vestiges of "feudalism" which existed in certain English colonies were swept away during the years 1776–1783. Alfred Cobban tries to show that the bourgeoisie, far from wishing to abolish feudalism, had been opposed to its destruction. Unquestionably some bourgeoisie had bought *seigneuries* and often collected the seigneurial dues and ecclesiastical *dîmes* which they held the right to collect with more rigor than the nobles. It would be especially bad grace to question it since Alfred Cobban has chosen his examples from the work of our students. But to go further and write that "the real historical fact which needs to be explained, therefore, is not the supposed 'abolition of feudalism by the bourgeoisie' but on the contrary 'their opposition to its abolition,'" presents us with a paradox. Can the fact that the deputies of the Third in the Constituent Assembly voted almost unanimously for the abolition of feudalism in some way demonstrate their opposition? Certainly subsequent to this vote they tried to soften the law and make the redemption of the monetary obligations profitable to their holders. But both the Legislative Assembly and the Convention, where the bourgeoisie formed a much larger majority than in the Constituent Assembly, actually completed the work of the latter and completely abolished without redemption all seigneurial rights. If the Revolution put an end to any regime, it was assuredly the "feudal regime," and the arguments advanced by Alfred Cobban against that evidence, although they are interesting and clever, will not persuade those who have worked to any extent in the documents of the time.

It is only after this first attempt at demonstration that Alfred Cobban raises the question, "Who were the revolutionary bourgeoisie?" The list of those he includes in the category does not provoke any major objections—it comprehends mostly "men of law," small businessmen and small and medium proprietors (landowners). Following M. J. Sydenham, Alfred Cobban affirms that the Girondins and the Montagnards came from the same social group, and the objections which have been raised against the former are still valid. Is the wealth of both groups known? The fact is that Sydenham has not done the essential research to give us precise information on this matter. Moreover, studies of the bourgeoisie at the time of the Revolution are still in their very early stages. In his Orleanist *Studies,*

Georges Lefebvre was able to give us only a superficial glimpse of the bourgeoisie of that city. Let us wait until Jean Sentou has published the major thesis which he is finishing up on the bourgeoisie of Toulouse at the time of the Revolution before making a judgment.

Next Alfred Cobban deals with the last two questions together. For him the peasant revolt did not arise as a result of the hostility of the peasants to the "feudal regime" but primarily as the result of conflict between town and country. Doubtless this was sometimes true, and on this point P. Bois has explained the attitude of the "Whites" of the west as being the result of the dissatisfaction of the peasants with the townsmen who supplied the seigneurs with their intendants, their judges and their tax collectors. But at bottom, was not the peasant attitude hostility to the "feudal regime"? It was only after the abolition of that, as called for in the *cahiers* and unanimously applauded, that the peasants then turned against the town dwellers with whom they found themselves in competition for the purchase of church lands. Continuing in his paradoxical way, Alfred Cobban writes: "The peasant revolt of 1789, then, far from being a revolt of the bourgeoisie against feudalism, is more realistically treated as a manifestation of the fundamental and age-old conflict of country against town." But it appears that one of the most characteristic traits of the Revolution in France, and the very condition of its success, was the alliance in 1789, especially between May and September, between the bourgeoisie and the peasantry. A peasant revolt alone in 1789 would probably have ended like the "Grain War" of 1775 without any result. A purely bourgeois revolt would certainly not have resulted in the abolition of the feudal regime.

Still in the same spirit, Alfred Cobban strives to demonstrate with the help of examples included in the works published by the Commission for Social and Economic History of the Revolution that it was the poor peasants and not the rich who were the supporters of the movement to divide up the common lands. That interpretation is diametrically opposed to that of most historians, and notably of Marc Bloch, who demonstrated the contrary in the last chapter of his *Charactères originaux de l'histoire rurale française.* It is the method of Mr. Alfred Cobban which leads him to these paradoxical conclusions: he draws from various documents this or that example favorable to his thesis, and immediately generalizes. With such a method one can prove anything. France at the end of the eighteenth century, like today, was characterized by extreme variations from one region to another, and even within one region one can find the whole gamut of opinions. It is imprudent to build a theory on a few isolated documents. Since Alfred Cobban has been willing to make use of the work of my students, I will take the liberty of calling attention here to the article of Gabrielle Richert, published in the *Annales historique de la Rèvolution française* of 1951, pp. 274–288. He will see there that the majority of the communities in the Haute-Garonne region in the Years II and III were hostile to the division of the common lands and favorable to the maintenance of the right of open pasture and the customary common rights of usage. Certainly I do not want to fall into the error which I have reproached Alfred Cobban for and deduce from the attitude of the poor peasants of the Haute-Garonne that of all France. I hope that a large number of investigations like that which Gabrielle Richert has undertaken will be carried out in other departments and in a variety of regions. I will be very surprised if their conclusions are not the same.

After having tried to provide responses to the four questions listed previously, Alfred Cobban turns to the problem of the *sans-culottes;* the one posed by Alfred Soboul in his thesis. I do not wish to summarize it again here because I have already expressed my views in a long account published in the *Revue Historique.* I do not always agree with Alfred Soboul, but in my estimation his thesis has profoundly revitalized the social and political history of the Revolution. The points on which Alfred Cobban criticizes Soboul are cause for sadness. He argues that the latter's only aim was to write the history of the Revolution, not according to the Marxist line (we have already indicated that Soboul's conclusions deviate from those of Marx) but according to the "Marxist-Leninist" line. Of greater interest is the deduction made by Cobban drawn from one of the fundamental conclusions of the theses of Soboul. Soboul, as is known, has shown that the *sans-culottes* did not constitute a true social class but rather a heterogeneous group which derived its relative cohesion solely as a result of political factors. Alfred Cobban wonders if the same situation might not have existed with respect to the social classes distinguished by historians as existing in eighteenth-century France:

aristocracy, bourgeoisie, artisans, peasants and all their subdivisions? Alfred Cobban does not recognize the existence of social-professional groups. For him the only distinguishable groups are the poor and the rich, with different gradations of wealth and poverty. This is a theory worthy of discussion, but not here for lack of space. We shall limit ourselves to observing that family and professional bonds are in general stronger than those which are based on wealth, and that simple common sense suffices to throw doubt on the validity of Cobban's theory.

Finally, and in conclusion, Alfred Cobban thinks that the Revolution was only an episode in the eternal struggle of the poor against the rich and that it was a failure because the rich for the most part maintained their position and even further consolidated it. Undoubtedly this was true, but not the same rich! The nobles, although they kept a part of their fortunes, little by little lost political power, especially after 1830. Upward social mobility was both facilitated and accelerated. The economic revolution which made possible the rise in the standard of living of a variety of social classes was in the last analysis made possible by the Revolution. Alfred Cobban thinks that the social history of the Revolution can be interpreted in a quite different way from that attributed to it by most historians up until now. That is undoubtedly true, but is the direction which Alfred Cobban undertakes to give it, valid? His book has above all two great merits, first that of forcing us to reflect on problems which were thought to have been solved, and secondly, that of stimulating us to study the social history of the Revolution making more use of the means and methods of modern sociology. Perhaps work now in progress will lead us to revise our conclusions. But at present we can scarcely follow Alfred Cobban in his interpretation.

Claude Mazauric

A MARXIST CRITIQUE OF COBBAN'S
SOCIAL INTERPRETATION

In the same book from which the earlier excerpts from Mazauric are taken, he includes a brief evaluation of the analysis of Alfred Cobban in his Social Interpretation.

A significant example [of a neo-positivist interpretation of the Revolution] is to be found in the various works of the British historian, Alfred Cobban. He takes the position that he sees no fundamental social cleavage underlying the political struggles of the Revolution from beginning to end. Practicing a rather unusual method which consists in using the anecdotal, exceptional or abnormal as opposed to the typical, the preponderant and the general, he goes as far, for example, as to refuse to recognize the common social origin of the peasant agitation in the countryside. And in his most recent book, *The Social Interpretation of the French Revolution,* despite a scrupulous attempt to be accurate in using the detailed facts in the works of his predecessors, he ends up by contradicting all their conclusions. In particular this is the case with respect to the antifeudal motives behind the peasant struggle, and the generally universal need of the peasant to free his small holding from monetary encumbrances. It is true that A. Cobban seems to imagine that the French peasants had no possibility of owning land—thus the suppression of the *dîme* would not have concerned them—when the clear fact is exactly the contrary. There was widespread peasant ownership even if we now know that it was diminished "in quality" by the juridical limitations of the feudal-seigniorial institutions of the Old Regime, as well as being diminished "in quantity" in the eighteenth century by seigniorial and bourgeois preemption. In addition, renters required to pay the *dîme* and seigniorial obligations among the payments called for in the terms of their lease obtained a substantial decrease in the amount they had to pay for rent as a result of the abolition of "feudalism."

From Claude Mazauric, *Sur la Révolution française: Contributions à l'histoire de la révolution bourgeoise* (Paris: Éditions Sociale, 1970), pp. 76–78. Reproduced with permission of the author and the publisher. Editor's translation.

A. Cobban similarly rejects the idea of a class alliance between bourgeois and peasantry. In support of this view his study uses as evidence a few peasant movements against bourgeois property, and the activities of the bourgeois militia in restoring order in the countryside. In this matter he confuses the two levels and the two phases of the peasant struggle; first joining with the bourgeoisie against feudalism, later on against (or in competition with) the bourgeoisie when attempting to extend their peasant land holdings. This makes one wonder if the work of Georges Lefebvre is still read!

Pushing his thesis further, A. Cobban sees the conflicts of the revolutionary era primarily as a political struggle for power. From this point of view, according to him things are clear, but they become obscure when one moves into the economic and the social realm. Certainly it is more difficult to analyze the relationship between the base and the superstructure than to deny its existence! Nevertheless, it is to this line, which represents a retrogression for most historians, that Alfred Cobban completely commits himself. Thus in responding to Dean Godechot who sharply criticized his book in the *Revue Historique,* A. Cobban tried to make the point that French historians, who are partisans of the social interpretation of the French Revolution, read social and economic history from a political context: "The error does not lie in seeing the Revolution as a political struggle for power, but in taking the political division as the basis for social history." He judges that consequently the outcome of such an approach, which in his eyes M. Godechot has fallen victim to, "is, inevitably, the kind of history which is irreconcilable with any serious social analysis." The context, the place and the circumstances of this statement—a colloquium on the problems of social stratification—leads us to believe that what A. Cobban calls "serious social history" can only result from applying those methods developed for the most part by American sociology for studying the social relations of autonomous social groups. But it is not by following these methods that one will arrive at any irrefutable proof of the falsity of the interpretation which most French historians, following the lead of Georges Lefebvre and E. Labrousse, hold to.

In fact, the indictment presented by A. Cobban arises very simply from a lack of study, because historical writing on the French Revolution has followed the opposite course from the one which he describes. Political history certainly has posed and still poses some questions, but these arose first in the nineteenth century as practical effects of the social and economic transformation introduced by the Revolution itself. Then in the twentieth century, the progress of social and economic history has led to the establishment of the theory of the social origins of political struggles for power as the most obvious and therefore the most studied. The real purpose of the Cobban approach, which is to separate the history of political struggles for power from their class basis, becomes clear when one reads, not without some appreciation for such frankness, the following comment: "Up to the end of the 1930s all serious historians of the Revolution were influenced by Marxism, even when they did not dogmatically follow a rigorous Marxist interpretation: since the Second World War its influence has largely been replaced by that of Marxism-Leninism. This has resulted in a major reorientation of historical thinking because it has shifted the emphasis from economic development and the facts of the social situation to the political struggle for power." Besides its being only approximately correct, are Jaurès, A. Soboul, E. Labrousse and Georges Lefebvre to be placed "before" or "after" 1930? This illogical description of a decline in Social Democratic reformism being compensated for by the rise of Marxism-Leninism will scarcely be applauded by those for whom Marxism is theoretically dead and buried!

Alfred Cobban
A REPLY TO THE ORTHODOX CRITIQUE

Historians have become increasingly interested of recent years in problems of social structure. Their researches in this field have often produced results which seem to run counter to accepted interpretations. They have in consequence sometimes found themselves talking at cross-purposes with more orthodox historians and frustrated by mutual incomprehension. The explanation of this failure of understanding is not necessarily the same for all periods. It is a reasonable supposition that in some cases it may result from the application of classifications relevant to one type of society to other societies in which they are quite inappropriate. Thus there is an obvious danger of confusion resulting from the use of such terms as *caste, ordre, classe* in the study of seventeenth-century Europe. For the period of the French Revolution, to which I am devoting this paper, however, this kind of misunderstanding either does not exist, or has largely been overcome. The history of the Revolution can be written without dependence upon any of these terms; and when they are used, as in the phrase "privileged orders," there is, it seems to me, little disagreement as to their meaning. This is not to say there is no conflict of opinion on the nature and significance of social factors in the revolutionary period, but I believe that here we have to look for a different explanation.

There has recently appeared an example of the conflict of views on the history of this period which provides an admirable illustration of its nature and causes. A short book which I wrote on *The Social Interpretation of the French Revolution,* as I anticipated, has aroused considerable opposition, sometimes not untouched with emotion. Its most thorough and fundamental *critique* so far is undoubtedly that published in the *Revue Historique* by my friend Godechot, who writes in the leading French historical journal with the authority of one of the most distinguished French historians of the Revolution, and who has moreover devoted his whole academic life to the study of the period between 1789 and 1815. The first thing that strikes one about his review is the almost total breakdown in understanding between author and reviewer. I will begin with a single point, which can be separated from the general argument. This is the question of *partage* of the common lands during the Revolution.

M. Godechot points out my error in this matter with the aid of an appeal to the authority of Marc Bloch. Now we have only to look at the chapter to which he refers to discover that Marc Bloch says precisely the opposite of what he supposes. There are other major issues on which what I myself have said is read by my reviewer in quite the contrary sense of what I supposed I was saying. My object in drawing attention to these apparent misunderstandings is not to complain of them, or even just to keep the record straight; but rather to attempt to explore the reasons for them, as well as for broader differences of interpretation, because I believe that they are relevant to the problem of the writing of social history.

If an historian of the highest competence reads into what appear to be quite simple statements something very different from their plain intention, it would be fair to suppose the explanation to lie in a deep-seated difference of presuppositions, which has the effect of changing the meaning of one set of historical judgments by translating them into a different world of historical thought. An examination of this particular failure in communication may therefore be of value as a contribution to the search for an explanation for the present lack of mutual comprehension among historians, not only of the French Revolution but of other periods.

Initially, the difference of opinion may seem little more than a matter of terminology, and it may appear, as for example it does to M. Godechot, as a lot of fuss about nothing. What I thought was a vagueness and uncertainty about the meaning of the terms commonly used for social description in eighteenth-century history seemed to me to present a serious problem to historians; but for M. Godechot there is no difficulty. The words that we use in describing French society in the eighteenth century, he says, *"doivent être parfaitement connus de tous les candidats à la licence, s'ils ont quelque prétention au succès.... Alfred Cobban enfonce des portes ouvertes."* [must be perfectly well-known to all candidates for a bachelor's degree.... Alfred Cobban is knocking down open doors.] This is doubtless true, if one is thinking of the kind of dictionary definition that can be given in two lines. On the other hand, if we wish to go a little deeper into the understanding of past societies we are hardly likely to be satisfied to remain on the level of the kind of history that any undergraduate knows.

Let us take some of these terms, to see if they are in fact perfectly understood. We all know, says M. Godechot, what *officier* means. But do we know the role of the *officiers* in French society, their functions and relative status, how these had been changing, and in what direction, during the course of the eighteenth century? There is a whole book to be written on this subject as a sequel to M. Mousnier's great work, and no inconsiderable or unimportant one.

Again, M. Godechot gives *manufacturier* and *ouvrier* as examples of
terms which are perfectly well understood. On the contrary, it seems
to me that they tell us practically nothing about the social position·
at the time of the Revolution of an individual thus described, except
that he is in some way connected with manufacture. He may have
been a wealthy employer or poverty-stricken wage-earner: without
further information we cannot possibly tell. This, I assume, is what
M. Soboul has in mind when he explains that, *"Il est ainsi le plus
souvent impossible, dans les documents de l'epoque, de faire le
depart entre le compagnon, le petit artisan, l'entrepreneur."* [It is
usually impossible from the documents to distinguish between a
journeyman, a simple artisan and an entrepreneur.]

In respect to the world of commerce, some interesting pages of
Brunot discuss the complicated, overlapping and changing meanings
of such terms as *commercant, négociant, marchand, trafiquand,
merchand en grand, grossier, marchand magazinier, regrattier, de-
tailleur.* The social terminology of agriculture was at least as imprecise as that of industry and commerce. Without knowing the details
of each specific case nobody could possibly guess the social and
economic position of someone described as a *fermier.* A *cultivateur,*
despite M. Godechot's confidence in the complete undergraduate
comprehension of the word, might be, during the Revolution, a
wealthy proprietor or a poor smallholder. We thought we at least
knew the meaning of *métayer,* until Paul Bois showed that in the
Sarthe a *métayer* was one of the richer peasants.

The first cause of misunderstanding will now be obvious. It consists in the belief that the imprecise language of contemporary
usage is adequate for the purposes of social history. Here I can
only echo the warning of M. Mousnier against the use of contemporary terms without careful examination and criticism. The variety of
meaning to be found in practically every single social term is useful
historical evidence. The very vagueness and overlapping of contemporary descriptions is significant. But this does not justify us
in using them for the purpose of historical analysis without an attempt to differentiate between their various meanings and to discover
the social realities behind them. Where they can be, and normally
are used, is in ordinary narrative and descriptive history, concerned to trace the main sequence of events on the great stage of
national politics. In this kind of history social analysis is an unnec-

essary complication, irrelevant to the task the historian has set himself.

The fact is that there is more than one kind of history, and we are here dealing with two different *genres*. One of these accepts the social terms of the past as adequate for its purpose, while the other tries to analyze them and break them down into what are believed to be more realistic elements. This opposition appears even more plainly if we turn from the more specific social terms to broader ones, such as the "régime féodal." A certain measure of agreement has been reached here. M. Godechot declares himself in perfect agreement that *"le régime féodal en France, à la fin du XVIII siècle n'avait guère des rapports avec ce qu'il était au XIII."* [the feudal regime in France at the end of the eighteenth century had scarcely any similarities to what it had been in the thirteenth.] But he continues, *"Est-ce une raison pour en déduire qu'il avait disparu?"* [But is that a reason to conclude that it had disappeared?], and his answer, to our surprise, is no. The significant point is the reason he gives for this answer: *"Aux yeux des contemporains il était très vivant."* [In the eyes of contemporaries it was still very much alive.] This cannot mean that contemporaries knew what feudalism was in the thirteenth century and by comparing this with their own conditions concluded that it was still alive. It can only mean that since they used the word to describe the contemporary situation we need not inquire further. Indeed this is what M. Godechot himself says: *"Qu'il soit peu justifié d'identifier les droits seigneuriaux et les dîmes avec le régime féodal, c'est certain. Mais peu importe, puisque les contemporains le jugeaient ainsi."* [That there is little justification for identifying seigniorial obligations and tithes with the feudal regime is certain. But that makes little difference, since contemporaries so identified them.]

Herein, evidently, is to be detected the difference between narrative history, which accepts the contemporary social vocabulary at its face value, and analytical history, which subjects it to critical treatment. But this is not the whole explanation. Why is it that many historians can still use words like bourgeois or *paysan,* can even, with M. Godechot, talk of *"l'alliance, en 1789, et surtout de mai à septembre, entre la bourgeoisie et la paysannerie"* as though these were meaningful phrases, whereas to others, like myself, it has seemed necessary to abandon them? Since it would be very wrong to try to claim that in such a major difference of view betwen reputable and serious historians either side is just totally and stupidly at fault, the only reasonable conclusion that I can see is that we are in fact starting from different premises, writing different kinds of history, and therefore inevitably reaching different conclusions. I believe, in fact, that a study of some of the major points at issue will demonstrate that this is so.

Let us begin with the statement already quoted that there was a peasant-bourgeois alliance, particularly from May to September 1789. Now clearly M. Godechot would not assert this unless it were a fact commonly accepted by historians. On the other hand, the evidence of conflict between the interests of the wealthier but non-noble social elements in the towns and the rural population is overwhelming.

The reader will already have noticed a second point of difference to add to that arising from differing attitudes towards contemporary social terminology. M. Godechot's belief in a peasant-bourgeois alliance is specifically referred to the period of May to September 1789. He appears to be willing to recognize that before and after these months there may have been a conflict. On the other hand, my own emphasis was on the long-range opposition of interests between town and country: this does not exclude the possibility of temporary and partial alliances between them. One kind of history, thus, is concerned primarily with the blow-by-blow account of the political struggle, while the other analyzes a social situation which changes more slowly and normally not from day to day or month to month.

When we look at the apparently contradictory facts of M. Godechot's history and of mine, a third difference also appears. The conflict between urban and rural interests is revealed in the *cahiers* and in the elections to the *États-Généraux,* but the conflict did not stop there. Sporadic outbreaks of violence in the countryside built up to a widespread movement during the spring and summer of 1789. There is ample evidence that the attacks of the peasant population were not confined to the property and rights of the privileged orders. Thus it hardly seems correct, from my point of view, to speak of the peasant-bourgeois alliance, even from May to September, or to say, *"C'est seulement après l'abolition de celle-ci que les paysans se sont retournés contre les citadins."* [It was only after the abolition of the feudal regime on August fourth that the peasants turned against the townspeople.] Furthermore, to repress the outbreak, in both town and country, the *Asemblée Nationale* called on the *milice bourgeoises,* which did indeed take very effective action, sometimes in the form of punitive expeditions into the countryside. The disturbances were put down, and those who were seized as guilty of the attacks were punished, often ruthlessly, by forces recruited from or by, and certainly representing, the better-off population of the towns—those who presumably are meant by the loose designation "bourgeois." How are these facts reconciled with the supposed peasant-bourgeois alliance?

The answer is that they are not: they exist on a different plane. The conflict between urban and peasant interests appears all over France in studies of local history: the alliance is demonstrated for M. Godechot by the vote of the Tiers in the Constituent Assembly, on August 4, abolishing feudalism. But over and above the social struggle scattered up and down the provinces of France, there was a general struggle between revolutionaries and counter-revolutionaries for the government of France. This, it seems to me, is the justification for M. Godechot's view. It was a struggle for power in the central government. Such struggles involve almost inevitably an alignment of forces on one side or the other. You were either *for* the Revolution or *against* it, and probably in 1789 most of those who did not belong to the privileged orders (as well as some of those who did) were *for* it, whether they could be described as *paysannerie* or bourgeoisie. In this sense M. Godechot is correct in saying that they were in alliance.

The third point to be noted is, therefore, the difference between history written in terms of the overriding political struggle and that concerned with the basic social conditions. One cannot for a moment question the importance of political history. Indeed, in discussing "social interpretation" of the Revolution I specifically recognized that the Revolution was, in large measure, a political struggle, waged for the government of France. The nature of a political struggle is to divide a nation into two sides. There is no incompatibility between accepting the existence of this simple political dichotomy and finding underneath the political struggle a much more complex social and economic nexus. The error does not lie in seeing in the Revolution a political struggle for power, but in taking the political division as the basis for social history. This, I believe, is the chief cause of the present misunderstanding, which is evident also in other historical periods, between historians brought up to see historical conflicts in terms of the struggle for political power, and those who are more concerned to study the social patterns and conflicts which political history naturally leaves on one side.

It is not difficult to provide further examples of the transfer of political categories into social ones. Thus it is obviously difficult for orthodox historians of the Revolution to believe that the so-called Girondins and the Montagnards could come from the same social strata. Their political opposition, it seems, must be assumed to reflect a difference in their social origins, even if there is no present evidence of this. Again, the concentration on political issues naturally produces a political vocabulary. M. Godechot rightly sees that the term *aristocratie* is, according to me, a political one. When the revolutionaries denounced aristocrats they did not necessarily mean nobles by this description. A noble might be a patriot, in which case he would not be an aristocrat, whereas a *roturier,* or even a peasant, might be, and sometimes was, denounced as an aristocrat. Similarly, as M. Soboul has shown, the *sans-culottes* of the Year II were identified, not by belonging to any specific social category, but by their political beliefs.

But when it is suggested that I also include *artisans* and *paysans* and all their subdivisions among political categories, this, of course, is absurd. The suggestion once again indicates a basic opposition between two different approaches to history. The responsibility for the misunderstanding must be mine, for failing to allow for the strength of commitment to the political interpretation of the Revolution in recent historiography. As I have said, one result of this is that the terms used to describe the major elements in the revolutionary struggle, while they possess social overtones, are essentially political. It is what one would expect if the Revolution was the product, as M. Labrousse said long ago, of a conjuncture of political and economic factors. This is true of terms like the *régime féodal,* the bourgeoisie, aristocrats, *sans-culottes.* But there is no reason to suggest that *artisans* or *paysans* are political terms, nor do I do so. The suggestion itself is indicative of the breakdown in communication and of a failure to appreciate the objection to the use of large omnibus terms, such as "bourgeois," in social history. Their defect is that they obscure significant social differences and stand in the way of a more adequate social analysis. It has truly been observed that the use of the word "bourgeois" has the effect of lumping together social categories at the very point where their differences become sociologically significant.

To sum up, the historical thought of the school of historians of the French Revolution represented by M. Godechot is conditioned by its primary concern with the political struggle for power. Insofar as it takes notice of social divisions, it superimposes the established political categories on them, and assumes that the broad, general terms of the political struggle are valid for the purpose of social analysis. This is in effect to identify social and political interests and tacitly to exclude the possibility that they might be in opposition, or even irrelevant, to one another.

The contradiction in interpretations of the Revolution now seems to be explained, but an explanation is still needed for the present predominance of political history. It is all the more remarkable in that the dominance of the political interpretation is very largely a development of the last twenty years. From the time of Jaurès up to the Second World War the economic and social history of eighteenth-century France and the Revolution was far from being neglected. It is in the last twenty years that there has been a fundamental change in historiographical direction, which cannot but reflect a change in the basic outlook of the leading historians of the revolutionary period. Such a change has indeed taken place. Up to the end of the 1930s all serious historians of the Revolution were influenced by Marxism, even when they did not dogmatically follow a rigorous Marxist interpretation. Since the Second World War its influence has largely been replaced by that of Marxism-Leninism. This has resulted in a major reorientation of historical thinking, because it has shifted the emphasis from economic development and the facts of the social situation to the political struggle for power.

M. Godechot seems to regard the suggestion that historians have been subjected to these influences as an attack upon them, as though it were wrong for an historian to possess a coherent social philosophy. I would not have drawn as heavily as I have done upon the works of Marxist or semi-Marxist historians if I had not recognized the value of their researches. Our differences of opinion lie on a different level of thought, which M. Godechot, perhaps, does not appreciate. If he did, I think he could hardly have written, if I follow him correctly, of Mousnier, Palmer, Ciampini, as well as myself, that our criticisms seem *"plus fondées sur un patri pris politique que sur un réel effort pour faire avancer cette histoire."* [to be based more on a political bias than on a real effort to advance history.] Obviously there is another failure in communication here, but again for the same reason. There is a great difference between attributing an opposition in historical interpretations to the holding of different social philosophies, and attributing it to a *"parti pris politique."* The latter, I cannot help feeling, is once more the result of the tendency to see history and the writing of history in exclusively political terms.

Finally, in his description of the end of the Revolution, as of the beginning, M. Godechot gives a political interpretation. How did the Revolution leave France? The wealthier classes, he agrees, still kept their predominance and had even strengthened it; though, he adds, if it was still the rich who ruled, it was *"pas les mêmes riches!"* [not the same rich!] The important point is that, *"Les nobles, tout en conservant une partie de leur fortune, ont été peu à peu écartés du pouvoir politique."* [The nobility, while keeping a part of their fortunes, have little by little lost their political power.]

On the political plane this verdict is quite clear. But as soon as we move from the sphere of political power to that of social relationships a fog of confusion descends. Having said that, after the Revolution, *"Les riches ont à peu près maintenus leurs positions et les ont même consolidées,"* [The rich have just about maintained their position and even consolidated it], he goes on to assert that *"l'ascension sociale a été facilitée et accélérée: la révolution économique, qui a permis l'élévation du niveau de vie des diverses classes sociales, a été finalement facilitée par la Révolution."* [Climbing up the social ranks has been made easier and quicker: the economic revolution which has made possible a rise in the standard of living of the different classes was in the long run facilitated by the Revolution.] The meaning here is not very clear. Can M. Godechot really mean that though France after the Revolution was still ruled by the rich, and even more effectively than before, it was now easier to climb into their ranks and this was the great achievement of the Revolution? And does he also mean, as he seems to say, that as well as a political revolution it was also an economic revolution, which raised the standard of life of all social classes? This latter statement is very difficult to reconcile with the facts of the social and economic condition of the French people after the Revolution. Lefebvre, for example, more realistically, had spoken of the "terrible condition" into which the working population was precipitated in the early decades of the nineteenth century. The only explanation of the contradiction that I can see is that Lefebvre was thinking of economic conditions, whereas M. Godechot is once again unconsciously transferring his political interpretation of the Revolution into the social and economic field.

The consistency of the interpretation of revolutionary history of which he is one of the most distinguished exponents is undeniable; nor would I deny its validity within its own sphere. I have said myself that the French Revolution was "primarily a political revolution, a struggle for the possession of power and over the conditions in which power was to be exercised. Essentially the revolution was the overthrow of the old political system of the monarchy and the creation of a new one in the shape of the Napoleonic state." The account of such a struggle is naturally a political narrative; the social terms to be used can be those that contemporaries used; the relevant social affiliations and oppositions are those that relate to the political struggles; national politics provides the basic divisions from which social classifications are deduced; political groupings and party labels are identified with social distinctions; changes in the balance of political power are taken to be equivalent to changes in social structure. The result is inevitably the kind of history which is irreconcilable with any serious social analysis.

The antithesis could not be demonstrated more clearly than it is by M. Godechot in the four pages which sum up admirably the political interpretation of the Revolution. For a social interpretation we have to turn to other historians—Jaurès, Sée, Bourgin, Mathiez, Lefebvre up to the 1940s, Labrousse, among others; and among more recent ones, Paul Bois, Saint-Jacob, Tilly, George V. Taylor, Reinhard and so on. Their work has not yet penetrated the fortresses of orthodox political history. Nevertheless progress is being made. *"Peut-être,"* writes M. Godechot, *"les travaux qui sont en chantier nous ameneront-ils à réviser nos conclusions."* [Perhaps the works which are now in progress will lead us to revise our conclusions.] I believe they will; indeed, I wrote my book under the impression that they should have done so already.

George V. Taylor

CAPITALISM AND THE ORIGINS OF THE FRENCH REVOLUTION

George V. Taylor (b. 1919), professor and now chairman of the Department of History at the University of North Carolina, until recently concentrated his research and writing on the development of capitalism in eighteenth-century France. Based on both archival and printed sources as well as the now more extensive monographic publications in this field, his study finally compelled him to take the position set forth in the excerpt that follows, in spite of its challenge to the orthodoxy currently established in France. Professor Taylor, having placed in question the traditional view of the bourgeois origins of the Revolution, has now turned to an in-depth study of the local cahiers of 1789 in order to try to gain new insight into the real aims and attitudes of the French people at that crucial moment in their history.

. . . There is no conclusive way of comparing the mass value of proprietary and business wealth in prerevolutionary France. Beginning with what passed in those days for statistics, supplementing them with estimates made by well-informed men who say little about their derivation, making inferences on assumptions which, though reasonable, can be endlessly debated, one concludes that the traditional modes of property—land, buildings, office, and *rentes*—accounted for more than 80 percent of French private wealth. This indicates a substantial preponderance for the proprietary sector. It is in no way astonishing. The day of heavy fixed industrial investment in factories and railroads, which would have altered the balance, lay far ahead. Meanwhile, most Frenchmen lived on the land, which yielded most of the taxable income and the gross national product. That is why the *économistes* not unreasonably attacked agricultural problems first, often to the neglect of the others.

For our purposes it is desirable to know the relative weight of the two kinds of capital not only for the society as a whole but in the upper Third Estate. Unfortunately, studies of the notarial records are not sufficiently advanced to show this. For the moment, all one can

From "Non-capitalist Wealth and the French Revolution," *American Historical Review* 72, 2 (1967): 486–496. Reprinted with permission of the author. Footnotes omitted.

do is count persons, and from this it appears that even in the most heavily commercialized cities the proprietors and professional men in the Third Estate outnumbered the merchants. At Bordeaux, the second most active port, there were 1,100 officials, professionals, *rentiers,* and property owners against only 700 merchants, brokers, and sugar refiners. At Rouen, a prime center of industry, banking, and maritime and wholesale trade, the administrative and judicial officers, professionals, and proprietors-*rentiers* outnumbered the merchants and brokers by more than three to one. At Toulouse, an agricultural, legal, and ecclesiastical capital, the ratio was about eleven to four, but the four included merchants who for the most part traded on small capital and in little volume and did much retail business, so that one hesitates to call them capitalists. There is, however, a further consideration. Because the merchants and industrialists owned, along with their commercial capital, considerable proprietary wealth, we could, with better data, divide them fractionally between the two sectors, and, by such a procedure, the share of commercial and industrial capital in the upper Third Estate would seem much lower than the impression we get by counting heads.

Soundings like these are merely straws in the wind, but they drift always in one direction. They confirm what seems to have been implicit in the consciousness of eighteenth-century France—that even in the well-to-do Third Estate proprietary wealth substantially outweighed commercial and industrial capital. This would not have surprised a Frenchman of the Old Regime and should not surprise us. The reason for stressing it here is to lay the ground for an assertion that is fundamental in analyzing the causes of the Revolution: there was, between most of the nobility and the proprietary sector of the middle classes, a continuity of investment forms and socioeconomic values that made them, economically, a single group. In the relations of production they played a common role. The differentiation between them was not in any sense economic; it was juridical. This situation, in the historiography of the Revolution, has received practically no serious attention and remains, in Orwellian language, an "unfact." The reason for this is that it contributes nothing to what Cobban rightly calls "the established theory of the French Revolution," the theory that the Revolution was the triumph of capitalism over feudalism. In that context the configuration of proprietary wealth that pervaded both the Second and Third Estates has no place and remains unwanted, unused, and therefore, in effect, unknown.

It deserves, however, to be recognized, and its claims are strengthened by bringing forward a second unfact: that a substantial number of nobles participated as entrepreneurs in commerce, industry, and finance. There was indeed, before the Revolution, a *noblesse commerçante,* though not, perhaps, the one that the Abbé Coyer called for in 1756. Provincial, military, and court nobles, peers, and members of the royal family invested in the General Farm, speculated on the Bourse, and developed and exploited mines, canals, and metallurgical establishments, including the great foundry of Le Creusot. On the other hand, there was, to reverse the phrase, a *commerce anobli,* a sizable group of merchants ennobled through the municipal offices of certain cities and the two thousand or more venal offices that conferred nobility on the buyers. For the most part, these ennobled merchant families were in a transitional stage. As enterprises were liquidated, or generations arose that were no longer trained for business, they dropped out of trade to live, as other nobles did, on their revenues. All the same, merchants or not, they were nobles and sat in the noble assemblies of 1789. To sum up, there were nobles who were capitalists. There were merchants who were nobles. As the proprietary wealth traditionally identified with aristocracy extended far down into the Third Estate, so the capitalism traditionally identified with the wealthy Third Estate penetrated into the second, and into its highest ranks.

This means that the old diagram by which we envision prerevolutionary society must be changed. There was a clear juridical boundary that separated nobles from commoners, and a commoner crossed it by registering a legal document, his letters of nobility. On the other hand, the frontier between capitalist and proprietary wealth ran vertically through both orders. The horizontal line marked a legal dichotomy, the vertical line, an economic one. To think of them as coinciding, even roughly, is to misunderstand the situation completely. The concept of two classes, at once economically and juridically disjunct, can be sustained only by ignoring the weight of proprietary wealth in the Third Estate and that of capitalism in the second, or, in other words, by continuing to ostracize them as unfacts.

From this follow two important conclusions. The first is that when the word bourgeois is used to indicate a nonnoble group playing a capitalist role in the relations of production it includes less than half the well-to-do Third Estate and excludes the proprietary groups that furnished 87 percent of the Third Estate deputation to the Estates-General. In other words, it embraces only a minority of the upper middle classes and explains almost nothing about the origins of the revolutionary leadership. In this sense it should be discarded as inadequate and misleading. But there are other senses, loaded with eighteenth-century implications, in which the word will continue to be employed because it alone translates what the documents have to say. One may, for example, speak of bourgeois who lived nobly on their revenues and comprised a fiscal category; these constituted a small portion of the Third Estate and counted entirely in the proprietary group. One may also speak of bourgeois as persons who, being inscribed in the registers of the bourgeoisie of a town, enjoyed what Anglo-Saxons call "the rights of the city," including political advantages and fiscal exemptions worth having, but in this sense the bourgeoisie included nobles and noncapitalist commoners and was not entirely of the Third Estate. Finally, one may adopt a peasant usage, applying the word bourgeois to townsmen who collected rents in and near the village and were felt to be an alien and adverse interest. All three meanings convey realities of the Old Regime and are useful on condition that one makes clear which of them he has in mind.

The second conclusion is that we have no economic explanation for the so-called "bourgeois revolution," the assault of the upper Third Estate on absolutism and aristocracy. No one denies that such an assault took place or that it left a powerful imprint upon French society. The struggle for the doubling of the Third Estate and the vote by head, the demand for a constitution and an elected legislature, the intimation of political equality in the Declaration of the Rights of Man, the liquidation of intendancies, provinces, parlements, fiscal inequalities, forms of nobility—all these, put in series with the emigration, the expropriation of church and *émigré* wealth, and the Terror, have to be made credible on some basis. By one of the unexamined postulates of current historiography we expect them to be explained by a conflict of social classes and the contradictions between a "rising" economic order and the order that it challenges.

The position taken here is that we have now learned enough to see that this cannot be done, that to divide the wealthy elements of pre-revolutionary society into a feudal aristocracy and a capitalist bourgeosie forces the concealment of too much evidence, and that the whole classic concept of a bourgeois revolution has become impossible to sustain.

This leaves in our interpretation of the Revolution a somewhat painful void. Our instinct is to fill it with a new class-struggle interpretation like Cobban's "revolution of the propertied classes," which explains some results of the Revolution but not, apparently, its origins. There may, however, be more plausibility in a political approach than in a reorganization of social categories. The gist of such an approach can be set down in two propositions that probably amount to the same thing. First, the struggle against absolutism and aristocracy was the product of a financial and political crisis that it did not create. Second, it was essentially a political revolution with social consequences and not a social revolution with political consequences. Because these assumptions suggest a backward step in historiography, it will take a few paragraphs to make them respectable.

The Revolution resulted from a bankruptcy that left the monarchy discredited and helpless. The disclosures of the first Assembly of Notables shocked everyone capable of reacting to public affairs, set off an expanding discussion of reforms, and raised hopes for a national regeneration. The government's reform program, which threatened privileges and seemed tainted with the supposed negligence and dishonesty of the Controller General Calonne, was rejected by the Notables. For more than a year the parlements and other constituted bodies opposed it. This resistance, the so-called *révolte nobiliaire,* taught the upper Third Estate the language, tactics, and gallantry of opposition. It made the convocation of the Estates-General inevitable. When in August 1788 this convocation was announced (along with a partial suspension of payments), there was thrust upon the nation a new political issue: whether royal power would pass to the privileged orders or would be shared with those who, until then, had been disfranchised. By inviting his subjects to advise him on how to organize the Estates-General, the king precipitated a landslide of publications that touched off a growing outcry for the doubling of the Third and the vote by head. This generated a political struggle between democracy, as Palmer has defined it, and aristocracy, substantially as he has taught us to understand it. The stakes were very high. They included the question of at whose expense the financial problem would be solved, and whether careers in the military, the clergy, and the judiciary, and, above all, in politics would be opened to commoners, rich and poor, whose main resources were talents, education, and ambition. In explaining the democratic assault on despotism and aristocracy it is unnecessary to conjure up a social struggle rooted in economic change. The paralysis of the monarchy, the apprehensions of the taxable groups and creditors of the state, and the hopes and ambitions of the professional classes, combined with the slogans, myths, and images generated by the struggle, seem quite enough. The revolutionary mentality was created by the crisis. It was, in fact, the writing of the *cahiers* that forced a crystallization of issues and their formulation in ideological terms. For the mass of the upper Third Estate, the schools of revolution were the electoral assemblies of 1789, not the salons and *sociétés de pensée* of the Old Regime.

What this interpretation restores is the sense of an unplanned, unpremeditated revolution that in many ways exceeded the aims expressed in the *cahiers de doléances* of March and April 1789. Take, for example, the abolition of nobility, which may be understood here as aristocracy constituted juridically as an order. If in the spring of 1789 the upper Third Estate had seen nobility as an intolerable institution it would certainly have called for its destruction. But this was never attempted until the revolutionary leadership had concluded, from more than a year of political experience, that the nobility was an incorrigible enemy of the new regime. Certainly there was friction in the quarrel of 1788 over how the new provincial estates would be constituted and whether nobles and commoners would deliberate there together. It was intensified by the dispute over how the Estates-General should be organized. But in the spring of 1789 middle-class feelings toward nobility were still benign. Far from wanting to abolish nobility, the Third Estate wished to rehabilitate it. One reads in the Third Estate *cahiers* of the major towns and cities that nobility was to be reformed, that nobles should be given opportunities to replenish their fortunes, and, still more remarkable, that nobility must be saved from adulteration by abolishing the venal offices and making ennoblement depend not on money but on service to the nation. Then came the quarrels and confrontations of 1789, the destruction of the constituted bodies, and the reform of the army and the church, which was dispossessed to protect the creditors of the state. These events made the opposition to the Revolution, inside and outside the National Assembly, formidable. In all three orders it developed considerable strength. On June 19, 1790, after a year of struggle, nobility, as such, was abolished in order to disarm and probably to punish the most conspicuous element of the opposition. Nothing in the *cahiers* forecasts such a decree. The intention to smash the legal basis of nobility and, along with it, the whole system of language, symbols, images, and formalities that reinforced the subservience of the lower groups, was a product of the revolutionary crisis, not a cause. To argue that it came about through long years of economic change, class formation, and the gradual growth of class consciousness in a bourgeoisie that played a capitalist role in the relations of production is not only out of keeping with the evidence, but superfluous.

The present crisis in the interpretation of the French Revolution results from the maturing of social history as a discipline. This specialty, in its present form, was virtually created in France. Its methods are as distinctive as the sources it employs, and its findings are most convincing when expressed in quantitative form. Applied to the history of the Revolution, it has yielded a mass of data on economic interests and conditions, standards of living, population change, corporate structures, social values, and the complex mentalities found at various levels of society. Much of this material disagrees with the vocabulary in use when the effort began. But the vocabulary is still in force. The problem is how to rescue the data from a language that misrepresents it and imprisons it in categories that can no longer be justified.

Although interest in the social history of the Revolution is very old, its progress as a specialty began during 1901–1904, when Jaurès published the first four volumes of the *Historie socialiste* and procured the establishment of the Commission of the Economic History of the Revolution. "It was Jaurès," Lefebvre once wrote, "who habituated historians to see [in the Revolution] a fact [that is] social and, consequently, of economic origin." Jaurès had no doubt that the Revolution was the political triumph of a bourgeoisie matured by the growth of capitalism, and, with an erudition that is astonishing, given the literature available to him, he rewrote the history of the Revolution on this theme. Lefebvre, who avowed a deep indebtedness to Jaurès, never renounced this view. In the first two paragraphs of *Quatre-vingt-neuf,* paragraphs that dominate the reading of the whole book, he identified the "primary cause" of the Revolution as a conflict between an aristocratic society, grounded historically in the ascendancy of landowners, and a new class, the bourgeoisie, enriched on liquid forms of wealth. In this passage Lefebvre left no doubt that capitalism was the economic basis of the bourgeoisie and the source of its growing power. Out of this socioeconomic configuration had come, he said, the ideology of the *philosophes* and the *économistes,* expressing the values and aspirations of a revolutionary class. These developments were fundamental. The royal bankruptcy and the aristocratic resistance that forced the king to convoke the Estates-General were treated as an "immediate cause" which explained many of the characteristics of the Revolution and why it began when it did.

Lefebvre's work, however, led him to modify considerably the original overview of Jaurès. Writing in 1932, he found that overview already too simple. As an explanation, he observed, it was credible only when supplemented with the financial crisis, the *révolte nobiliaire,* and the economic distress that produced the popular disturbances without which the Revolution could not have succeeded. In *Quatre-vingt-neuf,* passing well beyond the thesis announced in the preface, he described four revolutions: aristocratic, bourgeois, popular, and peasant. In *La Révolution française,* the synthesis that he contributed in 1951 to the series "Peuples et civilisations," he described an aristocratic revolution, a bourgeois revolution, and a popular revolution, the last being composed of a Parisian revolution, a municipal revolution, and a peasant revolution; all these were treated under the heading "L'avènement de la bourgeoisie en France." He was also troubled, far more than less perceptive historians, by the problem of relating the bourgeoisie, with all its diversity, to the derivation assigned it in Jaurès' writings and his own preface to *Quatre-vingt-neuf.* Twice he wrote that it was not "homogeneous." In *La Révolution française* he saw it as composed of bourgeois living on investments in land and, to some extent, liquid capital; holders of venal offices; financiers, maritime merchants, and manufacturers; a "middle class" or *petite bourgeoisie* of tradesmen and petty officials; and a bourgeoisie of intellectual capacities ranging from savants and artists to law clerks and office employees. The determinants of status, he believed, included birth, corps, vocation, and, occasionally, talent. In his last study, an analysis of the urban society of Orléans, he laid out social categories in terms of order, vocation, and wealth or income, but Soboul tells us that he was not satisfied with either the method or the results. It is not difficult to see why. Classification by wealth conflicted with classification by role, and both conflicted with classification by order. Nearly a fifth of the nobles who enjoyed revenues of more than five hundred livres per year, for example, were merchants and sugar refiners; "bourgeois" by vocation, they shared the privileges of the second estate. To put the matter another way, half the refiners and a third of the merchants named in the tax rolls of 1791 were nobles; giving priority to the system of orders, Lefebvre classified them with the nobility. The Third Estate he divided into a *haute bourgeoisie* and a large category called *moyenne et petite bourgeoisies,* but for lack of tax rolls did this entirely on the basis of vocations and corporate groupings. All nonnoble merchants, refiners, brokers, officials, and manufacturers were assigned to the *haute bourgeoisie,* although Lefebvre observed that, if the tax rolls had survived, some of them would have had to be demoted. On that principle, of course, the same documents would have elevated many professional men from the lower group to the higher. Finally, one reads that the *cahier* of the Third Estate of the *bailliage* was drawn up by the elite of the bourgeoisie, but that elite, a political entity, remains unreconciled with the socioeconomic groupings.

Apparently, what the emerging data have made impossible is to equate the identifiable leadership of the upper Third Estate—the "revolutionary bourgeoisie"—with a social class that played a common role in the relations of production, or, more precisely, owned the instruments of production in an emergent capitalist economy. Soboul, in his masterful study of the *sans-culottes,* faced a comparable situation. He found the *sans-culottes* a political bloc composed of diverse economic elements; he therefore pronounced them not a social class. The same step may now be taken with regard to the "revolutionary bourgeoisie." Jeffry Kaplow has, in fact, moved toward this solution by defining the bourgeois on juridical and political lines. They were, he says, well-to-do people excluded from the privileges of the nobles and from powerful positions in the state, the army, the church, and the parlements. Yet they had access, not enjoyed by the common people, to local political office. "They were beginning to become conscious of themselves as a class," he observes, "and shared a definite set of values." That is certainly true. Yet, if this is a social class, it is not one in the sense recognized by the last two generations of social scientists in this country. Nor is it the bourgeoisie as we commonly think of it.

Hexter has recently pointed out that one of the peculiarities of historical rhetoric is the use of words that he calls "evocative" because they signal the historian to summon up whole categories and sequences of associations with which professional thought identifies them. Terms like "aristocracy," "bourgeoisie," "feudalism," "capitalism," and "social class" have this quality. It is what gives them interpretive value. Each is freighted with implications that make it operative in the machinery of the bourgeois revolution model, so that, as Cobban points out, to accept the language is to accept the theory. In ordinary usage, whoever says "class" is heard to say "productive role," and whoever says "bourgeois" is heard to say "capitalist." Unless he adds an emphatic disclaimer, he should expect to be understood in this sense. But even emphatic disclaimers can be ineffectual if, as in the case of "class" and "bourgeois," special meanings have been welded on by more than thirty years of writing, teaching, and discussion. Under those circumstances, there is little prospect of revising professional usage. That is particularly true of a vocabulary which, among many millions of the world's people, has a content that is ideologically obligatory and is thereby frozen into alliance with an obsolete interpretation. Obviously, the project of solving this problem by giving new meanings to old words is more or less utopian. The phrases "bourgeois revolution" and "revolutionary bourgeoisie," with their inherent deceptions, will have to go, and others must be found that convey with precision and veracity the realities of social history.

Betty Behrens

"STRAIGHT HISTORY" AND "HISTORY IN DEPTH": THE EXPERIENCE OF WRITERS ON EIGHTEENTH-CENTURY FRANCE

Betty Behrens, sometime professor of history at Sydney Sussex College, Cambridge, besides having written an excellent general history of the Old Regime is the author of a brilliantly conceived and meticulously researched article entitled "Nobles, Privileges and Taxes in France at the End of the Ancien Régime," *which appeared in the* Economic History Review *in 1963. In this article she examines the validity of the orthodox view with respect to the incidence of taxation under the Old Regime. She finds this view (that the financial crisis of the Old Regime resulted from the privileged exemptions of the nobility) to be not correct on closer examination, even to the point that it seems probable that the French nobility were more heavily taxed than their English counterparts. The selection that follows was chosen not only because it is briefer than the article on taxation, but also because it deals with a wider spectrum of issues and interpretations relating to the Old Regime. It originated as a review of three books on the Old Regime written by defenders of the orthodox viewpoint.*

In 1955, an American scholar, Professor E. R. Tannenbaum, delivered an address to the American Historical Congress in Washington on the developments in French historical scholarship during the previous ten years. What principally struck him was French disenchantment with what, he tells us, is called "straight history" in English and *"l'histoire historisante"* in French. If we may believe him, these two pieces of academic jargon have the same meaning in both languages. They mean narrative history with the emphasis on political events—a kind of history that has fallen out of fashion because it has hitherto failed to take adequate account of social and economic causes. The interest of French historians, Professor Tannenbaum points out, has in consequence turned to these.

The phenomenon, needless to say, is not peculiar to France, but is characteristic of the age, reflecting our awareness that major political events cannot be explained merely in terms of the actions

From " 'Straight History' and 'History in Depth': The Experience of Writers on Eighteenth-Century France," *Historical Journal* 8 (1965): 117–126. With permission of the Cambridge University Press and the author. Footnote references omitted.

of the men in power, any more than the actions of private persons, as it has now come to be believed, can be explained merely in terms of their particular temperaments and desires. To a greater or less extent we are all seen to be creatures of circumstances, and the chief function of the historian has thus come to seem that of analyzing the circumstances which condition social and political action.

In England this new history is sometimes described as "history in depth," to distinguish it from the old or "straight" history which has been found superficial. Wickham Steed nevertheless once observed of the Germans that they dive deeper and come up muddier than any other nation, and since his day it has become increasingly plain that the deeper one dives the muddier one risks coming up. These are risks, it is to be hoped, that will one day be overcome, but in certain fields of historical writing, and particularly in French history in the eighteenth century, the auguries at the moment do not seem hopeful.

The second half of the eighteenth century culminated in the French Revolution, and even to contemporaries it was plain that here was an event which could not be explained merely in political terms but had its roots in social and economic conditions. The wish to understand these dominated much of the thinking of the time. The sites to be dug were prospected in the late eighties and early nineties of the century, particularly by Barnave in his remarkable *Introduction à la Révolution Française*. It is one thing, however, to have the hunch that oil is to be found, and another to locate the correct spots, to devise the tools, and to organize the labor for the job. On and off, this enterprise has been in progress in France for nearly two hundred years. It received a notable impulse after each of the two world wars of this century, and particularly after the second. It has, however, encountered great difficulties.

The writers of straight history had their terms of reference more or less prescribed for them by the major political events which they saw it as their function to describe and explain. The writers of history in depth have found themselves faced with a choice of subjects that has proved limitless; for now that it is believed that major political events may be largely caused by changes in the economy and the social structure, it has seemed to follow that they cannot be explained until the nature of the economy and the social structure, and the changes they have undergone, have been fully understood.

Matters of this sort, however, are even in the best of circumstances very difficult to fathom. They are peculiarly difficult in eighteenth-century France because of the lack of reliable data and the great differences in law, administration, custom, and economic conditions, between one district and another, that impede generalization. French ministers on the eve of the Revolution were acutely conscious that they lacked the data necessary to discharge even such minimal functions as were required of governments in those days; they habitually referred to the French administration as chaotic; even government revenue and expenditure could not be accurately estimated, so that it was possible for Calonne and Necker to engage in an impassioned and protracted dispute over what would today seem a pure matter of fact—the extent of the annual deficit.

How is the historian to proceed in these circumstances? Only, it has seemed in France, by pursuing every topic that seems worthy of investigation in each relevant locality separately. French history in depth in the eighteenth century has thus become a mosaic of bits and pieces. We have histories of *"Les Paysans du Nord,"* and of *"Les Paysans de la Bourgogne du Nord,"* of the nobility of Toulouse; of the Intendance of Alsace; of the Parlement of Dauphiné during the second half of the eighteenth century; of the magistrates of the Paris Parlement from 1715 to 1771; of the social structure of Paris in 1749; of this, that or the other trade, industry, or institution, in this that or the other town or *généralité,* in this that or the other year or period; and the writers of these works cannot generalize beyond the narrow limits of time and place which they have imposed upon themselves.

History, as Dr. Kitson Clark once observed, is thus being torn to pieces by the experts, and the experts do not seem to be much concerned with putting it together again. As the term used to be understood, history was held to be principally concerned with the evolution of political communities and with international relations. In some connection or other the emphasis was on political power. The modern preoccupation with sociology and economics, however, has deflected historians' interest from this question. They have been forced to trespass into fields belonging to other disciplines.

There they have found scholars who speak language[s] they had not previously used and only understood imperfectly. If at first they are suspicious, later they are often awed. In the end the two parties frequently reach a compromise whereby the sociologists and economists recognize that the historians can teach them how to find answers to some of their questions, but the historian accepts the terms of reference of the sociologists and economists. When he does this, however, he ceases to have a subject of his own, and becomes merely the exponent of a method applicable in many fields besides that formerly held to belong to history. As Professor Tannenbaum observes in the article referred to earlier, French historians are at present engaged in many studies unlikely to promote historical knowledge as it used to be understood—studies, as he puts it, "primarily concerned with systems, structures, and processes ..." which "tend to serve as demonstrations of hypotheses rather than as expository narratives."

The sensible conclusion to draw from this state of affairs might be that history as we used to know it is ceasing to exist, and this would be a plausible conclusion in relation to eighteenth-century France. The authors of the volumes in the Clio series on the eighteenth century refer the reader to a bibliography compiled in 1926 which contains the titles of 10,000 modern works on the period. But in 1926 the subjects thought suitable for study fell far short of what they do now, and the number of research workers was also much smaller; for there has been a great expansion in the universities everywhere, the Americans have entered the field in force and the writers of other nationalities in some numbers. The monographs in consequence proliferate and the cry continually goes up for more. If only, say Professor Germain-Martin and M. Bouvier, in their *Finances et Financiers de l'Ancien Régime,* we knew the sociology of the holders of the government debt. M. Méthivier, in the introduction to his book on the *Ancien Régime* discussed below, complains that the essential facts about French life before 4 August 1789 still sleep in the archives of the Hotel Soubise, and in the departmental and provincial archives. While, however, the questions and the answers multiply, the person who asks for a reliable general work on any period between 1660 and 1789 is referred to the series edited by Lavisse at the beginning of the present century. The serious reader, it appears, has no alternative except the unmanageable mass of monographs on the one hand, and on the other a survey written before the modern ideas had gained currency and the research inspired by them had begun.

No one likes to admit that the end to this state of affairs is not in sight. The pious hope is often expressed that some day all the questions will be answered and the pieces of the puzzle assembled in such a way that a new and convincing picture will emerge. It is, however, permissible to doubt if the hope is justified, for the number of monographs is already so vast, and their writers' approach so diverse, that no single person can hope to keep track of the conclusions.

Though, however, history is ceasing to exist for the scholars it continues to exist for the students. It remains a popular subject in universities, and the more the experts want to tear it apart, the more public opinion insists that the students should see it whole. It is left to the writers of textbooks to bridge the gap between these two attitudes.

The textbooks have thus acquired a prestige they never had before. In France as in this country scholars write monographs in youth but textbooks when they reach maturity. The purpose of these books is to provide students with the outlines of the subject and to keep the outlines up to date. They are concerned with history as it used to be understood—with the great events and their causes; and in relation to the eighteenth century they are at the moment the only kind of academic writing to aspire to this function. In the present circumstances, however, it is not a function they can fulfill adequately; for the new knowledge, fragmentary and disparate as it is, could only be unified (insofar as it is capable of being unified at all) in the light of some new principles which would enable the writer to place the various bits and pieces in some causal relationship to each other. The writers of textbooks, however, by definition, operate for the greater part with paste and scissors.

The nature of their tools determines their ways of proceeding. They have to adopt the conventional explanations that were formulated before the new knowledge became unmanageable. Except at the risk of incoherence they can only accept such parts of the new knowledge as they can fit into the conventional framework. They must discard the facts and theories which do not fit, or cannot, by means of judicious manipulation, be made to look as if they fitted.

In most important respects the conventional account now in vogue of the nature of the *Ancien Régime* and the reasons for its collapse dates back to the Revolution itself—to the version of the wrongs of the Third Estate as popularized by Sieyès and others, and to Barnave's analysis of the decline in landed and the growth in commercial wealth which undermined the power of the nobility and increased that of the bourgeoisie. These ideas were later taken up by Tocqueville, whose work, Professor Godechot tells us in another of the books reviewed below, had the merit of emphasizing that the Revolution sprang out of the class struggle. They have formed the core of orthodox doctrine since Mathiez set them out in volume I of his *Révolution Française,* first published in 1922.

This doctrine, broadly speaking, describes the *Ancien Régime* as characterized in its later stages by a growth in the wealth and self-consciousness of the bourgeoisie and by a decline in the wealth of the nobility; it portrays the bourgeoisie as eager for the power to which its economic position entitled it, and as hostile to the nobles' privileges; it portrays the nobles as not only clinging on to but as extending their privileges in what is commonly called the aristocratic reaction. It was one of Mathiez's principal contributions to show that the Revolution started not in 1789 but in 1787 with what he called, in a phrase that has passed into the language, *"la révolte nobiliaire"*—a revolt staged by the aristocracy against the government's attempts at reform.

This stock of ideas has received various additions since Mathiez's day, notably as a result of Lefebvre's discoveries about the aspirations of the peasantry and the part they played in 1789, and of Professor Labrousse's discoveries about the movements in the French economy—the boom that extended from the 1730s to the middle 1770s, and the slump that followed. None of this, however, disturbs the convention which, following Sieyès and Barnave, and Tocqueville with modifications and omissions, sees the principal cause of the Revolution in the class struggle between the bourgeoisie and the nobility—a struggle which the crown, supposed to act as arbiter between these two groups, failed to prevent because since the death of Louis XIV it had been unable to discipline the nobility.

Even in the skillful hands of Tocqueville, the argument in support of these ideas contained many contradictions, though the brilliance of the writing and the insight in other connections served to obscure them. It is not, however, so easy to obscure them now because much of the monograph literature has a bearing on them. The writing of textbooks on the eighteenth century is thus a hazardous enterprise which is avoided as far as possible. The century nevertheless has to figure as the conclusion to the work of Louis XIV and the prelude to the Revolution. What the textbooks make of it can be illustrated by three recent examples, none of them solely concerned with it, but all of them devoting a considerable proportion of their space to it. They are M. Méthivier's *L'Ancien Régime*, M. Soboul's *Précis de la Révolution Française,* and Professor Godechot's *Les Révolutions (1770–1799).*

All of these three writers subscribe to the new way of looking at things by providing chapters on the economic and social structure, which are followed by chapters on the political structure (mainly drawn from older works since this subject has not excited much interest lately). These are then followed by an account of the events leading up to the *révolte nobiliare* and the summoning of the States-General.

All three writers expound the orthodox doctrine. M. Soboul does so with the most enthusiasm but M. Méthivier is not far behind him. M. Méthivier tells us that *"La résistance des privilégiés à la réforme financière a rendu la Révolution inévitable."* [The resistance of the privileged to financial reform made the Revolution inevitable.] He speaks of *"l'irrésistible poussée bourgeoise"* [the irresistible drive of the bourgeoisie], and says that the nobility *"périclite devant la montée bourgeoise"* [was endangered by the bourgeois drive]. Professor Godechot conveys the same impression, though less emphatically. *"La structure de la société . . . poussé la bourgeoisie, qui detient la puissance financière, à vouloir exercer elle-même, et à son profit, la réalité du pouvoir. Grace au commerce maritime, qui avait pris son essor depuis l'exploration de l'Atlantique, au XVI siècle, la bourgeoisie était souvent plus riche, et même plus puissante, que la noblesse."* [The structure of society stimulated the bourgeoisie, who possessed financial power to want to exercise itself for its own benefit, the reality of power. Thanks to overseas trade which had been expanding since the exploration of the Atlantic in the sixteenth century, the bourgeoisie were often more rich and even more powerful than the nobility.]

While, however, the general conclusions are the same in all these three works, the supporting evidence and arguments are not. What any writer says in detail on any subject is more often than not contradicted by one or both of the other writers, and not infrequently by what he says himself in other parts of his work. Thus M. Méthivier tells us that there were no castes in French society, but M. Soboul, following Tocqueville, speaks of "véritables castes." Professor Godechot, in spite of his insistence in some places that the members of the bourgeoisie wanted power and prestige for themselves, points out in other places that they wanted titles—that is, they wanted to enter the aristocracy.

Or again, Professor Godechot describes the officials of the Parlements, and of the Establishment in general, as aristocrats. Much that M. Méthivier says conveys the same impression, but he nevertheless makes a point of saying that the officials of the Parlements were only in process of gaining admission to the aristocracy. M. Soboul uses a similar expression in one passage, but in another implies that they were bourgeois.*

Doubtless this confusion has arisen because for certain purposes of the orthodoxy it is convenient to see the magistrates of the Parlements as aristocrats (they led the *révolte nobiliare*) but for others to see them as bourgeois (they were professional men, who sometimes worked hard, and often accumulated fortunes which they administered carefully—all attributes at variance with the conventional view of the aristocrat).

Since the publication of Professor Bluche's admirable monograph on the magistrates of the Paris Parlement, however, which came out in 1960, one might suppose that no room had been left for argument. Professor Bluche shows that the vast majority of men who entered this Parlement between 1715 and 1771 possessed hereditary titles before they assumed office, and that the proportion of magistrates between these dates whose nobility was of *"ancienne*

---

* He speaks of the Intendants as having been selected *"dans les cadres de la haute bourgeoisie"* and as being hated in consequence by the nobility. This is an unusual thesis, for the complaint against the Intendants is generally that, with one or two notable exceptions, they identified themselves with the nobility in their *généralités*. To say that the Intendants were bourgeois is to say that the magistrates of the Parlements were bourgeois. For the Intendants always began their careers in the Parlement de Paris. Professor Bluche calls them *"Parlementaires de Passage"* because they saw office in the Parlement as a stepping-stone to a more distinguished career. At the end of the eighteenth century they were all nobles.

extraction" (that is, the most highly prized, unexceptional kind of nobility) was the same as among the nobility as a whole.

As this illustration demonstrates: of all the three writers here under discussion, it is Professor Godechot who walks the tightrope between the old conventions and the new knowledge with the greatest skill. Though the general tenor of his account is conventional, he nevertheless usually manages to avoid statements that can be easily disproved and arguments that plainly destroy each other. This feat, however, may only have been possible because his account is short, dry, and often ambiguous. M. Méthivier, who writes at greater length and with more eagerness to explain (and on occasions he seems to explain very well), involves himself in more contradictions. When it comes to M. Soboul, the reader can with difficulty suppress a sense of outrage at the indifference he shows to facts and logic.

In particular, he tells us, like everyone else, that by the end of the *Ancien Régime* the bourgeoisie was richer than the nobility. He adds (which Professor Godechot is careful not to do) that the wealth of the nobility was declining. The court nobility, he says (following Tocqueville and Mathiez) was wasting its substance in extravagant living, while the provincial nobility was "vegetating" in conditions often no better than those of its peasants. Later on, however, he points out (following Professor Labrousse) that throughout a large part of the century rents and the profits of agriculture were rising—a trend as Professor Labrousse emphasized which was to the benefit of the seigneur.

Here is a contradiction too glaring to be overlooked, even by the hurried reader; and indeed at this point any reader must begin to wonder what significance is to be attached to the observation—which all three writers make—that the bourgeoisie was richer than the aristocracy. It was of course more numerous. In the absence of figures what are we expected to deduce from the mere statement that its collective wealth was greater? It seems likely that the collective wealth of the peasants, of whom there were some twenty-two or more million, was greater than that of the bourgeoisie of whom there are said to have been about one million. If what is meant is that the richest people were bourgeois what is the evidence? Much cogent evidence points the other way. Mr. Robert Forster's *Nobility of Toulouse in the Eighteenth Century,* for example, shows that the richest people in that district were the twenty noble families whose estates he studied and who doubled their income from land in the second half of the century. In a study made for the *Annales* and published in 1961, a table which sets out the fortunes of the various social groups in Paris in 1749 shows that the people in the highest groups (that is, with fortunes of over 500,000 l.) were almost exclusively nobles. For those who dislike statistics there is Turgot's judgment on the distribution of wealth between the nobility and the Third Estate and the reasons for it. In his debate with Miromesnil in 1776 on the abolition of the *Corvée,* staged for the instruction of Louis XVI, Turgot said in arguing for the abolition of privilege in matters of taxation:

> *Une autre raison achève de rende ce privilège et plus injuste et plus onereux, et en même temps moins respectable. C'est qu'au moyen de la facilité qu'on a d'acquérir la noblesse à prix d'argent, il n'est aucun homme riche qui, sur-le-champ, ne devienne noble; en sorte que le corps des nobles comprend tout le corps des riches, et que la cause du privilégié n'est plus la cause des famille distinguées contre les roturiers, mais le cause du riche contre le pauvre.* [Another factor has the effect of making this privilege both more unjust and more onerous, and at the same time less respectable. That is the ease with which nobility can be purchased. There is no rich man who does not immediately become noble and as a result the body of noblemen includes all the rich men, and the controversy over privileges is no longer a matter of distinguished families against commoners, but a matter of rich against poor.]

M. Soboul, however, will not only have it that the bourgeoisie was the richest class in the nation; he must also have it (as indeed the conventional argument requires) that they were the most enlightened. The Enlightenment, he tells us, was a bourgeois movement. This is a proposition which M. Méthivier will only accept with qualifications and on which Professor Godechot is prudently silent. An hour or two spent with the *Biographie Universelle* would be enough to cast doubts on it. Though admittedly some of the *Philosphes* were of bourgeois or plebian origin, notably Rousseau, Voltaire and Diderot, Voltaire nevertheless acquired not only wealth but a title and an aristocratic way of life (including a marquise for a mistress) and many, perhaps most, of the famous *Philosophes* were born into the estate of the nobility. Condorcet was a marquis; his nephews Condillac and Mably were the sons of the Vicomte de Mably, Helvetius, appointed by the queen's favor, like many others with influence at court, to a high place in the tax farm, was the son and grandson of French noblemen, and his remoter ancestors were of the German nobility. His daughter (a famous beauty painted by Madame Vigée-le-Brun) married the Comte d'Andlau (whose ancestors had been knights of the Holy Roman Empire in 1100) and was a favorite of Marie Antoinette. Malesherbes was the great-grandson of the famous Chancellor of Louis XIV's reign—Guillaume de Lamoignon, Marquis de Basville, Baron de Saint-Yon and Comte de Launay-Courson, who could trace his ancestry back to the thirteenth century. Turgot's family was not much less ancient or distinguished. Diderot's most trusted and prolific contributor to the *Encyclopédie* was the Chevalier Louis de Jancourt, who came from one of the oldest families in France.

The writers who maintain that the *Philosophes* were bourgeois, and who are fond of quoting Sieyès in other connections, might quote him also in this one. How remarkable it was, he said, that the cause of the Third Estate was better defended by the members of the First and Second Estates than by its own members. For all his contention that the Third Estate was an exploited body which possessed all the talents and did all the useful work but received none of the rewards, Sieyès complained that it was servile. Many others among its advocates thought the same. Servan—the author of several inflammatory pamphlets—said, like Sieyès, *"Ils n'attendent de fortune que de leurs bassesses auprès de la Noblesse et du Clergé."* [They look to get ahead only through their servility to the nobility and the clergy.] Mirabeau said *"Le Tiers Etat est formé de tant de gens sans vigueur, de tant de campagnards accoutumés à la féodalite, detant de citadins qui ne pensent qu'à l'argent, de tant d'esprits bourgeois qui ne songent qu'à retirer quelques fruits des protections et du patronage de Messieurs tels et tels, qu'on tremblerait si l'ouverture des Etats les plaçait en même Chambre avec nos Seigneurs de toute espèce.* [The Third Estate is made up of so many people without drive, of so many country dwellers used to feudal rights, of so many citizens who think only of money, of so many of bourgeois mentality who think only of benefiting from the protection and patronage of such and such a gentleman, that they will tremble if at the opening of the Estates they find themselves in the same room with all kinds of noblemen.] Professor Egret, in his *Pré-Révolution,* provides many other quotations from well-known writers to the same effect. He has a section headed *"Le réveil du Tiers Etat,"* but dates this only from the end of 1788 when the *Ancien Régime* had already begun to collapse as a result of the *révolte nobiliaire.*

The orthodox doctrine would no longer be tenable if once it were admitted that the enlightened ideas, which provided the Revolution (a bourgeois society in the nineteenth century), with its ideology, were not principally the invention of bourgeois; that the bourgeoisie was not in any significant sense richer than the nobility; that the wealth of important sections of the nobility was increasing and not diminishing over a large part of the eighteenth century; and that until the *Ancien Régime* was already collapsing the *"irrésistible poussée bourgeoise"* expressed itself in a desire to enter the nobility and not to pull it down. In France, however, no one would accept all these propositions, though some writers might accept some of them, because the criterion for distinguishing noble from bourgeois on which they are based would not be generally acceptable. When it was said above that the richest families in Toulouse or Paris were noble, or that Helvetius, Condorcet, Condillac, Mably and others were noblemen, the criterion was a legal one. By nobility was understood the possession of titles and privileges recognized in law. To the English in the eighteenth century this would have seemed reasonable. It seemed reasonable in France in 1789 to the organizers of the elections to the States-General who based their electoral arrangements on this principle. But there are other points of view from which it seemed, and has continued to seem, unreasonable.

In England the legal and the social positions of the nobility more or less corresponded, but in France they often did not, because while hereditary titles after 1689 were rarely bestowed in England, in France they were always easy to get. Louis XIV sold five hundred titles in one month in 1696 and another two hundred in the course of 1702, not to mention all the titles that people acquired through the purchase of offices; and though in the eighteenth century new creations were not so common, they were still frequent. In these circumstances there naturally emerged the conception of the *bourgeois-gentilhomme,* the person who was a nobleman from one point of view but a bourgeois from others—a nobleman by virtue of his titles and privileges recognized in law; a bourgeois by birth, or occupation, or way of living or attitude of mind. In the eighteenth century people continually insisted and elaborated on these distinctions which were a powerful cause of social tension.

From the days of Sieyès onwards they have been a powerful cause of confusion in historical writing because they have made it possible for historians to call anyone they choose a bourgeois, regardless of his legal status which provides the only precise criterion. Thus it has been possible to call the tax farmers bourgeois, Helvetius included, because organizing the collection of taxes seems no profession for a gentleman, or because when in the time of Colbert the farm was set up more or less in the form in which it endured until the Revolution, its principal operators had been self-made men. This state of affairs, however, did not last. By the end of the eighteenth century the Company of General Farmers had become to a large extent "a kind of closed, almost family, corporation." The wealth of the General Farmers had always enabled them to buy themselves titles and to marry their daughters into the best families. In the course of time it enabled them to establish themselves in a high position in society. It also tempted the Crown to demand places in the company for royal favorites. In the end, as Duclos put it: *"La cour et la finance portent souvent les mêmes deuils."* [Often the court and financial circles were mourning the same person.]

It has also been possible to label the Intendants bourgeois, as Tocqueville did and M. Soboul still does, for similar though less plausible reasons, for they followed a profession, often like Turgot in a highly professional way. Turgot's long line of ancestors who had served the king in the robe and with the sword, or his sister who married a duke (he himself never married), seem outweighed by the nature of his official functions and the way he looked at them—by, for example, his numerous memoranda, which were stuffed with precise and complicated information about problems of agriculture and taxation, and might have been written by any modern civil servant but for the remarkable elegance and lucidity of the exposition.

Once, however, it has been accepted that it is permissible to argue in this way, it would not be difficult for one reason or another to classify as bourgeois a high proportion, perhaps even the majority, of those entitled to vote with the order of the nobility in the elections to the States-General; and this game can also be played the other way round. Like Professor Palmer in his *Age of the Democratic Revolution,* one can follow the revolutionary propaganda, in which aristocrat was a term of abuse, and classify as aristocrats various categories of people disliked at the time even though legally they belonged to the Third Estate.

Whatever merits these procedures may possess there seems one overriding objection to them. It is the objection against all arguments based on imprecise concepts or on concepts which change their meaning in the course of the discussion. They yield no clear and verifiable conclusions. So much confusion has recently been introduced into French eighteenth-century history that the central doctrine of the class struggle between bourgeois and aristocrats can now only be accepted as an act of faith; for no two people can agree on who the bourgeois and the aristocrats were; no one can formulate (and few even try to formulate) a criterion for distinguishing between them that can be followed consistently, and every argument is thus liable to be at variance with easily ascertainable facts.

In these circumstances it is plain that the conventional descriptions of the *Ancien Régime* and the explanations for its collapse need reformulating. In any case if this were not so, and if multiplying the monographs could only serve to elaborate conclusions reached during the Revolution itself by people without historical training and access to documents, but with an axe to grind, the task of the historian would seem to be futile. It would be utopian, however, to suppose that a reformulation will emerge of itself if only more people write monographs, and more operators with paste and scissors attempt to tinker up the outlines in the light of their conclusions. What is needed are some clear and useful concepts by means of which to organize such information as exists and to show where fresh research can profitably be undertaken.

The purpose of these observations is not to throw stones at the French, for their difficulties in writing the history of their country in the eighteenth century are not unique but only particularly acute. They are particularly acute in the first place because among the disorderly administrations that were typical of the age theirs must have been one of the worst; and the greater the disorder the harder it is for contemporaries, and therefore for the historians of later generations, to understand what was happening. But in the second place it is always particularly hard for a nation to rethink its history at the point when its main traditions were established, as they were in France at the Revolution.

These, however, seem to be merely local obstructions in the way of a task that is everywhere perplexing—that of understanding enough about the social and economic causes of the major political events to permit the rewriting of "straight history" in a plausible and illuminating way. If this is not done there will end by being no history at all; for everywhere the monographs multiply; everywhere they cast doubts on the conventional explanations of the various national histories, and everywhere in consequence these can only be repeated parrot fashion, or allowed to sink without replacement in the sea of uncoordinated and often contradictory facts; so that where "straight history" is thought unrespectable, as information accumulates understanding diminishes.

The curious fact thus emerges that the more loudly history is proclaimed to be a science, and the more interest the writers of monographs show in scientific techniques, the less scientifically historians tend to proceed in the discharge of what used to be held their specific function—the explanation of the major events. For whatever is meant by a scientific explanation, at least it is an explanation directly related to the situation to be explained. . . . It cannot be arrived at by adding together the conclusions of researchers who started from other terms of reference. Such an attempt, indeed, is incompatible with the use of a scientific method; for however that term is understood, at least it involves getting one's central concepts clear, and one's arguments coherent, and one's essential facts right, or at least not demonstrably wrong.

IV WHO INTERVENED IN 1788? A CASE STUDY IN THE ORIGINS OF THE FRENCH REVOLUTION

Elizabeth L. Eisenstein
WHO INTERVENED IN 1788?

*Elizabeth L. Eisenstein (b. 1923) received her Ph.D. from Radcliffe in 1953
and is a member of the history faculty at American University in Washington, D.C. Since her doctoral study of the socialist revolutionary F. M. Buonarotti as a link in the transmission of the radical social thought of the Revolution to the nineteenth century, she has extended her interest to the general
problem of the diffusion of ideas and especially the impact and role of the
printing press in that process. She has written several articles on that topic,
opening up new perspectives. The article reproduced here arose out of her
interest in the problem of the development of a revolutionary ideology as a
crucial factor in the initiation of the Revolution, and her annoyance at finding the orthodox view as reflected in Lefebvre's celebrated work to be so
unsatisfying.*

This paper is concerned with discrepancies in Georges Lefebvre's
presentation of the point at which, "strictly speaking, the Revolution
of 1789 began"[1]—more precisely with how the author locates revolutionary initiative at this point. Any such commentary on selected
portions of a single secondary text requires some sort of justification. For two reasons this particular exegesis seems worthwhile.
First, the point at issue is a strategic one in all interpretations of the
French Revolution. Second, the text is a widely circulated book by
a most eminent historian. Generally regarded as "the best introduction to the study of the Revolution available anywhere," the text
has, since R. R. Palmer's translation of 1947, become increasingly
available almost everywhere. Devoid of forbidding scholarly apparatus, relatively slim and readable, this English version is acces-
sible to the reading public at large. Widely used as a classroom
manual, it has also left its mark on high-level research undertaken
by political scientists, sociologists, and historians working in periph-
eral fields. Finally its outlines have been reproduced by the author,

From the *American Historical Review* 71 (1965): 77–103. With the permission of the
author. Some footnotes omitted.

[1] Georges Lefebvre, *The Coming of the French Revolution*, tr. R. R. Palmer (from
Quatre-Vingt-Neuf, 1st ed., Paris, 1939) (Princeton, N.J., 1947), p. 37. (Hereafter
page references to this book are given by numbers in parentheses following cita-
tions.)

himself, in his magisterial volume *La Révolution Française* and are thus impressed anew upon all those who become specialists in the field of French revolutionary studies. Puzzles resulting from the main features of Lefebvre's presentation are, as a result, even now being duplicated in a wide variety of other works.

Briefly stated, he presents the coming of the Revolution as a drama divided into four acts, with the aristocracy, the bourgeoisie, the urban populace, and the peasantry each, in turn, commanding the center of the stage. Each act is introduced by an analysis of the social structure and psychology of the group involved, followed by a narration of the episodes in which it played a central role. By employing a single framework, based on the social structure of eighteenth-century France, to sort out and order tangled, over-lapping episodes, the author has been able to compress a mass of unwieldy material into a terse and unusually lucid account. The clarity of his scheme accounts both for the popularity of the text and for its lasting impact upon a variety of readers. In his preface to the American edition the translator has summarized this impact:

> *On the debated question of who started the Revolution . . . he [Lefebvre] answers that all classes were in one way or another responsible; that the aristocracy, the bourgeoisie, the urban masses and the peasants, each independently and for reasons of its own, initiated revolutionary action (xiii–xiv).*

To suggest that the urban masses and peasants initiated "revolution-ary action" stretches the term "revolutionary" somewhat beyond its proper limits. Insurrections, *émeutes,* uprisings are not, after all, equivalent to revolutions. As a result, Lefebvre's answer is suscepti-ble to a somewhat different interpretation—not conveyed by his chapter headings but clear enough, nonetheless, from his analysis. This somewhat different interpretation is also given by the translator in his preface:

> *M. Lefebvre shows how all classes combined under the leadership of the aristocracy to overthrow the absolutist Bourbon regime. . . . Division there-after took place, for the aristocracy, being only human, hesitated to sur-render all the privileges of its position. The bourgeoisie came to the fore, taking advantage of popular insurrection in town and country. But the re-gime introduced by the bourgeoisie was not an instrument of class domi-nation; it had something to offer everybody and indeed postulated that no such things as fixed classes existed (xv–xvi).*

We have then two partly contradictory main themes. On one hand, each class separately and independently initiates revolutionary action; on the other, the aristocracy leads a concerted movement against royal absolutism and then, having paralyzed the royal power, is in turn paralyzed itself by independent action initiated by the bourgeoisie. This latter class is not thereafter paralyzed in turn by urban and rural uprisings. To the contrary, the last two acts merge with the second one, as all three classes collaborate, under bourgeois leadership, to bury the aristocracy "under the ruins of the Old Regime" (3). This second theme, already embedded in a rich and profuse historical literature, suggests that the sections devoted to the "popular" and "peasant" revolutions do not altogether deserve to be assigned equal weight as separate acts in the drama. In fact, the action initiated by the "bourgeois revolution" does appear to carry the author beyond the confines of his scheme—resulting in its abandonment toward the end of the book, where a section entitled "The Rights of Man and the Citizen" encompasses a less clearly focused political narrative of events from Bastille Day to the October Days.

Both themes appear most compatible in the earlier sections of the book. There they collaborate to impress upon the reader the importance of independent action initiated by the bourgeoisie when it "loudly demanded equality before the law" (37), acting in defiance of the Paris Parlement. We are concerned with the fact that the author's evidence does not substantiate his inference that this action was initiated by the bourgeoisie (however we define this difficult-to-define social sector). Here the order he imposes upon his material and the data he supplies work at cross-purposes with each other.

The point at issue comes, according to the author's scheme, when the Paris Parlement on September 23, 1788, ruled that the Estates-General should be constituted according to the precedent set in 1614. Up to this point the "aristocratic revolution" was proceeding without intervention from other social sectors and appeared to be successful in accomplishing its purpose. The Bourbon monarchy had been forced to concede constitutional limitations upon royal power, and, crippled by bankruptcy, forced to act in accordance with this concession: by reinstating the Paris Parlement and agreeing to convoke an Estates-General to determine fiscal policy. In prior decades, since the era of the *Fronde,* the political prerogatives of the intermediary orders had been weakened, those of the crown extended. A reversal of this trend after so long an interval of time may be appropriately classified as a "revolution." Major alterations in an unwritten constitution were being made. But one should note that this sort of revolution was not unprecedented. Prolonged experience, at home and abroad, could account for the behavior of the contestants in the struggle. As the author himself points out, these particular "beginnings of the Revolution" may be viewed as "the last offensive of the aristocracy." They represented, he says, "merely the crowning effort" of this class, the culmination of a struggle that had begun with the first Capetian kings (16). Similarly, earlier "times of troubles" had seen not only the coincidence of empty royal treasuries with noble sedition but also widespread outbreaks of urban *émeutes,* peasant uprisings, and even municipal insurrections.

If we agree with Lefebvre that the Revolution of 1789 begins "strictly speaking" with an orchestrated wave of protest over the issue of representation at the Estates-General, it is because this is the first large-scale response to the prolonged political and financial crisis that differentiates it from all preceding "times of troubles." The organization of this protest movement could not have been anticipated since it had no precedents in the annals of French state-craft. Its effectiveness in throwing the authorities off balance owed much to its coming from no familiar centers of sedition, no duly constituted groups in particular, but from many different amorphous groups who seemed to be at large. As the author notes, as late as "the summer of 1788 there was no reason to anticipate that the bourgeoisie would intervene in the name of the whole Third Estate in the conflict between the royal power and the aristocracy" (51).

It is this unanticipated intervention in the fall of 1788, made in the name of the whole Third Estate, that seems to lie at the heart of the question: "who started the French Revolution?" Who was responsible for this intervention? What scanty evidence the author supplies, relating to the social composition of the groups who intervened, does not bear out his implication that initiative passed from one class to another. This appears to be true however loosely or widely one cares to define the term "bourgeoisie" or even the much larger residual category "Third Estate." His evidence, to the contrary, suggests that a loose coalition of men drawn from all three estates provided the initial impetus for the protest movement and steered it through to obtain what is described as "The First Victory of the Bourgeoisie." On his own showing, intervention came from persistently undefined members of a shadowy "patriot party" led by a "Committee of Thirty," only nine of whose members are named. Not one of those named could be characterized as "bourgeois" or as members of the Third Estate. When leaders other than those belonging to this committee are mentioned, moreover, a sizable proportion turn out also to belong to the first two estates. In every passage describing political action the names of the real men who initiated this action are presented to the reader. (Some of their faces even illustrate the French edition.) But the blank-faced visage of the bourgeoisie is invariably substituted in analyzing the significance of this action, introducing it, summing it up, or generalizing about it.

Thus we are told about the first moves made to protest the Parlement's ruling: "In aligning themselves against the privileged classes, the bourgeoisie took the name hitherto claimed in common by all who opposed the royal power. *They* formed the 'national' or 'Patriot' party [italics mine]" (52). Who are *the real people* who took the initiative to form this more exclusive, class-oriented party?

> ... Great noblemen, the duc de La Rochefoucauld-Liancourt, the marquis de La Fayette, the marquis de Condorcet, and certain members of the Parliament, Adrien du Port, Hérault de Séchelles, Le Pelletier de Saint-Fargeau. These men, to take the lead of the movement, joined with bankers like the Labordes[2] academicians like the lawyer Target and jurists and writers of note, such as Bergasse and Lacretelle, Servan and Volney. The party organized itself for propaganda. Like the Parliaments and the Breton nobility before them, each man made use of his personal connections. Correspondents in the depths of the provinces did the same.... The general staff of the new party met in certain drawing rooms like that of Mme. de Tessé, soon to be Mounier's Egeria. Journalists harangued in the cafés.... (52–53).

[2] The earlier description of the aristocracy tells us (13) that a daughter of the banker Laborde became the Comtesse de Noailles, thus linking the Labordes with La Fayette's family circle. This sort of alliance of great nobles with the *haute bourgeoisie* points to the fallacy of dividing revolutionary leadership into aristocratic and bourgeois elements. It should be noted that financial connections linking both groups are not as significant as and do not necessarily correlate with social, familial, or personal affinities. Thus business associates may be excluded or snubbed—even down to the present—by aristocrats who prefer the company of members of their own class. D'Artois' investment in the Javel works (13) thus tells us nothing at all about his political or social orientation.

The phrase "to take the lead of the movement" is misleading. There was no "bourgeois" movement in the summer of 1788 organized by bankers, academicians, jurists, and writers for some great noblemen to join or to lead. There was no party to organize itself. None of those who "took the lead" could be depicted as "fellow travelers," climbing on a bandwagon that was already rolling. All of them were planning how to beat the drums and wave the banners in order to attract a procession, as they did by the winter's end. Although he sums the matter up—"the bourgeoisie from the first move showed shrewd political sense" (55)—the author, instead, describes how nonbourgeois leaders made the first moves, employed shrewd political tactics, utilized extensive personal connections, and expended much printer's ink in order to mobilize and organize resistance over the issue of "doubling the Third."

> The question is whether a central intelligence directed this orchestra of protest.... A directing role can apparently be attributed only to the Committee of Thirty of which unfortunately we know very little. It met especially at the house of Adrien du Port and its membership is said to have included the duc de La Rochefoucauld-Liancourt, La Fayette, Condorcet, the duc d'Aiguillon ... Sieyès ... and Talleyrand.... Mirabeau also came to the meetings. This committee inspired pamphlets, circulated models for the petitions of grievances, supported candidacies and dispatched agents to the provinces.... But the influence of the Committee of Thirty ... would be greatly exaggerated were we to imagine that everything done in every town was merely in execution of its orders. The state of communications allowed no such strict control. If the movement prospered it was because the local bourgeoisie proved its initiative ... (53–54).

Possibly the local bourgeoisie did prove its initiative in the provinces although one wonders about the social composition of those correspondents in its depths. Certainly it was not the Parisian bourgeoisie that took the initiative in their home town, but rather a socially heterogeneous, ideologically homogeneous collection of notables and nobodies drawn from the three estates. All that the Parisian leaders seem to have shared in common was that their private social circles overlapped and that they "unreservedly adopted the new ideas" (52). The point is not that everything done everywhere was done on the basis of orders from the Committee of Thirty. It is rather that, as the author tells us, what central organization the state of communications permitted *was* provided by this group. On the basis of what happened in Paris and judging from the other evidence provided it seems plausible that where local initiative did come, it came from similarly heterogeneous provincial groups.

A blurring of class divisions characterized the earlier common front formed against the royal power. The nobility did not monopolize provincial distrust of the court and the great town of Paris. Hostility to the centralizing Bourbon court and bureaucracy and defense of the local autonomy of provincial estates had cut across class divisions. "Particularism rather than privilege," we later learn, most persistently resisted the effort to liquidate *ancien régime* institutions (165). Class divisions, themselves, cut across the clergy and the legal profession. The multiple gradations and distinctions, the plural inequalities and privileges that led to overlapping and crisscrossing social groupings in *ancien régime* France do not, in short, lend themselves to a clear-cut dichotomy between any two large classes. This appears to be true with respect to the division of opinion over representation to the Estates-General. Members of the second estate were divided on this issue. A section of the Assembly of Notables, presided over by the Comte de Provence, pronounced after a very close vote in favor of doubling the Third (59). The Third Estate was, itself, by no means united on the issue of privilege. Much later in the book (a year later in time) we are told "since provinces and towns had privileges also, the aristocracy would not be without secret supporters within the Third Estate itself" (157). As "owners of manors or fiefs," as "managers, middlemen or lawyers for manorial lords" many bourgeois, it later turns out, provided aristocrats with "silent support" (161). The so-called "liberal" nobles and most of the parish priests provided constant support for the "patriot party." There is, then, no reason to assume, in the absence of evidence, that the protest against the Parlement's ruling was locally initiated by groups drawn exclusively from any one class or estate. What evidence is offered points in the opposite direction.

We had earlier been informed, in the first act of the drama, that

> the aristocratic class developed an organization for political action, ex-
> changing correspondence and passing instructions from town to town.

> *The Committee of Thirty, which was soon to take over the leadership of the Third Estate, seems to have originated as a center of parliamentary resistance (33).*[3]

If Parisian leadership of the Third Estate emerged from an organization developed by "the aristocratic class" (by heterogeneous groups of "notables" might be more accurate), why should not local initiative have emerged from a similar source? In fact, precedents established both by the royal ministers Calonne and Brienne, experimenting with newly formed provincial assemblies (24, 32), and by the "aristocratic revolution" in defense of old provincial estates, provided those who pressed the issue of "doubling the Third" with their main arguments. The case of the Vizille assembly—when "the aristocracy of Dauphiny got out of hand" (32) and after successfully defying the royal minister conceded "double representation to the Third Estate, vote by head and fiscal equality" (51)—is twice cited in this connection (51, 55).[4]

We are told also how the program to press double representation was executed:

> *the scheme was to overwhelm the government with a flood of petitions for which the municipalities whether willing or not were obliged to take*

---

[3] The author does not account for the apparent contradiction involved in a center of parliamentary resistance that becomes a center of resistance to parliamentary authority. This is only one of many puzzles obscured by the very clarity of his scheme. Since one-half of the puzzle belongs to the first act, the other to the second, the reader, like the author, is apt to forget that the pieces belong together. Thus the Breton Third Estate is, on papers 18–19, represented by nobles and privileged persons. On pages 60–61 this same privileged body defies the nobles and clergy until fiscal equality long demanded by it is granted. The fact that municipal oligarchs did have different interests than the hereditary nobles would, in this case, solve the puzzle created by overdramatizing the solid front composed of privileged status groups in the first act. But no such simple solution of the first-mentioned puzzle occurs to me.

[4] Nowhere is the analysis more puzzling than in the account (32) of this action by the Dauphiny aristocracy. "Still ... dissatisfied, *because* Brienne ... had granted double representation [italics mine]" and vote by head to the new provincial assemblies, this aristocracy demanded the return of their old estates. They defied his refusal to grant this request, "obtained the support of the bourgeoisie," and then at Vizille granted the very forms of representation that had, we were told, provoked their original defiance. By considering the issue of Versailles versus the provinces rather than that of aristocrats versus commoners this affair might seem less puzzling. Regional rivalries that crisscrossed social cleavages tend to find no place in the book, but they were of equal importance in determining the forms of conflict that set the stage for the coming of the Revolution.

responsibility during the autumn of 1788. At Dijon, for example, the matter was put through as follows: Some twenty "notables" [5] *met and decided to submit to their respective guilds and corporate bodies the questions of doubling the Third and of vote by head (56).*

Favorable response from roughly twenty out of fifty guilds, resistance from the municipal authorities overcome by an invasion of the town hall, and a petition sent to the king in the name of the Dijon Third Estate followed. Similar action occurred in the other towns of Burgundy. Who devised this "scheme," suggested to the original twenty notables in Dijon, elsewhere in Burgundy, and presumably throughout many other provinces in the vast realm of France that they canvass the guilds and force, by direct action, the signing of similar petitions by municipalities? "A directing role can apparently be attributed only to the Committee of Thirty" (53). In the one example offered we see that the burghers of Dijon were by no means unanimous in their response to the issue pressed upon them. Thirty or so guilds did not respond. Violence was required to force urban oligarchs to sign and send the petitions.

Evidence drawn from countless such towns, located in all the French provinces, would be required to determine precisely how members of the Third Estate divided on this issue. One would like to know, in the one example given, why some burghers and guildsmen (in particular the local lawyers' guild) responded favorably while others did not. But despite the evidence, bourgeois solidarity is blandly taken for granted. According to the author's scheme, in fact, the bourgeoisie moved to the center of the stage just as soon as the Paris Parlement pronounced its verdict.

... A wave of excitement passed over the bourgeoisie at the news that the Estates-General were to be convoked. For the first time since 1614 the king was authorizing the bourgeoisie to speak. At first no struggle was foreseen. ... The assembly at Vizille had left a deep impression by conced-

---

[5] As always, when specific examples come in the narrative, the blank-faced bourgeoisie disappears. In dealing with the issue of revolutionary initiative, social nomenclature which is vague appears to be more accurate than that which is precise. The closer one gets to the real men involved the further one is from clearly polarized class divisions. It should be noted that even craftsmen in some cases "counted as notables" (44), along with urban oligarchs, academicians, magistrates, and aristocrats.

ing double representation to the Third Estate. . . . Agreement seemed by no means impossible.[6]
But the outlook changed abruptly when the Parliament of Paris . . . ruled that the Estates-General should be constituted as in 1614. A clamor rose from one end of the kingdom to the other. Between night and morning the popularity of the Parliament vanished (51).

The state of communications, which did not permit Parisian organization to penetrate the provinces and left matters to local initiative, apparently proved more efficient in transmitting news of the Parlement's ruling. The question of who transmitted this news and how it was transmitted is, however, by-passed. The length of the interval between night and morning or *"du jour au lendemain"* is not discussed. On how the news was received, we are offered some undated comments by Weber and Brissot, told that Mme. Roland and Rabaut-Saint-Étienne "now took passionately to public affairs," and informed of Mallet du Pan's remark: "The controversy has completely changed. King, despotism and constitution are now minor questions. The war is between the Third Estate and the other two orders" (52). Mallet's remarks are dated. They came in January 1789, after three or more months of canvassing and campaigning on the issue of doubling the Third.

It seems to have been this canvassing and campaigning, accompanied by an outpouring of pamphlets that "astonished contemporaries" by their number (54), that accounted for the way hitherto quiescent subjects took passionately to public affairs in the the winter of 1788–1789. But disappointment at the Parlement's ruling and immediate action designed to reverse it came first of all from groups who had already been active in the first act of the drama. Indignation, defiance, and effective action from such quarters are, however, muffled by the author and detached from the public storm of protest.

---

[6] To suggest that agreement about representation seemed possible before the Parlement's ruling conveys a prior preoccupation with this issue before it was posed. The issues over which men might agree or disagree were still invisible during the two and a half months from July 5 to September 23, 1788, when the wave of excitement rippled over literate sectors of the public. It seems likely that no one, bourgeois or not, knew quite what to expect after learning an Estates-General would meet, that all sorts of vague hopes and plans were encouraged rather than specific expectations about how the orders would be represented.

As was to be expected, some of the privileged were inclined to grant the Third Estate a certain satisfaction of its pride. On December 5, 1788, the "nationals" in the Parliament of Paris prevailed on that body to declare, by formal order, that it had no intention of prejudging the number of deputies in the Estates-General, and that the number was not fixed by law (58–59).

"In private," we are also told, "some of the privileged expressed themselves definitely in favor of the Third Estate" (59). Presumably public expressions of such an attitude were not becoming to aristocrats. Yet something more than the tepid inclination to grant commoners "a certain satisfaction" is conveyed by a letter cited from one aristocrat to another.

Some think the nonprivileged, who are the base and pillar of the State, should be without sufficient representatives in an Assembly which is to regulate their destiny. This is really too insulting and will not work. In any case the thing has been seen through. It will be best to be careful of what is done. . . . But I perceive my dear count that I am repeating to you what you know and think (59).

This was, to be sure, a private letter. But the convictions contained in it were implemented by public action coming from the same privileged social strata, resulting not only in the Parlement's reversal of its ruling but also in the official decree of December 27 granting double representation to the Third Estate.

These moves did not occur without considerable opposition from many aristocrats, whose resistance, we are told, led "many bourgeois to become more radical in their ideas" (61). Along with the later behavior of the Breton deputies and a shift in Rabaut-Saint-Étienne's views, two illustrations of this change in bourgeois attitudes are offered. One is a famous pamphlet by Abbé Sieyès: *What Is the Third Estate?* The other is a famous printed speech by Count Mirabeau, eulogizing Marius for exterminating the order of the nobility (61–62). It is typically difficult to describe the social position of both authors in terms of conventional social nomenclature. Mirabeau was a "deserter from the nobility" who "had lived by his pen in the service of Calonne and Calonne's enemies" (71). Sieyès was a frustrated member of the second estate barred from a bishopric as a commoner whose "pamphlets made him an oracle" (69). In their service to the Committee of Thirty both "were certainly in contact with the Duc d'Orleans" (54). As publicists drawn from the first two estates who were ultimately elected to represent the Third, they are ill-adapted to illustrate changes in attitudes on the part of a single social class. They seem better suited to illustrate the more amorphous social strata to which "men of letters" (a formidable pressure group in its own right) belonged, and from which the attack on both despotism and privilege, the thoroughgoing assault on all the traditional ruling elites first came.

On the evidence provided then, sensitivity to a ruling that was taken as an insult to the nonprivileged was not confined to the bourgeoisie. The canvassing, pamphleteering, and circulating of petitions to reverse this ruling were neither initiated nor directed by the bourgeoisie. What precedents existed for a contrary ruling and what action was taken to obtain a reversal from the Parlement did not come from the bourgeoisie. Yet all of these measures receive the same treatment as the scheme that was put through in the fall of 1788:

> By such means, the bourgeoisie *set the "nation" into motion. Its maneuver was denounced then, and has been ever since. But the aristocracy, shortly before, had acted no differently. Every political movement naturally has its instigators and leaders.* No one has ever dared to maintain that the Third Estate, *invited to appear in the Estates-General, could have thought it natural to leave the aristocracy supreme in the assembly. Hence, what* the leaders of the patriot party *are blamed for is simply to have roused* the nation *to shake off* its *torpor and organize* itself *to defend* its *cause [emphasis mine] (56).*[7]

One must bear in mind that what is meant by "torpor" is the political passivity of quiescent subjects accustomed for hundreds of years to leave decisions pertaining to affairs of state to others. Otherwise one is apt to overlook the necessity of explaining how that torpor was shaken off. There was as yet no "nation" to be set in motion or, a more problematic issue, to rouse or organize itself. Since no evidence is presented concerning "maneuvers" by the blank-faced bourgeoisie—since scattered unorganized commoners

---

[7] The italics are employed to suggest ambiguity concerning the group whose behavior is involved, who set whom into motion, and who defended whose cause. At least four, possibly five or six collective terms are used: the bourgeoisie, the leaders of the patriot party, the Third Estate, the "nation," the instigators and leaders.

were not in a position to undertake such maneuvers—one is at a loss concerning the means by which they set "the nation" in motion. As already noted, the maneuvers of the leaders of the patriot party may be examined. It is not surprising that they appear similar to those employed by "the aristocracy, shortly before." For most of these leaders are the very same men whose tactics the author had described "shortly before"—in connection with aristocratic political organization—before he had them "range themselves" on the same side as the bourgeoisie. In fact, he shows them choosing sides before lines had been drawn, setting the terms of the debate, and canvassing opinion on it. How could they range themselves on the same side as men who had yet to be heard from?

To ask this question is not to ignore the fact that the policies pursued by the leaders would have proved ineffective had not support been forthcoming from men who had yet to be heard from. Of course such massive support from literate commoners was required for subsequent events to spin themselves out as they did. But we are concerned with who intervened rather than with all the unforeseen consequences of the intervention. Our question is designed to suggest the necessity of distinguishing between how contemporaries aligned themselves before the fact and how historians realign them after it. When this distinction is not made, the patriot leaders tend to be portrayed as "trimmers," siding first with one group and then (in many instances, after "deserting their class") with another. The evidence suggests, to the contrary, that they played a strategic role by not behaving as "trimmers," by their unwavering constant perseverance and willingness to exert steady pressure toward their chosen goal.

"No one has ever dared to suggest that the Third Estate could have thought it natural to leave the aristocracy supreme in the Assembly." The author himself shows that had the orders not been kept separate, it was feared that many members of the Third Estate would vote to be represented by aristocrats (55). What men thought "natural" before the French Revolution needs to be distinguished from what historians view as "natural" thereafter. Certainly few of the customs of the *ancien régime* appeared natural to men steeped in Enlightenment thought. But most of them probably appeared natural enough to men who were not. Both groups confronted what appeared by the late eighteenth century to be an "unnatural" vagueness about numerical representation in earlier meetings of the Estates-General. For, as antiquarians scouring the records discovered, the Third Estate, although officially summoned to send one delegate for each sent by the other two orders, had in fact sent many more than its share of delegates, outnumbering the clergy on one hand and the nobility on the other by different numbers which varied in each case (and which made little difference since there was also an unnatural agreement about consistently voting by order).[8] To follow the precedent of 1614 precisely was in this regard impossible. When the Estates-General had to be resurrected, after its demise more than a century and a half before, such vagueness concerning quantitative representation no longer came naturally to any party concerned. The fact that some eighteenth-century provincial estates had already doubled the Third and were voting by head suggests what France suffered by letting the Estates-General atrophy during the seventeenth and eighteenth centuries. In place of a relatively flexible institution that could accommodate social change, Frenchmen confronted only a brittle precedent that had to be either artificially reconstructed or deliberately broken. No one could escape this either-or issue. Every notable had to rethink and make explicit his view of how the body politic should be constituted. The resulting division of opinion involved conflicting concepts of a well-ordered commonwealth, incompatible opinions about how it should be governed, and rival ambitions about who should govern it.

Was this division congruent with the division between the first two estates and the Third? Did it not first of all divide those who had just emerged victorious in their long struggle with the crown and expected to exploit this victory to the full? Should we not look to the "liberal" aristocracy, even before turning to the bourgeoisie, for a "full consciousness of historic mission" shaped by "the thought of eighteenth-century writers" (50)? At least the men who thought

---

[8] Lefebvre points to the shrewdness of pressing the issue of doubling the Third while leaving open that of voting by head (55, 59–60). Indirectly he shows how the postponement of this latter issue was politically indispensable for the patriots (see pp. [198–199], below). But he never makes clear that when propagandists *did* stipulate "voting by head" or when, as in the Dijon case, the municipal authorities balked on this issue (56), the separation of the orders was taken for granted by *everyone* as far as the elections to the Estates-General went. Voting by head referred *only* to the procedure to be followed at Versailles—after the doubled Third had arrived there.

it unnatural to leave the aristocracy supreme in the Assembly, who at any rate posed the issue in this way to their fellow countrymen happened—many of them—to be marquis, counts, bishops, *abbés,* in short, members of the first two estates. Why did *they* think it unnatural to follow, as best one could, the precedent of 1614? The case could have been presented differently. Why did the leaders of the patriot party feel impelled to present it at all? That it presented itself, so to speak, to these leaders in this form, and that they felt impelled to enlist the support of like-minded compatriots, is what needs to be explained. The Parlement of Paris had decided the case otherwise. A recent analysis of the eighteenth-century robe nobility suggests why it was "natural" for this body to do so. But the Committee of Thirty seems to have originated in robe circles. Members of the Paris Parlement: Adrien du Port, Hérault de Séchelles, Le Pelletier de Saint Fargeau, and the unnamed "nationals" who obtained a reversal on December 5, 1788, worked hard and successfully to create a clamor against the ruling of the very body to which they belonged. It is this sort of purposeful action by active minorities, working both inside and outside duly constituted bodies, that one may unambiguously call "revolutionary." Since it could not be anticipated by contemporaries, authorities could not take measures to forestall it. Since it did not fit familiar formulas derived from prolonged experience with assassination plots and seditions during earlier "times of troubles" and since it could be traced to no court or cabinet, no foreign agents, no one class or group or region, new kinds of conspiratorial hypotheses would be woven to explain it (including those which involved impersonal agents set in motion by an invisible hand).

Instead of being isolated and studied, in *The Coming of the French Revolution,* the behavior of these active minorities, composed of like-minded individuals drawn from all three estates, is treated as marginal or inconsequential. Evidence pertaining to this behavior is invariably subordinated to the clear scheme of each large class acting independently in its own interests. Insofar as revolutionary initiative came from aristocrats, for example, attention is distracted from it and focused instead on the resistance of other aristocrats. Those who helped force the first conflict are made to appear as bystanders, or assigned secondary roles as supporting players in the second act. Those who behaved as stereotyped aristocrats . . . are assigned responsibility for not acceding to the will of "the majority," which historians in retrospect may fathom but contemporaries in prospect had not. Conflict came, we are told, because most aristocrats behaved in their customary manner and expected others to do the same. Concord would have come had they behaved otherwise. The men who did *not* form the first revolutionary pressure group are thus assigned a more strategic role in precipitating the conflict than those who did.

> *It is true that certain nobles had less narrow views. These men, in the Estates-General, were to ally themselves with the Third, take the initiative in surrendering privileges on the night of August 4 and vote for the Declaration of the Rights of Man and the Citizen. It is not that they had abandoned hope of keeping their leadership in the modern state, but rather that they were willing to count simply on the prestige of their names, the influence of their wealth and the claims of their own abilities. . . . The essential fact is that they consented [9] to being legally no more than citizens of France. But they were only a minority; otherwise the Revolution would have taken place by common accord.*
>
> *Should the Third Estate have contented itself, respectfully and submissively, with what the great majority of the aristocracy were willing to offer it? In any case it did not think so, and loudly demanded equality before the law. At this point, strictly speaking, the Revolution of 1789 began [emphasis mine] (36–37).*

Here the curtain comes down on the first act of the drama. An analysis of the social structure of the bourgeoisie sets the stage for the second. This analysis appears irrelevant to the rhetorical question concerning what the Third Estate should have done. Nor does it help us much in our effort to understand how the Revolution came. For what we must ask is what the heterogeneous, scattered, and politically unconstituted members of the Third Estate would have done had they not been presented with a most appealing and very clear alternative to respectful submission. It seems likely that whatever they might have thought and done and however widespread was a latent resentment of aristocratic privilege, had they not been provided with many identical petitions to get signed and

---

[9] On the author's evidence, they did not merely consent; they worked hard for this end. Nor did they merely vote for the declaration; they were the very first to propose it (La Fayette on July 11, 1789) (89). Along with other Committee of Thirty colleagues, they also played a prominent role in drafting it.

many similar pamphlets to read, local responses ot ‿ short-wave resonance would have resulted. There are, ᴇ many different ways of demanding equality before the law. were many more in the vast realm of France during the anᴜ ⸝ *régime* where justice before the law was dispensed differently in different regions and for different social groups, where there was no uniform law before which any kind of equality could be demanded.

If in the winter of 1788 a single demand sounded "loudly," it was because a sufficient number of similar petitions, singling out for protest the Parlement's ruling and singling out from among all the issues relating to composition, election, convocation, and procedure this ruling might raise, that of double representation for the Third Estate, were forced through scattered municipalities throughout the realm. Since local initiative was required to force through the petitions and since this occurred in many scattered areas, one may agree, roughly speaking, that a considerable number of commoners throughout the country were not content to submit respectfully to what the constituted bodies offered. But when one remembers the long list of earlier insurrections and seditions, it seems evident that a failure to submit to established authorities was not what distinguished the protest movement of 1788 from earlier "times of troubles." Such insubordination had hitherto been spread out over much longer intervals resulting in "sporadic" episodes, or, when occurring in shorter intervals, had involved so many bewilderingly various localized issues and incidents that historians, even in retrospect, have difficulty patterning and polarizing them. In the winter of 1788 protests came within a remarkably short interval and produced a remarkably uniform appearance. A considerable measure of central organization is suggested by the simultaneity of this action. The unprecedented use made of the duplicative powers of print largely accounts for the uniform character of the clamor.

This clamor, which rose from one end of the nation to the other, was made in the name of the Third Estate and appeared to come from that residual order of the realm. In some regions, we are told, "peasants and workingmen streamed into the halls and the whole Third Estate signed [or marked?] the petition" (56). Although they composed most of the nonprivileged, "the base and pillar of society," and although it was, as yet, by no means clear how the Third

Estate was to be represented, the participation of peasants and workingmen in this action is generally not regarded as evidence of revolutionary initiative. Whereas similar participation by a smaller residual category of literate commoners, who did not work with their hands and are diversely defined as "the bourgeoisie," is so regarded. Located in all the provinces of France, however, and presenting "an extreme diversity of condition" (46), this latter group were scarcely better situated than were their unlettered compatriots to ensure the uniformity and simultaneity that made the demands of the Third Estate sound loudly. They had yet to meet together, find some basis for a common accord, or discover how they differed.

On the other hand, the leaders of the resistance to the crown had already gathered in Assemblies of Notables and had already discovered how they differed. The activities of the Committee of Thirty appear inexplicable if we assume, as the author seems to, that the "aristocratic revolution" was made by men who fought royal despotism only with old feudal war cries or the more up-to-date *"thèse nobiliaire"* in mind. His evidence shows that it had also been made by men who had more "liberal" views about how a modern state should be governed; who had, in addition to their public concern, private personal ambitions. From this evidence, we also infer that these liberal notables moved in social circles that included talented commoners, preferred the latter's company, respected their judgment and competence rather more than that of many of their peers. Such men, it turned out, comprised a minority of the aristocracy. But they were not, for that reason, paralyzed, silenced, or rendered inactive. They were a sizable and powerful minority who had already combined in a loose coalition with a sizable minority of talented commoners who were particularly skilled with their pens. They had already created an organization for political action and correspondence throughout the provinces, had already laid the basis for a shadowy "national" or "patriot" party. They did not lose their initiative when thwarted. To the contrary, they initiated action as leaders of an independent coalition party.

In aligning themselves *against the privileged classes* the bourgeoise *took the name hitherto claimed in common by all who opposed the royal power.* They *formed the "national" or "patriot party." Those of the privileged groups who had unreservedly adopted the new ideas ranged them-*

selves on the same side. . . . The party organized itself *for propaganda [emphasis mine] (52).*

We would argue that "the party" did not organize itself any more than "the bourgeoisie" aligned themselves, took the name, or formed the party. Insofar as men were aligned, the party named, formed, and organized for propaganda, certain notables "who had less narrow views," who were "only a minority," played a leading role. Without the continuity of leadership they provided it would be less easy to speak strictly about the point at which the Revolution of 1789 began. Where there is "common accord" there is no place for revolutionary action. Exceptions in the form of atypical minorities may be dismissed as proving the rule more often than not. But they have to be considered when studying exceptional events. On such occasions one has to determine how rules are broken rather than how they are proved.

In concluding his account of "the first victory" achieved by the "bourgeois revolution," the author conveys always by indirection, that initiative remained in the same hands during the electoral campaign that followed the successful protest movement. The successful electioneering of the patriot party is contrasted with the failure of Necker and other royal ministers to draw up a list of candidates committed to a program of desired reforms. It is contrasted also with the clumsy, uncoordinated attempts at personal influence made, here and there, by the chairmen of bailiwick assemblies (66). "Since 1789 there have been political parties with much stronger organization than the patriots of that time but none has met with so little resistance on the part of the government" (67). Until 1789, however, the government had been engaged in mobilizing its forces against seditious elites: namely the parlements, provincial assemblies, municipal corporations (not to mention a variety of religious orders, the long arm of Rome, and of foreign courts as well). It had no experience with an independent domestic opposition party led by a loose coalition of aristocrats, ecclesiastics, men of letters and of the liberal professions mobilizing opinion against these elites and utilizing for this purpose the full power of the printing press, earlier turned against the crown by the parlements, now for the first time in France, released from the clandestine channels into which it had been forced.

What is surprising is that even a rudimentary political party could be organized, lists of candidates drawn up, platforms of reforms proposed in less than a year before the Estates had convened—not that subsequent parties would be more strongly organized or that the government failed to forestall this one. With respect to this problem, the author tells us, "The Committee of Thirty . . . assumed a lead whose extent it is impossible to determine" (66–67). On the other hand, he has no doubts,

> *It is hardly doubtful that enterprising bourgeois everywhere took con-*
> *certed action[10] to steer the town and bailiwick assemblies, with as many*
> *parish assemblies as possible in addition, by suggesting candidates and*
> *circulating models for petitions of grievances. The models were either*
> *received from Paris, or, more often, drafted locally (67).*

These "enterprising bourgeois" who suggested candidates and drafted local models, independently of those sent from Paris, are necessarily nameless. Two social groups are singled out as playing a predominant role: lawyers who "were very influential" and the village priests who "gave much aid." This is not the only instance, but it is the most transparent, where the vital distinction between being literate (as the village priests apparently were) and being "enterprising bourgeois" (as they surely were not)[11] is overlooked. This distinction is so vital to all theories pertaining to the coming of the French Revolution, or to the "rise of bourgeoisie to political power," that it seems worth pausing over. Because the electoral assemblies were also deliberative, we are told,

> *the most influential bourgeois, or those best informed on public affairs*
> *or most accustomed to speaking in public, namely the lawyers, . . . [domi-*

[10] However enterprising they may be, men who are located "everywhere" simply cannot take "concerted action" to steer an electorate toward a given slate of candidates. One group located in one place is required to see that all the others do not "steer" in all directions.

[11] Many bourgeois families sent one son into the priesthood as they sent another into law. But the former were more apt to be attached to cathedral chapters in towns than to village parishes. They were also apt to be the less enterprising among bourgeois offspring. Finally, to apply the term "bourgeois" to village priests as well as to "the upper level of the nobility . . . those conditions of life drew them to the bourgeoisie" (14) is to stretch this much-abused term beyond its already frayed limits. There is something wildly askew about a structural model that includes the top layer of nobles and the bottom layer of the clergy within the middle ranks of "the middle class."

nated] throughout the debates. In the bailiwick assemblies, the peasants lacking education and unable to express themselves, let themselves be docilely led. The result was that the representation of the Third Estate was made up uniquely of bourgeois (65).

In light of the vital distinction, we would argue that it was made up, almost uniquely (aside from three priests and a dozen noblemen [67]) of a nonprivileged literate laity. The acquisition of literacy, by whatever means and in whatever era since the sixteenth century, was the most important single determinant as far as the social composition of the Third Estate delegation went. As a group, literate commoners *had* no social structure or nomenclature—medieval institutions had not been designed to take them into account. But in countless villages and even in some small towns, they were nonetheless a very distinctive group. The village schoolmaster was yet to become as ubiquitous as the parish priest. The latter was out of the running as a delegate of the Third Estate. Lawyers "who lived in the villages or often visited them for manorial pleadings" (67) represented in some cases the only possible alternative.

One reason for so many varying definitions of "the bourgeoisie" is the impossibility of making this group, however regarded in terms of status, occupation, economic class, style of life, and so forth, congruent with the much more amorphous body of men who had, ever since the printing press, been rising from the ranks of a pre-literate population by mastering the written word. To whom else could this population turn but to such men when all the traditional literate elites—teachers, preachers, officers, bureaucrats—were out of the running? One may only guess how many more priests, aristocrats, or high magistrates might have been elected instead of the lawyers and other commoners who were, had not the former been eliminated from the running. Evidence is offered that the leaders of the patriot party feared the number might have been significantly large:

Seeming to fear the prestige of the privileged persons and to think them capable of imposing on commoners to the point of being elected to represent them, the patriot party often demanded, even later on, that each order be required to choose its representatives from its own members (55).

This is presented to show, not how elections were partly rigged by rigorously enforcing the separation of orders, but rather as evidence of "the moderation of the Third" despite the atypical "trenchant tone" of Sieyès' pamphlet. "The patriot party, in fact, by no means asked that the Estates-General be elected without regard to the three orders" (55). Of course it did not ask this. To obtain an overwhelming majority composed of the doubled Third, parish priests, and liberal nobles, working under the leaders of the patriot party, the electorate had to be insulated until after the elections. The abrupt accession to political power of the Third Estate depended very precisely on how demands for "equality before the law" were formulated and phrased. The sudden appearance of a commanding majority composed of hitherto politically quiescent unknown literate commoners (often described as the political accession of the "revolutionary bourgeoisie") paradoxically depended just as much on preserving the medieval tradition of separate and qualitatively differentiated orders as it did on pressing the issue of doubling the Third, while holding in reserve—until after the scene of action had shifted from the provinces to the capital—insistence on merging the orders and voting by head.

This majority was the freakish result of exploiting in less than a single year two wholly incompatible, thoroughly medieval and thoroughly modern, concepts of the body politic: hierarchical, heterogeneous, and qualitative; egalitarian, homogeneous, and quantitative. It involved keeping apart what, throughout the country, might have belonged together had procedures been consistently based on modern legal fictions: a rural, provincial electorate and their traditional governors and leaders. It also lumped together as a single unprivileged order groups that were in fact kept apart, not merely by traditional regional frontiers and social gradations, but also by a yawning literacy gap. Only the small minority that stood on one side of this gap—who belonged to the reading public served by Enlightenment authors and constituted the most atypical portion of the Third Estate—was thus singled out by a kind of unnatural selection or historical "accident" to represent at Versailles the entire nation. The atrophy of French representative institutions, encouraged by the crown, coinciding with the unevenly phased impact of literacy, which no one understood or controlled, produced this singular result. It was put together by historical circumstance, not by conniving politicians, none of whom probably clearly understood what had happened. But the patriot leaders did at least take full advantage of the opportunity offered them to exploit long-embalmed and newly resurrected fifteenth-century electoral procedures in the interests of recently developed eighteenth-century legal fictions and, thus, to overwhelm the old elites by a monstrous majority. Lefebvre so completely overlooks this that later in his account he presents the failure to merge the orders in the countryside immediately as evidence of a sociopolitical lag, impeding a thoroughgoing liquidation of the *ancien régime.*

> *The three orders, though united in the Assembly, had not disappeared from the social structure of the nation. It had not even occurred to the Third to force the election of a new Assembly, so that nobles and priests retained their seats though representing an infinitesimal minority of Frenchmen. . . . It cannot then be claimed that the Third contemplated a class rule (89–90).*

The nobles and priests who retained their seats have represented an infinitesimal minority of the population. The literate commoners did not represent a much larger one. Judging by earlier fears of the patriots, had an election of a new Assembly been forced right after the orders had been merged, more nobles and priests, rather than fewer, might well have been seated at Versailles.

> *Divide the human race into twenty parts and there will be nineteen composed of those who work with their hands and who will never know that there was a Locke in the world; in the twentieth part remaining, how few men are there who can read? and among those who can, there will be twenty who read romances to one who studies science. The number of those who think is excessively small and they do not think about troubling the world.* [Voltaire]

If we substitute eighteenth-century Frenchmen for "the human race," Voltaire's observation, ironic or not, appears to be well founded. The excessively small number of eighteenth-century Frenchmen who could read, who had heard of Locke, preferred science to romance, and could "think" were, most of them, surely not consciously thinking about troubling the world. They had never participated in noble seditions or popular *émeutes* before Voltaire's day; nor did they do so for a decade after his death. Their inner composure was possibly disturbed by silent dialogues with favorite authors whose messages tended to slip past inner censors much as they did, via clandestine channels, past outer ones. But whatever their fantasies—and no one can read the minds of book readers —they remained politically passive, probably the most orderly subjects of an occasionally disordered realm. Engaged, on the whole profitably, pursuing their diverse trades, occupations, and professions, they had, in fact, much to lose and little to gain from the disruption of domestic peace. Even after delegates drawn exclusively from this "excessively small number" of literate townsmen who "were for the most part mature men in comfortable circumstances . . . educated . . . proficient in some specialized calling . . ." (68) arrived at Versailles, six-hundred strong, the leaders of the patriot party had every reason to expect, if not peasantlike docility, at least solid support from these political unknowns. They had no reason to anticipate that future historians would regard their own role as subordinate to that of the deputies they dominated. At least another year would pass before their expectations would appear unwarranted. As the author notes, in discussing the National Assembly: "It is also characteristic that, at least at first, the most prominent leaders were men from the privileged classes" (69). From this fact, he suggests, the reader might judge "what a place the aristocracy might have retained in the state had it been willing to compromise" (69), whereas we would conclude, what a role some privileged notables played in the coming of the French Revolution because they were *un*willing to compromise. And what a role former members of the Committee of Thirty and their friends continued to play in the National Assembly. For not only Sieyès, Mirabeau, and Target elected to represent the Third, Talleyrand representing the First, but also such members of the second estate as La Fayette, Lally-Tollendal, Clermont Tonnerre, the Vicomte de Noailles, the Duc d'Aiguillon, Mathieu de Montmorency, Adrien du Port, Charles and Alexander de Lameth, are singled out as playing a prominent part in events and reforms down through 1790 (68).

On "the debated question of who 'started the Revolution,' " then, the author's evidence suggests that initiative came, beginning with the first Assembly of Notables called by Calonne in 1786 through the stormy year of 1789 and beyond, from a loose coalition of like-minded men drawn from all three estates. No conventional social nomenclature appears applicable to this group whose collective biography remains to be written. Judging by the frequency with which the same names turn up, in conjunction with the Committee of Thirty and the leaders of the patriot party, this group was not very large—roughly the same number as might appear in a composite portrait of our own "founding fathers" seems to be involved. Some sort of collective biography of these men appear to be indispensable to any understanding of how the Revolution of 1789 came. It does not pose the same formidable problems as attempting to analyze the entire social structure of eighteenth-century France. Yet in contrast with the remarkable dexterity he displays in handling the latter, almost insuperable problem, Lefebvre treats the former, more manageable, and equally relevant one in a remarkably slipshod fashion. Only three of his most "prominent leaders" are thus granted cursory sketches. The Marquis de La Fayette is curiously characterized as "the incarnation of the *bourgeois* revolution." His "romantic illusions and juvenile vanity" predominated over "political skill or realistic sense." He served more as a "symbol than a leader" (69). Abbé Sieyès, the "theorist" and "moving spirit of the juridical revolution," was "never known except to the bourgeoisie" (his services to the Committee of Thirty and contracts with the Duc d'Orléans notwithstanding?). Although he "was neither a speaker nor a man of action," he, "more than any other, seems to have led the Third in the early weeks" (69). The Comte de Mirabeau "never managed to overcome the distrust which was only too well justified by his adventurous past and venal habits." That he was capable of selling out to the court or to Necker, "all who knew him were certain." Because of this, "while he rendered the Third Estate great services, he never succeeded in controlling it" (70–71).

Clearly an aristocrat incarnating a bourgeois revolution who was not a leader but a symbol, a theorist who could neither speak nor act, and a corrupt adventurer must appear as somewhat marginal figures. Three literary stereotypes having been offered, the matter is summed up: "In summary, none of these men were able to dominate the scene to the point of personifying the Revolution of 1789 which remained the collective achievement of the Third Estate" (71).

What has been described, however, was the collective achievement of more than one marquis, one *abbé,* and one count—the collective achievement of Sieyès, Mirabeau, La Fayette *and* Talleyrand, Condorcet, Adrien du Port, Hérault de Séchelles, Le Pelletier de Saint Fargeau, the Duc d'Aiguillon, La Rochefoucauld-Liancourt, Laborde, Target, Volney, Mounier, and so forth. Insofar as a revolution such as that of 1789 may be personified or incarnated, this group of men did so. Insofar as concerted collective action was involved, these men conducted it.[12] As constant leaders of the patriot party who steered the protest movement of 1788 and the electoral campaign of 1789, who pushed through the transformation of the Estates-General into a National Assembly, who proposed and drafted the Declaration of the Rights of Man, who abolished all privilege on the night of August 4, they provided the basis for whatever unity or continuity may be perceived in the early phases of the French Revolution. Athough all his evidence points to this conclusion, it is not apt to be drawn by those who read Lefebvre's book, as the following citation suggests:

> *... Georges Lefebvre distinguished four overlapping revolutions ... without moving past 1789. Yet there is a rough kind of unity in the major changes of the early Revolution. That complex unity, in the last analysis, is probably best conveyed by the fabulous watchword Liberté, Egalité, Fraternité.*
>
> *One of the bases of this unity was surely the predominance of France's bourgeoisie in the events and reforms of the Revolution. There was continuity with the Old Regime in this respect. ... The bourgeoisie (the observation is at least as old as Guizot) was gaining strength and self-awareness throughout the eighteenth century; the Revolution swiftly augmented that class's political power. As Marx would have it, the "feudal" class system was crumbling, and the "capitalist" class system arising from its dust. As Marx would also have it, the bourgeois were the principal agents and beneficiaries of the Revolution.[13]*

As the author of this citation says, these are "unsubtle and largely commonplace generalities." To make them more subtle and esoteric, however, will not help clarify a necessary distinction between the groups who initiate a given course of action and those who ulti-

---

[12] To avoid misunderstanding, the qualification indicated by the term "insofar" should be underlined. There are many aspects to a revolution such as that of 1789 that Lefebvre deals with and my discussion has excluded. Throughout I have tried to isolate the problem of how to locate revolutionary initiative by examining who intervened in 1788–1789. Clarity and precision on this point seem to be required before undertaking any larger-scale analysis of other problems.

[13] Charles Tilly, *The Vendée* (Cambridge, Mass., 1964), 160.

mately may benefit from it. To locate agents by studying beneficiaries, to collect all the motives that might have led the latter to pursue the course of action that was, in fact, initiated by the former is at present an all too common way of dealing with revolutionary causation. Yet studying which groups presumably benefited from the French Revolution (a vexed question in itself) is not really the right way to go about finding out who started the Revolution or how it began. When a theory is contradicted by the data, one must change the theory, not brush aside the data. In this case the data relate to a specific course of action undertaken by particular individuals. It shows that "France's bourgeoisie" did *not* initiate the protest movement of 1788 and did *not* play a prominent role in the events and reforms of 1789. To analyze what was shared in common by the leaders who did play a prominent role, to ascertain the degree to which thy achieved or failed to achieve the goals they had in mind (as subsequent events showed, these goals were by no means uniform) would carry us far beyond the limits of this paper. Suffice it to say that unanticipated consequences more often than not result from a given course of action that is not grounded on precedent or prolonged experience. Here, at least, the revolutionary action initiated in 1788 proved unexceptional. It is thus most unlikely that La Fayette envisaged riding beside a ragged procession of hungry and angry women marching to Versailles, leading a "massacre" on the Champs de Mars, or languishing in an Austrian prison; that Le Pelletier conceived of being coupled with Marat as a Jacobin martyr; that Hérault dreamed of serving with Robespierre on the Committee of Public Safety; Condorcet of dying as a Girondin prisoner; Sieyès of serving as a consul with Bonaparte, or Talleyrand (and La Fayette again!) more than four decades later, helping to oust D'Artois and install the son of D'Orléans on the French throne—to single out only a few of the subsequent roles played by only a few of the figures offered us.

None of the leaders of the patriot party could have anticipated the subsequent roles they would enact in the drama. But they nonetheless did, by wielding all the considerable power and influence at their disposal, help determine the conditions under which the drama would be played out. Purposeful action directed toward desired goals is one thing; unanticipated consequences resulting from this action are another. This obvious distinction has to be stressed, in order to avoid entanglement in the empty and endless debate over whether the Revolution was "spontaneous" or "planned," the product of "circumstances" or "plot." The debate is empty because it is invariably held over a grand design, incorporating the full sequence of events which only began to unfold in 1789. This design is visible only in retrospect. It could not be foreseen by any contemporaries. Hence it could not have been planned or devised by any of them. The debate is endless because the sequence of events has no stopping point. It is still spinning itself out and will always be differently concluded for and by each successive generation. It is worth noting that those who weave conspiratorial legends or employ the *"thèse de complots"* are just as prone to ignore the real men who formed and led the patriot party as are those who insist on spontaneous mass or class action. In both cases, efforts to fathom a grand design result in perpetually unsatisfactory answers to the more limited range of questions which anyone curious about the coming of the French Revolution might be expected to ask: Who intervened in the conflict between crown and nobles in 1788–1789? How did they do so and why? To learn, for example, that many leaders of the patriot party were Masons or that their correspondents in the provinces belonged to "reading societies" does not get us very far. Or, rather, it leads us much too far with hints that we must look beyond a loose political coalition based on informal groupings of like-minded notables, in search of an invisible network controlled by a hidden hand (the Duc d'Orléans?) or manipulated by Protestants, aliens, libertine aristocrats, and would-be philosopher-kings. On the other hand, to be told that these leaders must have been, if not members of the bourgeoisie, then its agents, symbols, or incarnations and to examine the social structure of this ascending class in order to understand the behavior of these leaders does not get us very far either —or takes us much too far also in search of statistics pertaining to capitalist enterprise, industrial development, and landownership patterns. In both instances we are asked to look around, over, beyond, above, or below rather than at the assorted individuals whose group action we are curious about. What we have tried to suggest in the foregoing discussion is that evidence relating to this group action, undertaken by known individuals, using known means, to exert continuous pressure toward known ends is contained in *The Coming of the French Revolution.* But a static framework derived from a structural analysis is incapable of containing this sort of dynamic group action. Instead it keeps apart, as socially stratified, the very cluster of men who gravitated together, mutually attracted by political goals that appeared to be within their reach. By artificially segmenting this continuous group action, by arbitrarily assigning revolutionary initiative first to the class-oriented activities of the aristocracy, then to those of the bourgeoisie, the author has, thus, almost smothered his evidence.

This critique is best concluded with a brief tribute to the book that provoked it. Lefebvre has provided his readers with a remarkably succinct account of an unusually snarled series of episodes. He has employed a clear-cut scheme to unsnarl these episodes and has successfully used this scheme to isolate the most critical ones. He has, in our view, been more successful in isolating "the point at which strictly speaking the Revolution of 1789 began" than in isolating the group who played a strategic role in determining this point. But his failure, in this regard, would not be perceptible had he employed a fuzzier scheme. Nor could it be perceived if he had not, in this short and semipopular book, illustrated his general statements by specific examples—naming names and citing evidence— without regard for whether his facts fitted his scheme but with a scrupulous regard for their pertinence to the episode being discussed. Few historians have both the daring and the caution that are required thus to lay bare all possible discrepancies in their work. But then few have mastered their difficult craft so successfully.

Jean Égret

WHO INTERVENED IN 1788?—SOME FACTS

Jean Égret (b. 1902), longtime professor of modern history at the University of Poitiers, has been studying the history of the "Pre-Revolution" for more than thirty years. Starting as one must in studying the Old Regime at the local level, he did a detailed study of Dauphiné as well as some other areas

From Jean Égret, *La pré-Révolution française, 1787–1789* (Paris, 1962), pp. 325–337, 351–361. With permission of the author and the Presses Universitaires de France. Editor's translation. Footnotes omitted.

before moving on to the national level in his general work entitled La pré-
Révolution française, 1787–1789, *from which the following excerpt is taken.
Although Professor Égret's approach is political in the sense that he is
concerned with the actions and reactions of governmental authorities at the
local level, he is also keenly sensitive to the social and economic groups and
forces underlying the resistance to the royal government's efforts to deal
with its financial crisis in 1787–1788. His interest in the character of this
resistance has led him to study particular groups in depth—most importantly
the Parlements. The excerpt which follows presents the most accurate factual
information that we have about the individuals in the forefront of the opposition (not yet revolutionary) movement in the fall of 1788 and the first months
of 1789.*

The *Arrêt du Conseil* of July 5, 1788 had effectively granted the
political press a considerable degree of freedom, since it invited
all Frenchmen to give advice on the way to make the promised
Estates-General "a truly national assembly both in its composition
and in its effect." Barère, in his journal, confirms the decisive impetus which this appeal by the chief minister gave to the publication
of pamphlets. "The bookstore of Desenne at the Palais Royal," he
wrote, "is jammed with buyers and readers of these thousand and
one current publications." Such developments were further encouraged by the release at the beginning of September "of all the
bookstore owners, booksellers and hawkers who had been arrested
and imprisoned sometime previously for their distribution of pamphlets opposing the policies of the ministry of Brienne." A few weeks
later the correspondent of the *Gazette de Leyde* noted the reap-
pearance of those societies known as "clubs," which had been
closed by the authorities in August of 1787. He reported, "They have
just been reestablished by express order of the king, since they
cannot cause any uneasiness among ministers who carry on their
work openly and whose pure and beneficent intentions can only be
furthered by being examined and publicized."

In the memoirs of some aristocrats, Necker has been reproached
for his alleged complacency in this matter as though it were a crime.
They even accuse him of inciting this popular ferment. Malouet, who
was very close to Necker at the time, offers a seemingly well-sup-
ported categorical denial of this assertion when he writes: "I can
affirm that at that time I was a close confidant of Necker. . . . I would
therefore have been aware . . . not of any criminal projects since he

would not have confided them to me—but of any indications of intrigue, or in the private expression of his thoughts of some of the revolutionary opinions which were imputed to him. But in our private conversations he appeared to me to be completely at ease with his conscience, although unquestionably relying too much on his own capacities, and indecisive on several crucial points, but always seeking and desiring to further the public welfare and sincerely supporting the king."

Undoubtedly frightened but filled with respect for the manifestations of opinion which were becoming increasingly bold, Necker, according to the avocat-general, the Breton Loz de Beaucours, replied in January 1789 to the fears expressed by a deputation from the Parlement of Rennes, "while keeping his eyes fixed on the ground—eyes which I am told never look one straight in the eye: 'it is the awakening of a great people.' "

In fact this awakening was powerfully stimulated by a number of societies of which the most famous undoubtedly was the one which met in Paris at the home of a counselor of the Parlement of Paris, Adrian Duport.

The exact date of the founding of this "club" is made known to us by Mirabeau, who was one of its founders. He wrote to the Duc de Lauzun on November 10, 1788,

> Panchaud was to have spoken to you, sir, about our plan for a club to work for a constitution; several men of merit who have already joined are to meet today for the second time at the home of M. Duport, counselor in the Parlement, on the rue de Grand-Chantier. Your presence is very much desired and anticipated, and I believe that you will have no regrets about associating yourself with our views, for this conspiracy of honest men will go further than one might expect and just as far as the public interest, properly understood, may require; so come. It is worthy of you to support good citizens.

Montmorency-Luxembourg, who was also one of the first members of this society, gives some details about the way the club worked.

> Sessions were held every Sunday, Tuesday and Friday from five to ten in the evening and no one was admitted without the unanimous approval of the members of the society which at first included only twelve people. A president was chosen who sat at a table, posed the questions to be considered and kept order in the discussion by permitting opinions to be

expressed according to the order of seating. He also summarized the
discussion and announced the times of the next meeting.

Some of the principal speakers at the club were some of the publicists who formerly had supported the policy of the disgraced ministers (Brienne and Lamoignon) and who now decisively repudiated
their too-cautious proposals for reform. One of these was Condorcet
who, according to Charles Lacretelle, "served the government so
long as it opposed the Parlements, but later on became a relentless
enemy of the government." Duport, a former collaborator with Calonne, was preparing with Condorcet the publication of a defense of
American institutions. The illustrious avocat, Target, then fifty-five
years old, described as "an athlete of many years experience in
sparring at the bar, full of confidence and boldness and consumed
with ambition," addressed—with the support of the Society—certain
bold statements intended to influence the decisions of the advisory
Assembly of Notables which the king had just reconvened. Some of
the younger members of the Society already favorably thought of,
such as the lawyer Pierre-Louis Lacretelle and the counselor from
Metz, Pierre-Louis Roederer, exhibited the same assurance and elo-
quence.

Duport's professional standing naturally drew to his home several
members of the Parlement who had led the relentless war against
the government in the halls of Parlement. Some of them—like Robert
de Saint-Vincent and D'Eprémesnil—began however to draw back in
the face of the prospect of a revolution, which it seemed might be
more democratic than they wished. It was the influence of these
members of the Parlement in the Society which met at Duport's, and
the resulting second thoughts and equivocations which convinced
Mirabeau to take a step which seemed, reasonably, to foreshadow
his separation from the club. "I shall make tomorrow," he wrote to
Lauzun on December 4, "a very radical motion inside our Society
that it change its meeting place to a place where it can be more independent. We need to make every effort to escape from the tyranny
of the Parlement, and all those who have believed that they were
organizing a group of public-spirited citizens and not a reserve corps
for the Parlement, ought to join together to put a stop to this very
deplorable tendency."

The Marquis de La Fayette, naturally a very active member of the

Constitutional Club, did not share the distrust of Mirabeau for the young men of the Parlement whom he knew to be sincerely devoted to liberty: "Those whom I know in that body, and especially M. Duport whom I love tenderly, are honest men who are well-informed and patriotic; they are less sympathetic to the Parlement than many of the ministers, and none any more than I. Besides, my heart is pure, my mind is open, and my character is disinterested. I have two main supports: my conscience and the public confidence; if I should lose the second the first would still be sufficient." Along with La Fayette it is not surprising to find at Duport's house his brother-in-law, the Viscount de Noailles, and his friends, Castellane, Latour-Moubourg and Destutt de Tracy, all of whom shared the same hopes.

A young bishop named Talleyrand, two young noblemen, Aiguillon and Lauzun (who was in line to inherit the title of Duke and Peer, which he did when his uncle, the Duc de Biron, died on October 29), these young men, along with several other dukes who had become famous for their part in the revolt of the Court of Peers in May 1788, Aumont, La Rouchefoucauld, Luynes, Bethunes-Charost, Montmorency-Luxembourg, all these along with Marshall de Beauveau brought to the Society meeting at Duport's the luster of their reputations—or at least, of their rank and fortunes. Behind these prominent names one often finds there were well-informed publicists who helped them to overcome their inexperience and promoted their proposals. Mirabeau stood behind the new Duc de Biron; Roederer and Target behind Beauveau; Soulavie behind Luynes; Condorcet behind La Rochefoucauld; and Duport himself behind Montmorency-Luxembourg. But the latter, along with Bethune-Charost, already uneasy at the progress of the Third Estate, began to withdraw.

The club which met at Duport's was certainly the most influential of the numerous clubs, salons and political cafés where the issues of the day were debated. By the chance comments of some witnesses we get some insight into a few others. The Society which "had more members, was more influential and more active," if one is to believe Sieyès and which held its sessions at Masse's restaurant under the arcade of the Palais Royal, earned the name of the "Club des Enragés." There was also the debating society, more academic and more moderate, over which the Abbé Morellet presided every Sunday morning, as well as the closed and secret society with its mysterious countersigns and shadowy plans which Alexander Lameth makes known to us under the name of the "Society de Virofly."

These clubs published and disseminated the most famous pamphlets issued from Paris by the National Party, and particularly those of the Abbé Sieyès who prided himself on not belonging to any club. They established connections with the provinces in order to contribute "to the spread of common ideas so as to make possible a common will and a common effort," to use the exact expression of Rabaut-Saint-Étienne. There is no doubt but that they contributed to the widespread dissemination of the pamphlets written in Languedoc by the Count d'Antraigues, the pastor Rabaut-Saint-Étienne and the lawyer Albisson, and those from Dauphiné of the lawyer Lenoir-Laroche and Jean-Joseph Mounier as well as the pamphlets from Brittany of Volney and of Servan in Provence. And finally their members frequently belonged to the highest nobility of the kingdom and thereby exerted a direct and daily personal influence in the Court of Peers, at the Assembly of Notables, as well as in the salons of Paris and Versailles and up to the very threshold of power.

To the erudite dissertations which described the procedures followed in the past for the convocation of the Estates-General—procedures by which the conservatives tried to imprison the new assembly—the learned doctors of the National Party responded that in these matters there was no valid tradition or any "constitution." Target writes,

> *I conclude that a constitution has some significance in a nation which has had habitual rules of procedure, regular forms for the exercise of legislative and executive power and which regulates according to invariable forms, laws, liberties and customs where there is a mode of existence which never changes, a regular and invariable procedure for the forces which move the political machine. But can we say that up till now France has ever been in this advantageous position? Can we say that the convocation of the Estates-General has already been determined in precise constitutional form when there is no assurance of its return and it has been one hundred and seventy-five years since the nation was last assembled?*

They argued further that the mode of organization of the new Estates-General ought to arise out of the nature of things and not from history. All the writers of the National Party were unanimous in appealing to natural law, but none expressed it with more persuasive passion than the eloquent Rabaut-Saint-Étienne:

> What they call the Constitution of the State is nothing more than their own constitution and what they call the Rules of the State are nothing more than their own rules.... In order to justify these forms and these laws they point to their long existence; but the length of time of its existence proves nothing except that it is old. One appeals to rights based on long possession but past possession does not justify possession forever, because then nothing would change—not even abuses, since abuses are possessions also. An appeal is made to history; but our history is not our code of law. We ought to be wary of the mania for proving that which ought to be by that which is done, because it is precisely that which has been done that we are complaining about.

"Above all," Mirabeau wrote as early as August 16 to a correspondent, "let us be wary of erudition, let us be disdainful of that which has been done and not depend on it too much...."

In the struggle taken up against despotism, the threat of which was believed to have been reaffirmed during the last crisis (May 1788), it is remarkable that only the Count d'Antraigues—faithful to the spirit of the aristocratic revolution—pleaded for the return to the Parlements, in collaboration with the Estates-General, of that legislative power which Brienne and Lamoignon had taken away from them. The leader of the revolution in Dauphiné, Jean-Joseph Mounier, for his part condemned without appeal the theory of intermediary powers so dear to Montesquieu, who had provided the basis for the participation of the supreme law courts in public affairs. "The respect which I profess for the immortal author of the *L'Esprit des Lois* cannot keep me from voicing my opinion; I owe more respect to the truth than to Montesquieu, and I would have to say that this author who wrote for men of all nations has never been able to quite forget that he was noble, French and a member of the Parlement." Only grudgingly are the services which the sovereign courts have just rendered to liberty recognized. "When a poison has cured you," remarks the ex-Avocat-General Servan, "hurry and break the bottle for fear that it will kill you." The young, liberal members of Parlement who belonged to Duport's club resigned themselves to that partial forfeiture of power which would, however, leave them in the role of "guardians and watchmen of the public order." "This title is the only one," the counselor Huguet de Semonville admits, "which can be reconciled with full legislative power resting in the hands of the people. And one can be sure that the known patriotism of several magistrates, and perhaps of all, would compel them to refuse, even from the Estates-General, an extension of authority which they believed to be incompatible with both the rights and the well-being of the nation."

Some liberal writers, such as Beauveau, Demunier and Huguet de Semonville, who remained faithful to traditional French political forms, hoped to avert despotism by uniformly establishing provincial estates and stipulated periodic sessions of the Estates-General. Rabaut-Saint-Étienne and Mounier advocated the introduction into France of the English form of constitution. But Sieyès was already condemning it, in the name of sovereignty of the people, the only legitimate masters of legislative power. "Are these then," he writes,

> *true principles which include the idea of separating the legislative power into three parts, of which only one is supposed to speak in the name of the nation? If the nobility and the crown are not representative of the nation, they have no right to the exercise of legislative power, because only the nation can express its own will and consequently establish laws. All those making up the legislative body can vote on behalf of the people only if they have been properly authorized by them. But how is such authorization to be obtained when there is no free and general election?*

The privileges of the Old Regime were also put on trial. "War on the privileged and on privileges, that is my motto," Mirabeau declared on August 16, "privileges are useful against kings, but they are detestable when held against nations, and ours will never have a true public spirit until it is rid of them." And Target repeats, "Provinces, cities, courts, corporations and official orders, oppose your privileges to the king, withdraw them before France assembled. . . ." This explicit repudiation of all special interests was the fundamental article of the program of the party which declared itself to be "National."

D'Antraigues himself urged the privileged orders to voluntarily abandon their fiscal prerogatives: "Those privileges which isolate us and which have cost us so dearly have become odious to us. Past centuries have taught us that taxes levied by the Estates-General must be borne by all orders in the state; they have taught us that privileges are detrimental to the well-being of everyone, because they are obstacles which prevent the formation of useful cooperative groups. But it is also necessary for the people to have only a single and identical interest in order to achieve the permanent victory of liberty and law and to save the republic." All the liberal nobles were equally generous, but Sieyès was uneasy about the danger of a maneuver which might deceive the Third Estate, if that concession was intended only to serve the purpose of a backfire: The nobility could be suspected of wishing to mislead and wishing, by seeming to promise the Third Estate equality, to get it to alter its current demands and especially to distract the order from the absolute necessity of demanding more power in the Estates-General. The nobility seemed to be saying to the Third Estate: "What is it you want? That we pay the same as you do? That is fair. We will pay. Leave in force then the old set-up in which you were nothing, we were all, and in which it has been so easy for us to pay only what we wished to."

There were some other inequities, actually, which the Third Estate would tolerate no longer, the bitterness against which can be found expressed in the *Mémoire pour le peuple français* by the ex-Jesuit Cérutti. "It is said that the people conspire on all sides against the nobility, the clergy and the judges. This is the nature of the conspiracy: barred from the best positions in the army, they are allowed only to die; excluded from the top ranks of the clergy, they are there permitted only to work; excluded from important positions in the courts, they are only allowed to practice law; excluded from a legal share of legislative authority in the Estates-General, they are to be allowed only to pay on their knees."

The fact that the National Party included both bourgeoisie and gentlemen, explains the condescension with which the most influential leaders of that party—Target and Mounier—while condemning *privileges,* accepted the right of precedence and distinguished, as Condorcet wished, the "legal prerogatives of the nobility," which they repudiated themselves, from the "public esteem in which they are held," which they accepted as natural and just. More independent and more radical, Sieyès refused even to make any concession in favor of honorific privileges: "For me, I will say frankly, I find them to be only one more vice and one which seems to me to be the greatest of all. It is that they tend to degrade the great body of citizens, and certainly it is no slight evil to degrade men. It is not easy to conceive how one could consent to allow twenty-five million, seven hundred thousand men to be humiliated in order to ridiculously honor three hundred thousand."

*   *   *

If Lacretelle and Roederer—like Malesherbes in his memorandum to the king—wished to abolish at once any distinction between orders in the Estates-General, the chief writers of the National Party contented themselves with calling for the orders to join in common sessions while granting the Third a representation at least equal to that of the first two orders. The most moderate of all—the Abbé Morellet—explained that double representation for the Third—which was not necessary in 1614—had become so by 1789:

> *At that time in 1614, the privileges of the clergy and the nobility were not in question, at least not publicly. Their mournful effects had not yet been felt to the same degree. The people, less affected by the methods of taxation, and less oppressed by them, accepted with more patience an inequity which did not reduce them to the miserable situation in which one sees them today. The nobility and the clergy also had their griev- ances, but they did not make complaints about the Third Estate and were not held responsible for the grievances of the people. Today the busi- ness situation, and the enormous weight of the public debt, mean that the only possible resource is a more equal division of the tax burden be- tween all citizens and all orders of citizens. Or to put it another way, the situation requires the abolition of all privileges which stand in the way of a fair assessment on all citizens. The question, the debate, is then be- tween the Commons on the one hand and on the clergy and the nobility on the other. It must be decided. How can the court which is to judge the question be composed of two judges having a common interest against a single judge having an opposing interest?*

On the matter of a just ratio between the orders, as a precondition of all reform, the Patriots were intransigent. They urged the Notables to be reasonable on this issue and assumed almost a threatening tone: "It is a matter of the fate of the nation"—declares Target— "and so much is at stake, that all uncertainty is a danger, all anxiety a torment, and all truth a duty."

*   *   *

It is certain, moreover, that the great majority of these publicists sincerely respected the king: "A king," writes Lanjuinais,

is a magistrate, but the highest one and the most necessary of magistrates, above all in an extended realm like France. He is the head of the family without whom it would be scattered; he is a center of unity without which there would be only a disordered mass of incoherent groups of people. The king then is the supreme motive force, the depository of the executive power, and he gives to the laws to which the nation has consented the seal of public authority. He is the essential support of the people, the foundation stone of the structure of our whole society.

"The fact is, and it can be counted on," writes Mirabeau, to the Duke of Lauzun on November 14, 1788, "that in the National Assembly I shall be a very zealous monarchist. . . ."

And Pierre-Louis Lacretelle agreed also: "The august monarchy suits both our geographical situation and our moral character; our views and our principles do not look for its destruction; we seek to regulate it only in order to strengthen it."

Mathieu Dumas, the brilliant thirty-five-year-old officer, who at that time shared all the hopes of the young military nobility, describes thus the illusions which gave birth to the National Party:

One spoke of the establishment of a new constitution for the state, as a job easily done, as though it were something natural. In the intoxication of those days of celebration and hope, we scarcely paid any attention to the obstacles which had to be surmounted, before the first foundation of liberty could be laid and before one could establish these principles which the spirit of the court, the privileged orders, the great corporations, and the old customs all repudiated. . . .

The extent of the movement generated by the Third Estate across the kingdom in the last months of 1788 astonished even the leaders of the National Party themselves.

Actually they placed little hope on the will to resist of a class so susceptible to the numerous means of seduction possessed by the first two orders. "They expected no more from fortune than to serve and no more distinction than the usual humiliation at the hands of the nobility and clergy," Servan states, "on the one hand benefices, on the other judicial offices, all the power of gifts, the seductiveness of promises and illusions of hope were like chains in the hands of the nobility and the clergy with which to shackle

the Third Estate, which accepted them while kissing them, sometimes as honorable, sometimes as sacred! By what means finally
were those who were capable of knowing their rights and defending them to be drawn away from that part of the Third Estate which
was unaware of its own abilities!" And Mirabeau says, "The Third
Estate is made up of so many people without vigor, with so many
country people accustomed to feudalism, of so many citizens who
think only of money, of so many bourgeois spirits who think only of
getting some benefit from the protection and patronage of the noble
mister such and such, that they would tremble if the opening of
the Estates-General put them in the same room with our noblemen
of all kinds."

In addition, could one expect of a rich member of the bourgeoisie,
impatient to become ennobled, that he abandon his highest hopes?
Mably, whose complete edition of *Observations sur l'histoire de
France* was published three years after his death, had no illusions
on this point:

> *It would require a concurrence of circumstances of the most extraordi-
> nary kind to change the national view that the Third Estate amounts to
> nothing in France because no one wishes to be included in it. All the
> bourgeoisie, in our nation, think only of removing themselves from their
> situation and of buying offices which confer nobility; and when one finally
> achieves that goal, he no longer considers himself to be part of the com-
> mon herd. The people are, actually, the only part of the population with-
> out credit, without consideration, and without fortune which can do
> nothing for itself.*

The avocats (lawyers) of the town of Nuits in Burgundy prove
this correct when before the assembly of all the inhabitants on
December 31, 1788, they declare that "the privileges of the nobility
are a true property which are all the more worthy in that we are
not excluded from them and that we can acquire them. Great deeds,
valor, courage, personal merit, offices, fortune are all equally ways
of attaining them. Why then would one suppose that we would
think of destroying the source of emulation which, like a compass-
needle, guides our efforts?"

The conservative upper nobility itself, however, provided its
adversaries with leaders by refusing to accept among its representatives in the provincial Estates those whose nobility was not sufficiently up to its requirements. This was the case in Brittany for nobles

who were not nobles by birth, and in Provence even for men of noble birth who did not possess a *seigneurie*. Jacques Cottin, a great propertyowner in Santo Domingo, seigneur of a parish in Brittany, ennobled by purchase of the office of Secretary of the King, but excluded from the provincial Estates, became, at thirty-four years of age, in November 1788, the moving spirit of the Commune of Nantes, a resolute group which gave a decisive impetus to Breton patriotism. At Aix, a counselor in the Parlement who was twenty-nine years old by the name of André, a nobleman of birth but without *seigneurie*, initiated a request sent to the municipality on December 21, 1788 calling for—against the aristocratic provincial Estates which refused to admit him into its ranks—a meeting of a Constituent Assembly made up of all three orders.

The recently ennobled—as they did also in the Assembly of Notables—joined with those hereditary noblemen, who, in a movement where generosity and ambition were united, were already serving as leaders of the French Third Estate, and provoked these reflections from Abbé Sieyès:

> *I am not surprised that the two higher orders have furnished the first defenders of justice and humanity. Talent is developed exclusively from intelligence and long nurture. The members of the Third ought for a thousand reasons to excel in it, but enlightenment with respect to social ethics ought to appear first among those men who are in the best position to grasp the broader relations within society and among whom the original ties are less commonly broken, because there are some sciences which relate as much to the soul as to the mind.*

One also should not fail to appreciate the importance in the awakening of the new ambitions of the bourgeoisie of the municipal campaign stimulated by projects for the reestablishment or reform of the provincial Estates, and which preceded or accompanied the great national debate on the representation of the Third Estate in the Estates-General. In this movement, in which the people of Provence had taken the lead since their assembly at Vizelle, the inhabitants of Dauphiné had become most important as their proceedings at that point held everybody's attention and stimulated emulation. They had obtained the much-desired right to frame a constitution for their province in a consultive assembly, which had sat at Romans from September 10 to 28, 1788. They met again at the beginning of

November, in order to consider the reply of the government to the proposal which they had presented. It was at the same time when the second Assembly of Notables was itself beginning its work. By that coincidence, Jean-Joseph Mounier, the leader of the revolt in Dauphiné, was put in a position to give to all of France, in the form of a letter addressed to the king on November 8, formal notice of the great trial then in progress. In it he called for both double representation for the Third Estate and the vote by head:

> *The Commons include the greatest portion of your subjects, and the one which pays the most in taxes, which possesses the most property, and it is they who bear the brunt of all the abuses. . . . If the orders and the provinces are kept separate they will be simply different bodies; it will no longer be the nation itself expressing itself through its deputies.*

Instructed by manifestoes of this kind and by those patriotic pamphlets stimulated by the appeals of these Notables belonging to the defeated minority at Versailles, or by the advance of fellow patriots associated with the National Party and led at the same time in the provinces by spontaneously formed groups, a few of which are known (the Committee of Nantes for Brittany, for example, and that of Dijon for Burgundy); by all these means the Third Estate of the town was awakened, throughout all France.

* * *

The simplest expression—and the least convincing—of this reawakening were the spontaneous resolutions of various municipal bodies addressed to the sovereign. An example of these was the letter of November 4, 1788 written to the king, in which the mayor and the town councilmen of Dieppe (six members) requested an "adequate representation" in the Estates-General. After this request was criticized by leading citizens of the town as being too modest, the municipal officers made it explicit in a new letter of December 2 that double representation was what was wanted. Such manifestations could easily have the allure of being a formality quite reconcilable with profound indifference in a town not tormented by political fever, but carried out by scrupulous municipal officials in order to satisfy their consciences. This is why the leaders of the National

Party judged them to be fundamentally inadequate. One of the most moderate, Malouet, wrote to the municipality of Riom on December 18: "As the only means of resistance can and must be no more than passive resistance, there must be a striking degree of unanimity among the groups and individuals participating in the deliberations, and to give expression to that unanimity, it is necessary that insofar as possible the resolutions be supported by all the inhabitants living in the city and its districts."

The regular and most impressive procedure recommended by the National Party was to associate all the corporations and subordinate communities of the town, in a proceeding presided over by the municipal council. Such was the procedure followed at Rouen, which provided a sort of model of this kind. The movement began at the lowest level between November 22 and 29, when the members of the various communities and corporations along with individual citizens covered with signatures a memorandum which presented the general view of the Third Estate with respect to its representation in the convocation of the Estates and to the mode of deliberation in the Estates once convened. The municipal government formally received the memorandum, adopted it and designated two council members to carry it to the king.

For the sending of a petition to the municipal council could be substituted, a more-or-less general assembly, organized and presided over by the standing municipal council. This assembly could be official if it were provided for under the municipal constitution. It was such a reenforced general council, composed of 210 members, which the vigorous demand of the commercial corporations imposed on Toulouse on December 8, 1788 in the face of the timidity or opposition of the chiefs of the city council (*Capitouls*). And it was in equally large assemblies, but less regularly composed, that the municipalities of Nancy, Montauban and Angers received the view of the Commune.

At Paris, where the municipal government had lost all representative character and attempted to hold itself aloof from the movement, it developed outside of it. Dr. Guillotin, "a celebrated doctor and regent of the medical faculty of the University of Paris," set down at the beginning of December the text of a petition. On the initiative of a nobleman of recent origin, Claude-Etienne de la Frenaye, head of the mercers' guild, the petition was adopted on December 10 by the officers in charge of the six guilds of merchants, before being proposed on the thirteenth for consideration by the members of the guilds of which a single one—that of the wine merchants—rejected it. Simultaneously the petition was deposited with the notaries so that it could be signed by all those citizens who wished to support it. It was this which stirred up . . . the uneasiness and the now impotent anger of the Parlement of Paris.

The example of Alais and other villages of Languedoc proves that the Third Estate was sometimes strong enough and well enough organized to disdain the relatively discreet form of the petition and to bring together—except for one reluctant municipality—general assemblies which affirmed with all necessary vigor the point of view of the unprivileged.

Beyond the boundaries of the towns, the Third Estate attempted to organize its manifestations throughout the provinces. The deliberations in Dijon on December 11 were followed in the course of the next month by deliberations in sixteen other Burgundian towns. The appeal of Rouen was heard and reiterated by twenty-five Norman towns. In the traditional provincial estates of Provence, the Third Estate was made up of the mayors of thirty-six cities or privileged towns and by the consuls of certain communities designated by roster, in each of its twenty administrative units (the *viguries*). In November and December, nineteen cities and towns and nine *viguries* indicated to the Assembly of Notables the views of the Third Estate as to its future representation in the National Assembly. There was the same manifestation of the views of the Third Estate in the twenty-four dioceses constituting the traditional structure (in this instance a civil and not a clerical unit) of Languedoc. It was particularly notable in Upper Languedoc, around Alet; and in Lower Languedoc around Uzes, Beziers and Nîmes. It found its most perfect expression in the diocesan assemblies of all three orders such as the one held at Uzes on December 23, when 577 deliberators led and inspired by the Third, expressed their demand, "with respect to both the organization of the assembly of the Estates-General and the proposed changes in the constitution of the Estates of Languedoc."

                              *   *   *

The multiformed power of this movement, betraying an unsuspected degree of rancor, astonished the Assembly of Notables and inspired in it that desperate resistance to the demands of innovators that we have already noted: "It is known," wrote a generally well-informed journalist on December 30, 1788, "that the number of requests from provinces, towns, communities, and corporations which demand representation for the Third Estate equal to that of the first two orders is immense and is estimated at more than 800, without counting those arriving daily from all directions."

Necker and even certain intendants like Bertrand de Moleville in Brittany, Amelet de Chaillou in Burgundy, and Lefevre de Caumartin in Franche Comté have been blamed for the complacency which is supposed to have benefited these municipal manifestations. But while one might agree that this complacency may have supported the movement, who could still maintain that they provoked it?

More appropriately the preponderant role played by some leaders in the most striking manifestations of this kind has been emphasized. The Norman lawyer, LaFoy, and the member of Parlement Gressent, both noblemen, formally denounced two members of the municipal government of Rouen: the first councilman, LeCouteulx and the retired lawyer, Thouret, as being the real authors of the *Mémoire présénté à MM. les Maire et Echévins . . . par les Communautés, Corporations et Citoyens particuliers.* "They had an office," Gressent notes, "where the workingmen went to sign and were given for their trouble a printed copy of the memoir and sometimes some money."

Who can doubt that the demonstrations of a Third Estate for so long quiescent were not always as spontaneous as appearances might lead one to believe? One should not, on the other hand, underestimate the rapidity with which the bourgeoisie became aware, in those decisive months in the fall of 1788, of the legitimacy and the necessity of its struggle. Nothing is more instructive in this regard than to see in the course of the pages where he sets down successively each day the notes from his reading, the birth of a true revolutionary feeling in Hardy, the little bourgeois sexegenarian of the rue Saint-Jacques, fashioned, to tell the truth, in the demanding style developed as a result of his long acquaintance with the parlementary rhetoric, to which for such a long time he had been so partial. On the eleventh of October, after having read the already old *Mémoir*

of the Provençal Pascalis, *On the Contribution to Common Charges,*
he wrote,

> *One ought to give him credit for having so well demonstrated, so solidly
> established, and so energetically defended the rights of the Third Estate
> and the interests of the poor, which have been sacrificed up until now to
> the pride of the big shots, the nobility and the clergy, while at the same
> time they are made the prey of the cupidity, let us say even the voracity,
> of the bloodsuckers of the tax-collection service and of finance.*

Two months after, having read and admired in the meantime certain manifestoes of the Bretons and the Dauphinese as well as
the commentaries of Target, Guillotin, and Cérutti, he is indignant in
commenting on the *Mémoir of the Princes of the Blood,*

> *One might suspect that one is seeing here the effect of their fear that in
> spite of their alliance with the clergy they have exhausted all practical
> means of preserving for themselves and all the rest of the nobility their
> old privileges—those odious exemptions which have lasted to the pro-
> longed or perpetual detriment of the true interests of the Third Estate,
> whose cries and loud reclamations they wish to continue to stifle.*

To the accusations of plotting and spreading false information
made by the aristocracy against the leaders of the National Party
whose maneuvers they denounced, Servan responded with good
humor,

> *There exists now in France a seditious plot of about twenty million sub-
> jects of all ages and sexes who ask only to be united to their king against
> two or three hundred magistrates, a few hundred great seigneurs, and the
> little sacred legion of bishops and other consorts who, in the name of
> the convocation of 1614, wish to reduce the people to the most extreme
> state which they call rightly,* the last previous state of things.

And further,

> *These* maneuvers!... maneuvers *hatched with finesse and cowardice in
> all the town halls, in all the public places, in all circles; in short those*
> maneuvers *for which the whole Third Estate was responsible.*

By the very moderation of its demands, the movement in the
towns and cities was able to rally the immense majority of that

timorous class for double representation of the Third, deputies of the Third to be limited only to members of that class, deliberations in common and the vote by head. Sieyès in praising them compares this "timid insufficiency" with the unconsidered boldness of the writers without a mandate. Malouet perfectly expressed the spirit and the reason for it in the directions which he addressed to the town of Riom:

> *Note well that in the stormy position in which the nation finds itself, and by that I mean the Third Estate, it would be dangerous to risk a setback in the face of the pretensions of the clergy and the nobility. It is necessary therefore to make one's way forward only cautiously, placing the feet carefully at each step on an unshakable foundation. That is why it is so essential to defend oneself from all appearance of heat in our demands, refusals and decrees. It is in order to be firm to the point of inflexibility that I ask you to be prudent.*

In addition, the most confident deference was everywhere affirmed with respect to the sovereign: "It was then," wrote a witness, Charles Lacretelle, "that there appeared to be renewed, in a most solemn manner, the old alliance which the kings had made with the people."

Jeffry Kaplow, Gilbert Shapiro, Elizabeth L. Eisenstein

CLASS IN THE FRENCH REVOLUTION: A DISCUSSION

Jeffry Kaplow (b. 1927), now living in France and still pursuing his study of revolutionary France, was an assistant professor at Columbia University when the following commentary was written. His detailed study of a French town during the Revolution, Elbeuf during the Revolutionary Period: History and Social Structure *(Baltimore, 1964), ideologically is in the French orthodox tradition of such studies. His introduction to a book of readings on the*

This article by Jeffry Kaplow and the following items of Gilbert Shapiro and Ms. Eisenstein all appeared as a unit in the *American Historical Review* 72 (1967): 497–522. Reproduced without reference footnotes with permission of the authors and the editors of the *American Historical Review*.

Revolution, which he edited, entitled New Perspectives on the French Revolution *(New York, 1965), also reflects this viewpoint. Accordingly his critical reaction to Ms. Eisenstein's challenge to Lefebvre's thesis concerning the origins of the Revolution is understandable.*

In her review article, "Who Intervened in 1788? A Commentary on *The Coming of the French Revolution*" Professor Eisenstein sought to show that Georges Lefebvre's claim that it was the bourgeoisie who initiated revolutionary action against the parlements in September 1788 is not supported by the evidence. This revisionist view calls for several comments.

First, it should be noted that Eisenstein is really a new kind of revisionist. Unlike some of her predecessors, she refuses to throw out the concept of the bourgeoisie, although she maintains that it is a "difficult-to-define social sector." Her own view is much more radical—that the existence of a bourgeoisie, however defined, is irrelevant to the discussion, for the theory of class from which the concept proceeds is

> *a static framework derived from a structural analysis . . . incapable of containing this sort of dynamic group action [that is, the action of the national party in the fall and winter of 1788]. Instead it keeps apart, as socially stratified, the very cluster of men who gravitated together, mutually attracted by political goals that appeared to be within their reach. By artificially segmenting this continuous group action, by arbitrarily assigning revolutionary initiative first to the class-oriented activities of the aristocracy, then to those of the bourgeoisie, the author [Lefebvre] has, thus, almost smothered his evidence.*

Now this argument, ingenious though it may be, sins in two ways. First, it sets up a theoretical straw man, and, second, it neglects to make use of evidence gathered by scholars since Lefebvre wrote in 1939.

Any theory of class analysis that proposes a static model is fundamentally ahistorical and therefore inapplicable to the matter at hand. Lefebvre and his successors—George Rudé, Albert Soboul, Richard Cobb, and others—many of whom approach the history of the French Revolution from a Marxist or neo-Marxist standpoint, are aware of this and are at pains to stress the constant evolution of classes, their inner complexity, and the interaction that takes place between them and their social environment. They would, I think, agree with Eisenstein that there was no clear-cut dichotomy between any two large classes in old-regime France. I suggest that their use of words like "nobility" and "bourgeoisie" does not in any way imply a belief in the homogeneous nature of the two groups or in their political solidarity, as Eisenstein seems to infer. Certainly, the distinction between noble and bourgeois in the eighteenth century was not so absolute as that between capitalist and proletarian in the nineteenth, for instance. And the internal cohesion of each class has also gained much in the telling. There were nobles of the robe and nobles of the sword, those of the court and those who resided in the provinces, the rich and the poor, the officeholders and those deprived of participation in government. The members of the bourgeoisie also differed from one another according to criteria of profession, wealth, residence, and status, to name only a few. Furthermore, there were surely nobles who played bourgeois roles (by holding capitalist investments, for instance) and bourgeois who became noble, but did not give up the activities nor the attitude of mind that made them bourgeois. In the light of this, is there any meaningful sense in which the bourgeoisie and the nobility can be said to have been fundamentally opposed to one another? Indeed, there is. Each represented a different stage in a complex set of socioeconomic relationships, the one feudal, the other capitalist. The dichotomy is not between the purely feudal relationships of Charlemagne's time and the industrial capitalism of the nineteenth century, both of which terms are historically anachronistic when applied to our period. But the conflict remains, and associated with it is a set of political choices. Contrary to what has been said and repeated a thousand times, these choices were not centered around the narrow conflict between aristocracy and democracy, still less around a particular set of political institutions, but rather around the questions of who should rule and, more important still, who should have access to the levers of power. The choice between Parlement and Parliament was less important than that between the stasis of a noble-oriented society based on birth, privilege, and honor, on the one hand, and the dynamic society of the bourgeoisie with its watchwords of talent, intelligence, and productivity, on the other.

Now it would be a grave error to assume that belonging to a given class automatically determines one's political attitudes. This sort of crude determinism has long been out of fashion with historians of the French Revolution, and the use of it constitutes another instance of Eisenstein's straw man technique. To expect the nobility to act in defense of its interests (as it did, for the most part) is one thing; to hold that each noble will respond to a given stimulus like Pavlov's dogs is quite another. While the first expectation is borne out by the facts, the second is shown to be indefensibly mechanical.

The author's argument falls into two main parts: first that " 'France's bourgeoisie' did *not* initiate the protest movement of 1788 and did *not* play a prominent role in the events and reforms of 1789"; second, that this leading role, usually attributed to the bourgeoisie, was in fact played by a heterogeneous group of men "mutually attracted by political goals that appeared to be within their reach." On the first point, she holds that there is no evidence to prove that "protest against the Parlement's ruling [of September 25, 1788] was locally initiated by groups drawn exclusively from any one class or estate." That is true enough if the emphasis is placed on the word *exclusive*. The fact is that the bourgeoisie did intervene in numerous provincial cities. Although they were not alone, they did constitute the new element in the struggle, not having previously played any but a passive role. Every bourgeois did not participate in the movement equally, and some—like the representatives of privileged towns in Brittany or some guild members in Dijon—even opposed it. For that reason, they would soon be removed from positions of authority and replaced by bourgeois of a politically more radical sort. For someone who insists that it is indeed the struggle over representation in the Estates-General that distinguishes the Revolution from all preceding "times of troubles," Eisenstein is curiously blind to the agitation led by these men. What is surprising is not that some bourgeois remained outside of politics but that so many did in fact rally to the national cause. As Michel-Joseph-Antoine Servan, the former *avocat général* of the parlement of Grenoble, put it:

> Ils [le Tiers État] n'attendent de fortune que de leurs services et de distinction que de leurs bassesses auprès de la Noblesse et du Clergé. Les bénéfices d'un côté; les offices de judicature, de l'autre. Tout ce que les dons ont de réel, tout ce que les promesses et les illusions de l'espé-

rance ont de séduisant; que de chaînes dans les mains de la Noblesse et du Clergé pour accabler le Tiers État, qui les reçoit en les baisant, tantôt comme honorables, tantôt comme sacrées! Que de moyens enfin d'enlever à la partie du Tiers État qui s'ignore elle-même, celle qui serait capable de connaître ses droits et de la défendre! [Égret, see above pp. 215–216.]

The chains of subordination are hard to break. The bourgeoisie, like many another oppressed class since that time, had internalized the portrait drawn of it by the Establishment, and that is a situation less conducive to revolution than to Uncle Tomism.

Because this was true, the liberal nobility in the Committee of Thirty rendered the bourgeoisie a great service by making propaganda in favor of the good cause. Why did they do so? We cannot say without undertaking biographical study of the individuals involved. That many of the Thirty were members of the robe engaged in a struggle with the monarchy may be one reason. Mirabeau's desire to strike a blow against the society that had effectively disowned him may be another. Adherence to political goals or the charisma of leadership may have to be taken into account. In any case, the constant reminder that certain aristocrats did in fact go so far as to support the doubling of the Third proves nothing whatsoever about the class nature of the struggle of 1788. Nor will it do to kick in an open door by arguing, as Eisenstein does, that the clergy was in fact not a class. Mallet du Pan was a more accurate journalist than the author thinks when he wrote, in January 1789, that " 'The war is between the Third Estate and the other two orders.' " What he—and, I would argue, most of his contemporaries —meant when they spoke of the clergy was that portion of it made up of great abbots and bishops, but certainly not the parish priests. In the Third Republic, a priest was a priest, and that was that, but that was not the case in the old regime.

Let us now look more closely at the specific issue at hand: the doubling of the Third. A significant section of the bourgeoisie wanted this change, as did some aristocrats. It will not, however, do to play with the evidence in order to show that there were no essential differences between the attitudes of the two classes. Thus, it is true that the First Bureau of the Assembly of Notables of 1788 voted, under the leadership of the Comte de Provence, for the doubling, but Eisenstein neglects to quote the second half of Lefebvre's sentence to the effect that this was done "on condition that each order in the Estates-General should remain free to accept or reject the vote by head"—a provision that effectively took the guts out of the resolution. Furthermore, she argues, without a shred of evidence, that the patriot leaders used old electoral traditions to keep the issues of the doubling of the Third and the mixing of the orders separate until after the elections, so that the Third Estate would be free of representatives of the clergy and nobility, who normally would have been elected in the place of the "literate laity." Even if this were true—and it presupposes a centrally organized electoral campaign whose existence is not proven—it would say nothing about the vote by head. Mixing one estate with another for the purposes of debate does not automatically imply voting as individuals. If we are to believe Mirabeau, it may well be that some parlement members of the Committee of Thirty were not just using a tactic in desiring to keep the issues separate, but were actually expressing a preference: "yes" to the doubling of the Third, but no farther than that on the democratic road.

There are a couple of other points that have to do with the use of evidence. Eisenstein accuses Lefebvre of contradicting himself on two occasions. The first concerns the third order of the provincial estates of Brittany. The Third Estate was made up of privileged persons, but they nonetheless defied the first and second estates by refusing to sit until fiscal equality was granted. How can one explain the apparent paradox? If we consult Jean Égret, we find that the persons in question, privileged though they were, acted daringly, precisely because of the presence in the meeting room of some twenty-nine municipal deputies and several *commissaires adjoints* from Nantes, who represented the revolutionary force of the Breton bourgeoisie. Another example: Lefebvre is guilty of contradiction in arguing that the central organization of a revolutionary movement was inhibited by uncertain means of communication, while at the same time stating that news of the Parlement's September ruling spread quickly. To this it must be said that the spreading of news and the organizing of revolution cannot be lumped together when discussing the problem of communications. To spread the news of a parlement's action was perfectly legal and above board; to organize a revolution is to engage in clandestine activity.

Newsboys and revolutionaries have not the same access to transportation facilities.

The Third Estate was indeed represented in the Estates-General by members of the literate laity—who also happened to be bourgeois. I would be the last to say that our concepts of class in preindustrial societies could not stand sharpening and, perhaps, redefinition. But it is a quibble to take Lefebvre to task for his use of the expression " 'enterprising bourgeois' " when speaking of those responsible for drawing up the *cahiers* and suggesting candidates. Most of them were not entrepreneurs, but they were enterprising.

In my view, it is impossible to discuss the making of the Revolution solely in terms of who was responsible for a given set of actions at its beginning, without making reference to the program and accomplishments of the Revolution as a whole. But even if we permit Eisenstein her approach, it must be said that she has failed to make her point. When she says that "There is something wildly askew about a structural model that includes the top layer of nobles and the bottom layer of the clergy within the middle ranks of the 'middle' class," she is accusing only herself. She has lumped these people together on criteria of political ideas and literacy. No one else has ever done so—at least not on the basis of a social definition. What Lefebvre and his followers have undertaken to prove is that the French Revolution was a bourgeois one, in that it was made by bourgeois for the benefit of the bourgeoisie—or, if you will, in the name of an ideal formulated by the bourgeoisie and identified with the well-being of humanity as a whole. The facts show that the bourgeoisie was active, that it had ideals, although its members differed among themselves on specific issues within the general framework and, of course, on the question of means. They were not alone, but they were dominant. All our questions have not been answered, but a foundation has been laid. Is it not possible, at long last, to go on from there?

Gilbert Shapiro

Gilbert Shapiro, now professor of history and sociology at the University of Pittsburgh, is one of those rare scholars who manages to bridge the gap between two disciplines—a difficult feat even for two fields as closely related as sociology and history. Trained initially as a sociologist, Professor Shapiro became interested in the prospect of applying quantitative techniques used in sociological studies to historical research having a sociological dimension. Applying his techniques to the cahiers *of 1789, he has published several articles on his findings and on his methodology. In order to carry on his research Professor Shapiro has had to become expert in the history of the French revolutionary era and has had to adopt an interpretive framework. Clearly he has found the orthodox tradition of Soboul and Lefebvre congenial, and it is against this background that he criticizes Ms. Eisenstein's analysis of Lefebvre's interpretation.*

During the past few decades, studies of the French Revolution have flowered. A wide consensus seems to have been developing, muffling the traditional conflicts of rival ideological schools in a mass of documentary evidence. Empirical studies of theoretically crucial issues were pursued by new techniques, particularly in economic history and in the study of the social origins of participants in various revolutionary groups and activities. In the wake of such a wave of progress it is, I suppose, both healthy and inevitable that we should witness a wave of skepticism. Elizabeth Eisenstein's review article on Lefebvre's *The Coming of the French Revolution* is best understood as one instance of this reaction, along with Alfred Cobban's important volume, *The Social Interpretation of the French Revolution,* Richard Cobb's wide-ranging attacks on new methods in history, at the 1966 meeting of the Society for French Historical Studies and in the *Times Literary Supplement,* and George Taylor's brilliant contribution to the session on the French Revolution at the American Historical Association meeting in San Francisco and published in this same issue of the *American Historical Review.*

Despite some serious differences in their approaches, Eisenstein's main purpose is, like Cobban's, to show how a traditional Marxist approach to the French Revolution is contradicted by the growing body of evidence (which, paradoxically, has been largely collected by "Marxists"). Outside of China and Albania, it is difficult to imagine anyone objecting to this ambition. As "Neo-Marxists," whether sociological theorists (such as Ralf Dahrendorf or Norman Birnbaum) or historians of the Revolution (such as Lefebvre or Albert Soboul), become more "Neo" and less "Marxist," it becomes difficult to distinguish their theoretical position from ordinary good sense. It the *Communist Manifesto,* we find a simple (or simpleminded) view of both the French Revolution and revolutions in general. Social structures (such as "feudalism") are built by ruling classes (such as the nobility) to protect their collective interests, only to be overthrown by rising groups (such as the bourgeoisie), both groups being defined simply by their productive roles. Neo-Marxism, however, has moved to the mere expectation that we will find in history social groups, variously defined, struggling for power and, thereby, continuously changing social structures.

Like Cobban, Eisenstein presents Lefebvre's views as if he were a simple-minded Marxist, who shows the "bourgeoisie" as having created the Revolution (or seized control from the aristocracy) in its own interests. Since I, on the other hand, have found his writings the most important impetus to the de-Stalinization of our view of the Revolution, at least one of us, clearly, is reading his works incorrectly. At a time when the non-Marxist Crane Brinton was excluding data on the prevalence of Jacobin Clubs in rural areas on the grounds that peasants only did what they were told by representatives on mission, Lefebvre was, for the first time, placing the peasant on the revolutionary stage as an actor in his own right, responding reasonably to the pressures of his own social, economic, and political situation. Again, while he gives perhaps more importance and less definition to the bourgeoisie than this group warrants, Lefebvre's primary emphasis is clearly upon the fact that, at its various stages and in various ways, all of the groups constituting eighteenth-century France somehow participated in the making of the Revolution.

A learned friend has recently described Soboul's Marxism as a kind of frame. The picture that he provides of the Revolution can be regarded as valid, valuable, even beautiful, but it is placed in an inappropriate Marxist frame. The frame does not detract from the picture, which could be removed from this frame and placed in another without changing its value.

The analogy suggests that the broad theoretical assumptions and the significant conclusions of the work are radically divorced from its empirical details. Since, in the social studies even more than in the fine arts, the frame really matters, as it provides the linkage between any particular historical study and those general views of man and society that justify the scholarly effort, Cobban and Eisenstein perform for us a truly valuable service. They are strongest when (in the classic tradition of Anglo-Saxons dealing with continental thought) they confront a simplistic Marxist statement with historical fact. For example, while he was certainly aware of it, Lefebvre neglected or refused to draw the full historical lesson from the prominence of nobles and clergy in the leadership of the struggle for doubling the representation of the Third Estate, during the winter of 1788–1789. Or, again, instead of assuming (as do both Cobban and the Marxists) that those who profited most from the Revolution must be those who produced it, Eisenstein insists that we approach these as two separate empirical issues, with proper respect for the unanticipated consequences of purposive social action, or the "ironies of history."

Two concerns, however, restrain my enthusiasm for these achievements: the danger that, in stereotyping Lefebvre's before a superior synthesis is presented, we will feel that we need no longer read him (any more than we still read Marx); and the even more important danger that we will accept an alternative theory of history, with its associated methodology, as misleading as the Marxist view which is introduced in the implicit assumptions of the critique. The critics' views of Lefebvre may be misleadingly partial, and their underlying ideas of social change and their views of historical method may simply lead us into new errors, or, what would be as bad if not worse, sterile negations.*

We have already referred to Lefebvre's introduction in his early work of the peasant as an independent actor on the revolutionary stage. His *Grande Peur* and *Paysans du Nord* had some importance in the conception of those recent works by Paul Bois and Charles Tilly, which have cured us of thinking of the peasant of the west as

---

* Unlike Eisenstein, Cobban explicitly regards Lefebvre as a "Marxist." *(Social Interpretation,* II.) The difference, however, is only a superficial one in the etiquette of intellectual debate in England and the United States. While he uses the term "Marxism" or (worse) "sociology" to attack Lefebvre's fundamental theoretical approach, she speaks of "a static framework derived from a structural analysis," a description that, to my mind, bears no resemblance to anything in Lefebvre or Marx. The point is, however, that they seem identical in their ideas of what Lefebvre thought of the Revolution: as a successful effort by the bourgeoisie to break the bonds of feudalism so that capitalism could flower.

a rural supersitious dolt simply following the rule of nobles and parish priests. They force us now to analyze his behavior as a political man in light of such objective conditions of his social and economic life as the purchase of land by the urban rich. This is hardly a Marxist approach in any narrow sense. It attributes mind and historical significance to the peasant, which Marxism has never done in theory or practice. It sees the process of urbanization as significant as productive relations, and, in the determination of the lines defining historically relevant groups, it takes residence as being equally as important as ownership of the means of production.

Lefebvre's later work seems to me to have been aimed at an empirical synthesis, rather than a *parti pris*. He can probably be more effectively criticized for having presented a flat, eclectic picture, without indications of the relative importance of the various historical events and processes he describes and analyzes. Non-Marxist positions abound in this mélange: for example, "France remained a nation of agriculture and handicrafts. The development of capitalism and of economic freedom met strong resistance on French soil" could have been written by Cobban. Perhaps *The French Revolution* is the only text in which we could find an author using both Augustin Cochin's study of the conspiracy of privileged groups in Brittany and C. E. Labrousse's analysis of the *conjoncture économique* at the dawn of the Revolution. Elsewhere, he expresses great admiration for Alexis de Tocqueville and even Hippolyte Taine. It is precisely his breadth, which encompasses the results of serious empirical work of any school, that provides, within his own work, the ammunition for critics of his general position regarding the importance of the bourgeoisie.

Without some organizing principle, such an eclecticism would leave the reader disoriented, with a mass of facts and interpretations, but no clear ideas of the meaning, the sources, or the consequences of the Revolution. Lefebvre finds the mortar to hold his structure together in two distinct themes. The first is the retention of the Marxist view of the overriding significance of the bourgeoisie in a drama having many other participants, the primary point of criticism of Eisenstein and Cobban, to which I will return presently. The second, which cannot be ignored in any estimate of Lefebvre's intellectual orientation, or his relationship to Marxism, is the set of ideals of the Revolution, which, though formulated by the bourgeoisie, aimed at the universalistic assurance of the Rights of Man and the Citizen. While analyzing the contents of the Declaration in terms of the interests of those who drew it up, and of their constituents, and the historical circumstances and pressures of the moment, Lefebvre ultimately turns to its abstract, universalistic message as the profound meaning of the Revolution, even assimilating it to the Christian tradition: "The Church promised salvation to all without distinction of race, language or nation. To this universalism the new thinkers remained faithful. They secularized the idea of the Christian community, but they kept it alive." Lefebvre takes no pains whatever to resolve this idealistic view of the meaning of the Revolution with his idea of the prominent role played by the bourgeoisie, perhaps because he saw no contradiction in the notion of a particular group as the agent of a universalistic ethic. Written at the impending death of the Third Republic, the closing passage can hardly be taken as the work of a simplistic Marxist: "It is therefore more difficult to live as a free man than to live as a slave and that is why men so often renounce their freedom; for freedom is in its way an invitation to a life of courage and sometimes of heroism, as the freedom of the Christian is an invitation to a life of sainthood."

Lefebvre was certainly a Marxist, but he was also a demographic determinist, a constitutional theorist, an intellectual historian, and a humanistic moralist. He was, above all, an empiricist, and the pity would be if an attack on one facet of his work, however valid, should be taken as a basis for rejecting or, worse, ignoring the rest.

The validity of the attack is, however, still on the agenda. Eisenstein and Cobban conclude that there is no basis for the Marxist description of the Revolution as an act of a "bourgeoisie" in opposition to the restrictions of a "feudal" system. Taken as a dogma (as it sometimes has been), this is unacceptable, but, taken as a hypothesis, I believe that the necessary theoretical and empirical work for its evaluation remains to be performed. This work would be built, as are the critiques of Cobban and Eisenstein, around a limited number of questions: What is the "bourgeoisie"? What is "feudalism"? What is a "revolution," and what is "social change"? And what is to be accepted as historical evidence?

The critics raise questions about both the identity and the historical role of the bourgeoisie. Both seem particularly incensed at the use of a concept referring to people of highly varied occupations, wealth, and social origins. Lefebvre himself makes clear the heterogeneity of the French bourgeoisie, in contrast, for example, to that of Russia, where Catherine was apparently able to identify it clearly enough to grant it corporative autonomy and exemption from military service. The diffuse character of the concept, as used both by contemporaries of the Revolution (such as, notably, Antoine Barnave) and by Marxists and those they have influenced, leads Cobban and Eisenstein almost (but not quite) to wish to do without it entirely. At one point, Eisenstein is carried away:

> *Finally, to apply the term "bourgeois" to village priests as well as to "the upper level of the nobility ... whose conditions of life drew them to the bourgeoisie" ... is to stretch this much-abused term beyond its already frayed limits. There is something wildly askew about a structural model that includes the top layer of nobles and the bottom layer of the clergy within the middle ranks of the middle class.*

If the son of a bourgeois family enters the clergy, the clergy is not thereby "bourgeois," nor does Lefebvre ever designate it as such. As for the nobility, the full quotaton reads: "At its upper level, the nobility *tended to suffer amputation of a minority* whose conditions of life drew them to the bourgeoisie and gave them liberal ideas." I have italicized the passage that fills the ellipsis in her quotation because it is important. To say that a minority (Mirabeau may serve as an example) is amputated is not to say that the nobility, or any part of it, is to be included in the reference of the concept of the "bourgeoisie." It is to say the opposite: that having entered the bourgeoisie, the minority is no longer considered in law or public opinion as "noble." In both the case of the priest (who, after all, had to come from somewhere outside the clergy!) and the *noble dérogé,* Eisenstein confuses the origins of an individual with the structural position of a group. Her differences with Lefebvre here are not over historical facts, but over the proper procedures for the construction of social concepts and the analysis of social events.

Since the "bourgeoisie" contains a wide variety of groups (although not as wide a variety as Eisenstein thinks), it is certainly, from one point of view, difficult to define. But that which is difficult to define may, in fact, exist, and even have great historical significance. Indeed, the lack of precise definition may even be an important part of the historical situation: Tocqueville makes much of the lack of *cultural* differentiation in France between the upper levels of the Third Estate and the nobility. "They differed only in their rights" is his summary of a situation he regards as explosive. This he contrasts with developments in England where the social, legal, and kinship lines between noble and commoner were more ambiguous, and with Europe east of France, where differences in culture and style of life rendered stratified groups more identifiable, and differences in prerogatives presumably more acceptable. I suggest that, in this context, both contemporaries and Marxists have generally meant by the "bourgeoisie" nothing more complex, nor better defined, than the "upper levels of the Third Estate," which is to say the wealthier, more urban, more educated, less privileged members of the society. I believe that such a definition is workable since we can usually identify those who belong to the group and proceed to study the role of such people in the events of the Revolution.

One can readily see their very minor role in the *leadership* of the movement that intervened in the conflict between the aristocracy and the monarchy in the winter of 1788 to insist upon the doubling of the representation of the Third Estate. But this does not mean that they did not play an important role. Eisenstein is correct in emphasizing that those who made the Revolution need not have been those who profited from the Revolution, but I would go one step further: those who, at any given moment, led the Revolution were not necessarily those who made the Revolution. This point bears upon the more general question of the contexts of political action as relevant historical material, to which we will return below.

While Eisenstein's critique is directed almost exclusively at the identity and significance of the "bourgeoisie," Cobban also takes up the nature of the "feudalism" against which, in the Marxist view, the bourgeoisie are supposed to have taken up arms. His position is unambiguous: "If 'feudalism' in 1789 did not mean seignorial rights, it meant nothing." And since, Cobban continues, these rights were destroyed by action of the peasants against the wishes of the bourgeoisie, many of whom had vested interests in them, there was no bourgeois revolution against feudalism. *Quod erat demonstrandum.*

One almost hesitates to examine so elegant an argument for fear of disturbing the peace. Like so many of the concepts used in the social studies, "feudalism" has had a varied history. Carl

Stephenson, for example, refuses to use it unless he can visualize a man in full armor on a horse. But the term has been used much more loosely, by participants in the revolutionary events, by scholars, and by political activists with a large number of pejorative connotations and institutional denotations.

As a conscientious scholar, Cobban inquires: in the institutions of eighteenth-century France, what remains with sufficient historical continuity with the medieval system of land tenure and its associated obligations, to warrant the application of the term "feudalism"? He finds only seigneurial rights and privileges. But this, whether correct or not, is irrelevant to his purpose, which is to evaluate the "social" or Marxist interpretation of the Revolution. For that purpose what we need is not a historically justifiable definition of feudalism for the eighteenth century, but rather an idea of the meaning intended by those, like Marx, Jean Jaurès, Albert Mathiez, Albert Soboul, or Daniel Guérin, at whom the critique is aimed.

For these people, I am sure, the term refers to all those institutions of the old regime providing special rights, privileges, or powers to the first two orders of the realm, or to privileged groups of commoners, including (besides seigneurial rights) privileges in legal processes (such as *committimus*); exclusive access to careers in the church, the military, and the diplomatic corps; deferential rights to church pews, the wearing of swords, and the use of weather vanes; recreational privileges such as the rights to hunt, fish, and keep pigeons and rabbits; the rights of assembly and political representation; and, perhaps most important, tax privileges, exemptions, and advantages. The fact that many of these, the seigneurial rights particularly, came in later years into the hands of *roturiers* does not change their designation as "feudal."

What is important in the Marxist view is not the historical sources of these social arrangements in medieval life, but that, along with such later innovations as venal offices, royal grants and pensions, tax farming, and governmental and guild restrictions on freedom of production and distribution, they functioned inappropriately for the demands of the "capitalist" (read "modern") world. Where they are most wrong, and Cobban's critique is most powerful, is not here, but in identifying the needs of the modern world, to which the "feudal" old-regime institutions were inappropriate, with the demands of modern industrial production. The evidence indicates that these needs are to be found much more readily in the consequences of agricultural innovation, demographic pressures, urbanization, and foreign and colonial trade, with their associated military adventures and fiscal pressures.

Cobban denies the charge he attributes to Lefebvre, that he had intended to deny the existence of the Revolution in his inaugural lecture. If a man is the final authority on his own intentions, and if Lefebvre did make such a charge, we must accept that Lefebvre made a mistake; but it was a mistake easily made. At every step in his argument Cobban takes pains to show the similarities of post-revolutionary France with the old regime. For example: "Looking at the economic consequences of the Revolution as a whole, they seem astonishingly small for such a great social and political up-heaval." This conclusion is reached by the examination of data on the rate of industrialization and trade during a period of twenty-five years of internal and external warfare. I find it hard to understand how he could write: "Finance, in fact, traversed the Revolution little changed except in personnel," unless, somehow, the unleashing of the assignats on a society profoundly distrustful of paper money since the John Law debacle could be regarded as unimportant. He doubts that there was a "permanent change of personnel in the upper ranks of society." To investigate this, "It would be interesting to know to what extent, in different parts of the country, the noblesse kept its lands during the revolution. . . . We know also that there were many purchases of *biens nationaux* by nobles, sometimes even on behalf of *émigrés. . . .*" Also, the abolition of venality of office is not to be taken too seriously because the officers were compensated, and, "Moreover, many of the former *officiers* seem subsequently to have obtained salaried judicial and administrative positions not dis-similar from those for the loss of which they had earlier been com-pensated."

I would hold that a society that has changed from one in which industry and commerce are regulated by a multiplicity of Colbertian mercantilist regimens and administrative agencies as well as priv-ileged corporate guilds and in which internal trade is hampered by a multiplicity of prohibitions and tariffs, to a free national market economy, has undergone a fundamental change—a revolution—even though, temporarily, industry and trade do not expand under the pressures of continual warfare. Even if every noble becomes a landlord in fee simple, I would contend that a revolution has occurred in the stratification system of the society. The same biological humans, or their descendants, are to be found in leading positions, but they are different social beings, with different rights, duties, and functions: they pay taxes like everyone else (or avoid them under the same rules as everyone else); they appear in the same courts (even though with better attorneys); they sit in legislative assemblies if elected, not in constitutive assemblies by right of birth; if they wear different clothes or enjoy better career chances, it is because they command more resources and not because they are given monopolies in law or by discriminatory administrative practice. Finally, a society with a bureaucratic administrative staff, responsible in a hierarchy to central authorities, is a very different society from one in which many of those who must be charged with the day-to-day administration of executive decisions hold property in office, even if all the biological individuals filling the bureaucratic slots were once venal officers. (Ask Turgot, or Napoleon; or read Max Weber.) Cobban never claims that there was no French Revolution, but Lefebvre's charge is essentially sound; he gives us a large number of specious reasons to believe that *plus ça change, plus c'est la même chose,* based largely upon a wholly inadequate theoretical conception of what constitutes social change.

My final point, directed more at Eisenstein, is perhaps the most important, since it bears upon the most general questions of historical method. In the closing paragraphs of her critique she takes a methodological position which, I believe, is directly contrary to the very idea of a social history. She attacks both conspiracy theorists and "those who insist on spontaneous mass or class action" as equally prone to "ignore the real men who formed and led the patriot party.... In both instances we are asked to look around, over, beyond, above, or below rather than at the assorted individuals whose group action we are curious about." This passage only makes explicit the underlying methodological source of a number of serious errors earlier in her paper: her unwillingness to examine the social contexts of political action while pursuing her favored (and necessary) method of "collective biography."

She writes, for example, "Up to this point [September 23, 1788] the 'aristocratic revolution' was proceeding without intervention from other social sectors. . . ." But during the June crisis following the Lamoignon edicts suppressing the parliamentary powers, there were "popular" disorders in Toulouse, Dijon, Pau, and, notably, Grenoble (the "Day of Tiles"). Nobles rarely riot. From the point of view of social history, this is "intervention" of a most important sort. Since she cannot see this as "intervention," she can cite the Vizille assembly, at which the Third Estate was given the vote by head with double representation and fiscal equality, as an instance of liberal provincial aristocratic "initiative." She is puzzled by this action, since the same people had earlier rejected similar forms proposed by Brienne for the new provincial assemblies. Perhaps her puzzlement would disappear if she would look not only at the ideas and group memberships of the people who signed the papers, so to speak, but also where *they* looked, around them, at the actions of those with whom they were allied, or whom they feared. In fact, the "Day of Tiles" took place at Grenoble only six weeks before the Vizille assembly, a fact that we may not ignore any more than could the aristocracy of the Dauphiné.

The fact that all political actors (and not only elected delegates) have, in a sense, constituents goes far to explain those occasions in which we find them taking actions that violate their deepest personal convictions. Sometimes, as in the case of the Vizille assembly, since the constituents are off stage, we must proceed by comparing the plausibility of their influence with the fantastic notion that the assembly was unaware, or uninterested, in the violence in the streets only six weeks earlier. As Kaplow shows, however, in another case she is puzzled because her methods blind her to the relevance of a literal constituency physically present in the assembly hall: the democratic position taken by the privileged representatives of the Third in the provincial estates of Brittany.

This inability to see political actors in relation to their constituencies, and not merely as expressing their personal beliefs, leads to some strange interpretations of the convocation. The elections are said to have been "partly rigged" because only a handful of *bailliages* chose to send nobles or clergymen as representatives of the Third. The privileged orders were "eliminated from the running." But this was a choice of the assemblies. They were eliminated from the running because they were slow horses, not because they were unfairly scratched. The fact that the *cahiers* contain demands for a legal restriction that the delegates of the Third be chosen from members of the Third is irrelevant; such demands must necessarily refer only to future convocations. Finally, Eisenstein seems to be led to a most astonishing confusion between the statistical concept of "representation" and the political concept. "The nobles and priests who retained their seats may have represented an infinitesimal minority of the population. The literate commoners did not represent a much larger one." This is nothing more than a bad pun. The delegates of the Third represented over 95 percent of the population, which they did not resemble any more than Ted Kennedy resembles me. They were given *cahiers* expressing the desires of their constituencies and, at times, mandates limiting their range of choices in legislative actions, and committees of correspondence to keep them responsive to the desires of their constituents. It was undoubtedly the will of the vast majority that the delegates be atypical precisely in such qualities as literacy and knowledge of public affairs in the hope that they would serve the interests of their constituents not only more reliably than a noble but also more competently than a *maître Jacques.*

A proper appreciation of the relevance of social contexts in the formation of political decisions would reveal to Eisenstein the possibility of a high degree of convergence in the types of delegates chosen, and of grievances expressed, without any central direction or undercover campaign. Hence, I cannot agree with the theory underlying her claim that, "However enterprising they may be, men who are located 'everywhere' simply cannot take 'concerted action' to steer an electorate toward a given slate of candidates. One group located in one place is required to see that all the others do not 'steer' in all directions." Indeed, unless local communities and their leaders faced, to some degree, common situations and problems, there is little reason to expect them to pay attention to Parisian opinions in their choice of delegates or model *cahiers.* In fact, many did not. Eisenstein quotes, but nevertheless ignores, Lefebvre's statement that most models were drafted locally.

The most serious of those errors deriving from her unwillingness to examine the contexts, and, particularly, the constituencies, of political actors is her erroneous interpretation of the events of the night of August 4. She explicitly regards the abolition of "all privileges" on this date as the work of a limited number of leaders of the patriot party who cut across the lines of estates and social classes. In this case, the facts are established and clear. The dramatic gestures of the privileged on August 4 only endorsed a *fait accompli;* to a great extent their privileges had already been destroyed by peasant uprisings, municipal revolutions, and the Great Fear—disorders in which, among other things, the records of seigneurial obligations were often destroyed. The decision to abjure that which they had already lost was made the previous night in the Breton Club, where over a hundred deputies participated, most of whom were recruited from the upper levels of the Third Estate. Naturally, if this particular gesture, designed to reestablish civil order and political stability, were to have effect, it must be set off by the action of those with the status of the Duc d'Aiguillon or the Vicomte de Noailles. Eisenstein takes these symbolic figures as independent actors, ignoring both the caucus that obviously prompted them and the mobs that prompted the caucus.

A similar analysis would explain civil rights legislation today by the actions of a small, socially heterogeneous group of students, ministers, congressmen, and Supreme Court justices, with nothing in common except the reading of the Fourteenth Amendment, affected neither by urban crime nor by protests in the streets of Watts, Harlem, Selma, Philadelphia, Rochester, or Chicago. Malcolm X actually feared such an interpretation. He once asked his autobiographer, Alex Haley, to deliver a message to the latter's brother, a state senator. "Tell your brother for me to remember us in the alley. Tell him that he and all of the other moderate Negroes who are getting somewhere need to always remember that it was us extremists who made it possible." The continuing task of the social interpretation of the French Revolution, to which Lefebvre's contributions remain of first importance, is to find the links between the actions of those in the alley and those in the palace.

Elizabeth L. Eisenstein

A Reply

Mr. Kaplow and Mr. Shapiro have raised several issues that need further clarification. I wish they had looked harder at the particular issue raised by my "Commentary." Where they do touch upon it, they stay in the provinces; although, in following Lefebvre, I focused on Paris. In the provinces, moreover, they skip over the places where, following Lefebvre, I spent some time (Dijon, for example). That I was following Lefebvre's account and not making up my own, scrutinizing a single text and not synthesizing many, has been overlooked. Let me restate my purpose. I did not set out "to show how a traditional Marxist approach . . . is contradicted by the growing body of evidence" or to compare this evidence with Lefebvre's approach (however labeled). As both my title and first paragraph make clear, I did try to show how presentation of a strategic point in a single influential book was contradicted by the author's own evidence. In view of this stated purpose, I am unrepentant about the second of my two sins detected by Kaplow and wish to lodge a complaint instead. By taking my exegesis as if it pertained to something other than a particular text, both critics have smudged the clearly defined limits of my commentary and blurred the sharp focus I sought to obtain.

My remarks about a "static framework" are thus applied (by Kaplow) to a "theory of class." He goes on to object that this theory theoretically makes room for evolution and complexity. Shapiro makes a similar objection. My remarks did not pertain to any abstract concept or to the use of it made by other historians, or by Lefebvre, himself, in his other works, They referred to how a particular narrative describing political action was interrupted at a crucial point by a chapter devoted to class structure, thereby breaking the thread of the narrative, distracting attention from a group that supplied continuous leadership, and artificially separating members of this group. I see nothing contrived or theoretical about this point and wish Kaplow had discussed it. In the guise of objecting to a "straw man technique," he has, instead, injected into my discussion several higher order abstractions—the very ingredients I tried to leave out. Whether the dichotomy noble-bourgeois is congruent with the dichotomy feudal-capitalist is certainly disputable. I would side with George Taylor and Betty Behrens on this dispute, but that is beside the point. I happen to be more curious about the location of revolutionary initiative in 1788–1789. Here I did object (and still do) to making a "blank-faced bourgeoisie" responsible for initiating action. But that class membership automatically determines political responses or that noblemen act like Pavlov's dogs was not imputed by me to Lefebvre. Such straw men are not of my making any more than are the passages I cite from Lefebvre's book.

Fortunately Kaplow does get down to specifics. His tactics remain evasive, however. In dealing with the protest movement he passes over Parisian leadership, beginning instead with unevenly documented provincial developments. Surprisingly, he seems to agree with my speculations about socially heterogeneous local leadership. He then states, as if posing an objection, that some bourgeois did intervene in numerous provincial towns. But this seems entirely compatible with heterogeneous local leadership. While they were not alone, he goes on, these bourgeois did constitute a new element in the struggle. Now this is an argument that is not in Lefebvre's book and hence was not discussed in my commentary. It should nonetheless be considered. I would hold that some bourgeois had also previously been active in the so-called "aristocratic revolution." The new element in the struggle was, I still think, the injection of a new issue: defiance of the Paris Parlement's ruling. The social composition of groups responsible for mobilizing opinion on this issue has, in my view, some bearing on theories about the "class nature of the struggle of 1788." Why should evidence on this point prove "nothing whatsoever" about such theories? If a theory is so framed that it cannot be invalidated by any evidence, I regard it as useless and barren. At all events, I welcome Kaplow's use of my own argument that many traditionally submissive commoners had to be roused into action even if he finds me "curiously blind" in the process.

Space limitations require a very cursory review of other points raised by Kaplow (I am following his order throughout). (1) The first estate is simply not equivalent to the second in any century. It compounds confusion to regard it as such. (2) The "guts" were not removed by a tactic that made passing the resolution possible, since the gut issue was doubling at the time the section voted. That it was a shrewd tactic not to press voting by head is persuasively argued by Lefebvre. (3) Objections to the view that patriot leaders favored the separation of orders to prevent commoners from electing privileged persons should be directed against Lefebvre's account. Presumably, he had "shreds of evidence" in mind when he wrote the passage I cited. (4) I point to contradictions on many more than two occasions. The particular footnote singled out by Kaplow contains another more important puzzle than the one he has unwittingly misconstrued.[1] The second contradiction he mentions does involve a major issue, and I hope more thought will be given it. The spreading of news about the Parlement's ruling seems to me entirely relevant to the "organizing of revolution." Given the way news was circulated in eighteenth-century France, references to "newsboys" seem anachronistic. Kaplow's distinction between "clandestine" and "legal" news distribution does not hold up. The private couriers and agents of the Parisian leaders had access to the same transportation whatever messages they carried. According to Égret, Volney's *Sentinelle du Peuple* "gave the real signal for the bourgeois revolution" in Brittany. This was not a clandestine periodical. Indeed Bretons thought Volney was a government agent. But Volney had been dispatched to Rennes by the Parisian leaders, according to Lefebvre. (6) An objection to the inclusion of parish priests, often recruited from the peasantry, within the category of "enterprising bourgeois" is not, I think, a quibble. (7) Of course one cannot discuss the making of the Revolution solely in terms of who was responsible for a given set of actions, whether one considers the

---

[1] See my "Who Intervened in 1788?" [p. 177, above]. The major puzzle was how a center of parliamentary resistance became a center of resistance to parliamentary authority. The minor one involved the Breton Third Estate portrayed earlier as composed exclusively of nobles and privileged persons but later as having "*long* demanded" fiscal equality. Both critics miss this contradiction (possibly I should have italicized "long" in my original citation). Both object that I missed seeing how pressure groups forced the "privileged" deputies to defy the first and second estates in late December 1788. This defiance, however, involved new political as well as old fiscal demands. These old demands for fiscal equality, I repeat, come oddly from an assembly of "nobles" until one realizes that municipal oligarchs are not really equivalent to nobles. Here, as elsewhere, Egret's treatment resembles Lefebvre's. Compare his description of the mayor of Nantes as a noble who led the privileged Nantais faction in "The Origins of the Revolution in Brittany (1788–1789)," in *New Perspectives on the French Revolution: Readings in Historical Sociology,* ed. Jeffry Kaplow (New York, 1965), p. 142, with description of the same man as one of five *roturiers* attending an Assembly of Notables in *Pré-révolution,* p. 341.

"whole Revolution" or any of its less problematic phases. I pointed this out myself. The question is: should one discuss the making of the Revolution (in whole or in part) by excluding the problem of who was responsible for initiating action or by disregarding evidence pertaining to this problem? (8) If I have failed to make my point, I wish Kaplow would show me how or where. The discursive footnote (about a skewed model) he goes on to discuss is clearly not the place to look.[2] (9) His peroration significantly rephrases a statement made previously in his introduction to his volume of readings. There (version *A*) he holds the Revolution was bourgeois "because the bourgeois initiated it and emerged triumphant from it." Here (version *B*) he says, more ambiguously, it was because the bourgeoisie was "active . . . had ideals . . . [and] were dominant." To make my position clear, I will comment on these two versions. *A* contains two statements that can be detached and separately tested. Reserving judgment on the question of outcome, I find that the evidence does not support the assertion about initiative. *B* offers an opening for further discussion, namely, when, how, or by what means did commoners become politically dominant. Finally, I share with Kaplow the desire to "go on from there," but am puzzled by his phrase "at long last." As Behrens points out, the sites to be dug for the foundation he mentions were already prospected by Barnave and Sieyès. Historians have been going "on from there" ever since and will undoubtedly continue to do so for many more decades. It is

---

[2] Both critics have misfired in taking this footnote as a target. (See [p. 196 above] of my "Who Intervened in 1788?") Shapiro hauled out the heaviest artillery and made the worst blunder. I deliberately left out the ellipsis he fills in to avoid misleading a reader who might not consult Lefebvre's whole paragraph. Presumably, Shapiro did consult the paragraph. He was nonetheless misled by the phrase "amputation of a minority." It does not apply to the "lower level" where "the nobility *also* suffered from attrition," unclassing themselves "like Mirabeau" ("déclassé" is, incidentally, confused by Shapiro with "dérogé"). The "amputation" excludes Mirabeau et al. and refers to the "upper level," that is, to rich prestigious lords who acquired "liberal ideas" and English Whiggish ambitions. (See Lefebvre, *Coming of the French Revolution,* p. 14.) Surely a "skewed model" results when a group exhibiting no signs of downward mobility and personifying the "haute noblesse" for contemporaries is arbitrarily amputated by a later historian. Kaplow is merely wrong in saying I lumped the top layer of nobles with the bourgeoisie on the basis of political ideas, since Lefebvre did this. In lecturing me on why I am confused about a point he has muddled, Shapiro is infuriating as well as wrong. As for parish priests, the "quibble" noted in point 6, above, accounts for my assertion (queried by Kaplow) that Lefebvre placed them among bourgeois merely because they were literate. Shapiro somehow misconstrues my remarks about recruitment and ignores my basis for asserting that Lefebvre places them among "enterprising bourgeois."

only those of us who are dissatisfied with the results of this work —seeing not a "wave of progress" but a proliferation of false issues—who are deterred from contributing further to it.

This brings me to Mr. Shapiro's excursion into the field of French revolutionary historiography. I have no space to unravel the tangled web he has woven, but must express dismay at having my article set within such an inappropriate context. Fortunately Behrens has provided a different, more suitable one. Insofar as my piece enters into his account, Shapiro begins by misconstruing my main purpose. He goes on to opine that I read Lefebvre's works incorrectly without knowing my views on these works. Had I chosen to appraise the lifework of a prolific historian instead of analyzing portions of an influential text, I would have written a very different article. Even while he neglects the French historiographical tradition upon which Lefebvre draws and the Robespierrist cult that runs, like a red thread, through his work, Shapiro worries about my exaggerating the "Marxist" element in Lefebvre's *oeuvre.* In fact, he stresses it much more than I would—and clearly much more than I did in the actual article I wrote.

Shapiro asserts that this article contains a "number of serious errors" all derived from a presumed blindness to "social context." Since I had tried to avoid errors and had looked at social context, I was troubled by this indictment until I examined the counts upon which it was based. To put the matter bluntly, he has blundered too often in posing his objections to make possible a fruitful debate. One blunder, based on careless reading, has already been described. . . . Another involves his bringing up the "Day of Tiles" without first doing homework in straightforward political history. His presentation of this episode points to the fallacy of ascertaining "methodological positions" before posing simple questions such as: who? what? when? where? how? The Grenoble *émeute* of June 7, 1788, as described by Égret, was instigated by judicial aids to protest royal action against the local parlement—a popular protest in a town economically dependent on legal business. It formed part of the "aristocratic revolution," involved the issues of Versailles versus the provinces, and happens to support my footnote on the Vizille assembly. According to Égret, it had no repercussions outside Grenoble and "obtained no result"—a "fantastic notion" according to Shapiro. Égret views the Dauphinoise revolution as the work of a "coterie" led by Mounier. Shapiro asks me to look where members of the Vizille assembly looked. "The multitude never had any influence on our assemblies," remarked Mounier. The often cited remark: "I am their leader, I must follow them" may be applicable to 1848 but not to 1788. This possibility should be considered when distinguishing between those who led and those who made the Great Revolution. Historians cannot afford to be tone deaf to the music of time.

To "see political actors in relation to their constituencies" requires, first of all, finding out who the former were. Such an attempt, I am told "is directly contrary to the very idea of a social history." Any kind of history, in my view, is incompatible with premature leaps in the dark. A look at the composition of pressure groups formed within and without duly constituted bodies has convinced me that some premature leaps have been made in the wrong direction. How does it undermine social history to point this out? If I had dealt with the Breton assembly of December 1788 (and I did not) I would not confuse deputies with constituents, but would examine the different pressure groups that were present.[3] Of course an argument based on misconstrued footnotes is bound to engender unnecessary confusion, but difficulty with fine print is not the only source of such confusion. Shapiro has also misread my meaning to produce a "bad pun," divined the will of the peasantry in accordance with his thesis rather than historical veracity, and imputed to me his own "strange interpretations of the convocation."

Unless degree is specified, it is meaningless to say that "local communities . . . faced, to some degree, common situations. . . ." Common denominators are required for modern social analysis. Historical imagination has to be exerted to prevent the search for such denominators from distorting conditions prevailing in earlier

---

[3] In Provence, according to Egret, revolutionary initiative was displayed by "members of the nobility not possessing fiefs." Instead of trying to decide whether they were "political actors," representatives, or "constituents," it seems preferable to look at them as a pressure group. It would be useful to know, in the Breton case, how the social composition of the recalcitrant faction in Nantes (led by a rich new noble) differed from that of the "revolutionary" faction (led by a rich new noble). I would single out three different pressure groups gathered in the hall who forced action from recalcitrant spokesmen for forty-two Breton towns: (1) twenty-nine deputy commissioners from different towns; (2) fourteen extraordinary deputies from Nantes; (3) a group of local "jeunes gens" who threatened to pelt uncooperative deputies from the galleries. (See Egret, "Origins of the Revolution," pp. 161, 144.)

eras. Not neglect of social context but caution about historical context leads me to worry about such distortions when thinking, back across two centuries, about situations in *ancien régime* France. The possibility that "a high degree of convergence" could occur "without central direction" is one that I did not ignore. I examined it with some care when discussing the single demand that "sounded loudly" during the protest movement of 1788–1789. Shapiro ignores this discussion and accuses me of ignoring the subject I discussed. Having added insult to injury, he throws in a discourse on methodology for good measure.

To find my "most serious" error he again passes over the events I did discuss and hits upon one I did not. He takes a glancing reference out of context from a long sentence about the group that "provided the basis for whatever unity or continuity may be perceived in the early phases of the French Revolution." The reference was, admittedly, too fleeting and should be emended: "who *helped to abolish* all privilege" conveys my meaning properly. This emendation does not alter my point that continuity of leadership was demonstrated by Lefebvre's account of the night of August 4. Target read the proclamation; Noailles was "in on the secret"; Aiguillon was already active as a member of the Committee of Thirty in the fall of 1788 and deserves, no more than any other of its members, to be regarded as a mere "symbol." The Breton Club grew out of a protest movement that had been initiated and orchestrated by Parisian leadership and was linked with this leadership. To detach members of its caucus from those who implemented its decision in public the next night or to regard the latter as mere figureheads manipulated by the former is to draw an unwarranted inference that does not agree with prior developments and has nothing to do with "facts that are established and clear." Neither the Breton Club caucus nor peasant uprisings provided the revolutionary movement of 1788–1789 with unity and continuity. A leadership that cut across estates and social classes probably did. Consistent to the end in ignoring this issue, Shapiro concludes by offering his views on the present civil rights movement.

In his discourse on methodology and social context, he has inadvertently misconstrued political history and misread Lefebvre's account. He has also falsified my argument, playing carelessly with textual context to do so. More important and dismaying, his whole paper—beginning with remarks about Albania and China, going on to de-Stalinization and Ted Kennedy, ending with Malcolm X's "auto-biographer"—reveals a reckless disregard for historical context. I object to his stating that my position on any issue is "directly contrary to the very idea of a social history" as I object to his delivering his opinion of the Day of Tiles "from the viewpoint of social history." For one thing social history has no viewpoint, although social historians have many. For another, Shapiro is not a historian; he is a sociologist. There are many occasions where too much has been made of this distinction and some where it cannot be drawn at all. But this seems to me one of those exceptional cases where it should be drawn as emphatically as possible.

The most fitting summary of my general position on the objections raised by both critics has been provided by Behrens in [the concluding paragraphs of] her review of three recent French books [see above, p. 173 and the Conflict of Opinion].

Suggestions for Additional Reading

Ever since Marxian theory achieved scholarly respectability in the last decades of the nineteenth century there has been increasingly wide acceptance in scholarly circles, even among those who felt themselves to be uncommitted to the Marxist cause, of the view that social and economic history are so inextricably intertwined that, while it may be possible to study some kinds of economic history without reference to the prevailing social structure, it is impossible to write meaningful social history without a thorough knowledge of the economic patterns (mode of production, etc.) underlying it. Rather than argue the validity of this assumption at this point the following suggestions for further reading will include those works on social and economic history that are most directly relevant to the issues raised in this volume. It is not intended to be all-inclusive but will hopefully provide adequate resource material for the student who wishes to pursue the subject further in a serious way. Although many of the important studies have been translated (or were originally written in English), the really serious student will have to be prepared to arm himself with a good French-English dictionary and dig in.

Because the controversy has now been going on for some time and continues at a high pitch, several articles directly related to it have appeared since the contents of this volume were established. As it happens all of them except one offer a further challenge to the orthodox view. First and most useful from the point of view of providing an overall survey of the controversy is John F. Cavanaugh, "The Present State of French Revolutionary Historiography, Alfred Cobban and Beyond," *French Historical Studies* 7 (1972): 587–606. Although critical of orthodoxy, this article gives an excellent impartial review of the subject and has some interesting and constructive suggestions about new interpretive theories. A similar article by a French scholar, G. Lemarchand, "Sur la société française en 1789," *Revue d'Histoire Moderne et Contemporaine* 19 (1972): 73–91. The other two articles, although written independently, both challenge the orthodox view in fundamental ways. W. Doyle, who has written several articles on the Old Regime and especially the Bordeaux area, asks the question, "Was There an Aristocratic Reaction in Pre-Revolutionary France?" *Past and Present*, No. 57 (November 1972), pp. 97–122, and directly challenges the Establishment by answering in the negative. The second article, by Colin Lucas, "Nobles, Bourgeois and the French Revolution," *Past and Present*, No. 60 (August 1973), pp. 84–126, also questions the Lefebvrian view concerning the precise character, aims and roles of these two classes on the eve of the Revolution. While it relies primarily on secondary materials, so much has become available in the last twenty-five years that it is not surprising that a fundamental revision of the older view can now be called for.

Among the general works on the social and economic history of the Old Regime, the one that still stands preeminent after more than a century is Alexis de Tocqueville's *The Old Regime and the French Revolution*, available in several editions and translations. Although some of his data, as well as some of his theories and conclusions, have now been superseded, it remains a kind of classic example of social history. Another general work that is now a half-century old but still useful, particularly because it is available in English, is Henri Sée's *Economic and Social Conditions in France during the Eighteenth Century* (New York, 1927). For a view of one important aspect of the economic background of the Revolution the editor's earlier reader, *The Economic Origins of the French Revolution: Poverty or Prosperity?* (Boston, 1958), includes translations of portions of several important French works including the authoritative and indispensable work of C. E. Labrousse, *La crise de l'économie française à la fin de l'ancien régime et au début de la révolution* (Paris, 1944). A more recent work of synthesis of that author is *L'histoire économique et sociale de la France*, Tome II (1660–1789) (Paris, 1970), written in collaboration with the famous F. Braudel.

Other general studies dealing with the social and economic history of the Old Regime are R. Mandrou's *La France au XVIIe et XVIIIe siècle* (Paris, 1967); the now somewhat outdated study of Philippe Sagnac, *La formation de la société moderne*, 2 vols. (Paris, 1945–1946), and of course Georges Lefebvre's now classic *The Coming of the French Revolution*, trans. R. R. Palmer (Princeton, N.J., 1947). Good discussions in English of the social and economic aspects of the Old Regime will be found in the two volumes of *The New Cambridge Modern History* dealing with that period: J. O.

Lindsay, ed., *The Old Regime, 1713–63* (Vol. VII), and A. Goodwin, ed., *The American and French Revolutions, 1763–93* (Vol. VIII), (Cambridge, 1957 and 1965 respectively). Another useful work in English is the collaborative work of J. M. Wallace-Hadrill and J. McManners entitled, *France: Government and Society* (London, 1957). Two other books in English that include brief but important portions dealing with the question of the social origins of the Revolution are Norman Hampson's *A Social History of the French Revolution* (Toronto, 1963), and J. Kaplow's *New Perspectives on the French Revolution: Readings in Historical Sociology* (New York, 1965). The latter includes English translations of three important articles by French scholars on the issues of the social origins. These will be noted in the appropriate places in this listing. There are two recent general works of great importance for this issue by two leading French scholars, P. Goubert's *L'Ancien Régime,* Tome I, *La société;* and Albert Soboul's *La Civilization et la Révolution française, I, La crise de l'Ancien Régime* (Paris, 1970).

Below the level of these broader, general works, the more specialized studies tend to be concerned either with particular social groups or classes, or with specific aspects of economic life with special social relevance, or with aspects of either or both of these in particular limited geographic areas. These works will be listed and discussed in that order.

Following the traditional breakdown of classes in the Old Regime, aside from the traditional histories of the First Estate there are two recent excellent books emphasizing the social aspects of the order of the clergy. The first of these is J. McManner's exemplary study, *French Ecclesiastical Society under the Ancien Régime: A Study of Angers in the Eighteenth Century* (Manchester, 1961). The second is Norman Ravitch's *Sword and Mitre: Government and Episcopate in France and England in the Age of Aristocracy* (The Hague, 1966). An insight into the views of the clergy on the eve of the Revolution is given in articles by J. Égret, "La dernière assemblée de clergé de France," *Revue Historique* 219 (1958):1–15; and M. G. Hutt, "The Curés and the Third Estate: Ideas of Reform in the Pamphlets of the French Lower Clergy in the Period 1787–1789" *Journal of Ecclesiastical History* 7 (1957): 70–85.

There is no satisfactory scholarly study of the nobility under the *Ancien Régime.* One has to make do with brief accounts such as the

chapter relating to France in the comparative study of European
nobility edited by A. Goodwin, *The European Nobility in the Eighteenth Century* (London, 1958), or his article in the *John Rylands
Library Bulletin* for 1965, "The Social Origin and Privileged Status
of the French Eighteenth-Century Nobility," or with the short article
by R. Forster in the *American Historical Review* 67 (1965): 681–691,
entitled "The Provincial Noble, A Reappraisal." A book that has been
frequently referred to as a source of information about the nobility,
even though its principal concern is opinion *about* the nobility and
not the Second Estate itself, is Henri Carré's *La noblesse de France
et l'opinion publique au dix-huitième siècle* (Paris, 1920). A more
recent treatment of the same subject by A. Decouflé, "L'aristocratie
française devant l'opinion publique à la veille de la Révolution," in
Etudes d'histoire économique et sociale du XVIIIe siècle, R. Besnier,
ed. (Paris, 1966), adds almost nothing new.

Fortunately we are beginning to get some excellent monographs
dealing with the nobility of specific geographical areas. A model of
its kind which provided much of the data for the article mentioned
above is the perceptive and pioneering study of the nobility of Toulouse by Robert Forster, *The Nobility of Toulouse in the Eighteenth
Century: A Social and Economic Study* (Baltimore, 1960). A second
book of equal quality by Forster concentrates on one family, *The
House of Saulx-Tavannes: Versailles and Burgundy* (Baltimore, 1971).
A comparable and even more ambitious study of the Breton nobility
is that of J. Meyer, *La noblesse bretonne au XVIIIe siècle,* 2 vols.
(Paris, 1966). Of great importance, of course, was the relationship
between the nobility and the government. This has been fruitfully
explored in several recent books, although D. Dakin's book, *Turgot
and the Ancien Régime in France* (London, 1939), set a standard
difficult to maintain. The important relationship between the two
principal groups of the nobility, robe and sword, was studied for the
early years of the century in some detail by F. L. Ford in his *Robe
and Sword: The Regrouping of the French Aristocracy* (Cambridge,
Mass., 1953). Since by 1789 all the *intendants* were nobles, Vivian
Gruber's analysis of the social origins and background of the royal
intendants entitled *The Royal Provincial Intendants* (Ithaca, N.Y.,
1968) contributes a great deal to our knowledge of the social history
of the Second Estate.

We are fortunate in having several very good studies relating to the question of access to the nobility in the eighteenth century. The best are those by François Bluche. In collaboration with Pierre Durye the process of ennoblement by purchase of office is examined in *L'Anoblissement par charges avant 1789* (La Roche-sur-Yon, 1962). Bluche studies the social origins of the members of the Parlement of Paris in the eighteenth century in *L'Origine des magistrats du Parlement de Paris au XVIIIe siècle* (Paris, 1956). Jean Égret had attempted to do a similar but much briefer analysis of the background of the *magistrats* in an article which appeared in 1952, "L'aristocratie parlementaire française à la fin de l'ancien régime," *Revue Historique* 208 (1952): 1–14. The traditional view of the economic role of the nobility has been more and more questioned in recent years in the works of Taylor and Forster. Relevant to this is an article by G. Richard, "Les corporations et la noblesse commercante en France au XVIIIème siècle," *L'Information historique* 20 (1957): 185–189. Especially important is the article by M. Reinhard, "Elite et noblesse dans la seconde moitié du XVIIIème siècle," *Revue d'Histoire Moderne et Contemporaire* 3 (1956): 5–37. Of special interest on this topic is the article mentioned above by Ms. Betty Behrens, one of the contributors to this volume, "Nobles, Privileges and Taxes in France at the End of the Ancien Régime," *Economic History Review,* 2nd series, 15 (1962–1963): 451–475.

The Third Estate, of course, had several important subdivisions. The most important of these, even if not the largest in number, was the bourgeoisie, however broadly or narrowly that term may be defined. An American scholar, Ms. Elinor Barber, published *The Bourgeoisie in Eighteenth-Century France* (Princeton, 1955) in which she undertook to apply current sociological analytical theory to the relatively meager sociological data then available from traditional sources relating to the bourgeoisie in eighteenth-century France. Accordingly the value of the book depends on one's judgment about the theory and its premises. The best discussion of the problem of defining the meaning of the term "bourgeoisie" in eighteenth-century France is to be found in the opening chapter of Philip Dawson's outstanding study of one particular subgroup of that bourgeoisie, the provincial magistrates in the revolutionary situation. His *Provincial Magistrates and Revolutionary Politics in France, 1789–1795* (Cambridge, Mass., 1972) offers an invaluable example of the kind of sociological analysis that we must ultimately have for all subgroups in the Old Regime and the Revolution if we are to be able to arrive at sound generalizations that can provide a firm base for new interpretive theories. An earlier article by Dawson, "The Bourgeoisie de Robe in 1789," *French Historical Studies* 4 (1965): 1–21, provides much important information to supplement the now badly outdated work of F. Delbèke, *L'action politique et sociale des avocats au XVIIIème siècle* (Louvain, 1927).

Because of the great diversity of regions under the Old Regime most detailed studies of various groups are limited generally to some particular traditionally defined geographical area. There are some general studies of subgroups within the bourgeoisie, however. There is an excellent recent study of the financiers, *Les gens de finance au XVIIIe siècle* (Paris, 1972), by G. Chaussinand-Nogaret, as well as an earlier study, *Finances et financiers de l'ancien régime* (Paris, 1964), by J. Bouvier and H. Germain-Martin. Actually, as the work of Chaussinand-Nogaret and others has shown, this group, as well as the tax farmers described by G. T. Matthews in *The Royal General Farms in Eighteenth-Century France* (New York, 1958), and Y. Durand in his *Les Fermiers-généraux en France au XVIIIe siècle* (Paris, 1971), could have been included above with the nobility since so many of them had achieved that status by 1789. Another recent and very valuable work in this general area is that of H. Lüthy, *La Banque protestante en France de la revocation de l'Edit de Nantes à la Révolution,* 2 vols. (Paris, 1959–1961). Of more specific relevance to the question at issue here is G. Chaussinand-Nogaret, "Capital et structure sociale sous l'Ancien Régime," *Annales E.S.C.* (March–April 1970): 463–476. On the economic activity of the bourgeoisie, see George V. Taylor, "Non-Capitalist Wealth and the Origins of the French Revolution," *American Historical Review* 72 (1967): 469–496, of which an excerpt appears in this volume. Professor Taylor has also written earlier two important articles, "Types of Capitalism in Eighteenth-Century France," *English Historical Review* 79 (1964): 478–497, and "The Paris Bourse on the Eve of the Revolution, 1781–1789," *American Historical Review* 67 (1962): 951–977.

As indicated above, by far the most popular form of social and economic study of the Old Regime is that dealing with a specifically defined geographical area. Those that focus on cities, towns and villages generally are primarily concerned with the bourgeoisie, even though they do include some discussion of other groups.

Prominent among these is the final contribution of the great Georges Lefebvre, his study of Orleans and its environs on the eve of the Revolution, *Etudes Orleanaises: Contributions à l'étude des structures sociales à la fin de XVIIIe siècle,* 2 vols. (Paris, 1962). A pioneering effort to develop a methodology for social history is to be found in the study of A. Daumard and F. Furet, *Structures et relations sociales à Paris au milieu de XVIIIe siècle* (Paris, 1963). Bordeaux has also been studied by F. G. Pariset and others in a much more traditional approach, *Bordeaux au XVIIIe siècle* (Bordeaux, 1958), as well as by M. Lhéritier in *La Fin de l'ancien régime et la préparation des Etats généraux (1787–1789)* (Paris, 1942). Thanks to the efforts of J. Godechot, Toulouse has been rather extensively studied, beginning with his own article, "L'Histoire économique et sociale de Toulose au XVIIIe siècle," *Annales du Midi* 78 (1958): 363–374, and one by M. Thoumas-Schapira, "La bourgeoisie toulousaine à la fin du XVIIIe siècle," *Annales du Midi* 67 (1955): 308–318, and concluding with the study by J. Sentou, *Fortunes et groupes sociaux à Toulouse sous la Révolution* (Toulouse, 1969). An early work of G. Lefebvre but published posthumously was his study of *Cherbourg, à la fin de l'ancien régime et au début de la Révolution* (Caen, 1965). Although primarily concerned with the revolutionary period, a model of its kind as a study of a town is J. Kaplow's *Elbeuf during the Revolutionary Period: History and Social Structure* (Baltimore, 1964). A similarly useful study is that of O. Huften, *Bayeux in the Late Eighteenth Century* (Oxford, 1967). There are two older articles on the important Breton area, M. Brevard's "La Municipalité de Brest de 1750 à 1790," *Annales de Bretagne* 31 (1915): 101–120, and H. Sée's "La rôle de la bourgeoisie bretonne à la veille de la Révolution," *Annales de Bretagne* 34 (1920): 402–425. Of particular relevance to the problem of social origins is the article of L. Trenard, "La crise social Lyonnaise à la veille de la Révolution," *Revue d'Histoire Moderne et Contemporaine* 2 (1955), which fortunately is included in English translation in J. Kaplow's *New Perspectives on the French Revolution,* along with an article by Y. Lemoigne on Strasbourg in the eighteenth century, as well as the key article by M. Vovelle and D. Roche, "Bourgeois, Rentiers, and Property Owners: Elements for Defining a Social Category at the End of the Eighteenth Century."

There are a large number of important works on geographical

divisions larger than towns or cities. One of the best is the study of Régine Robin entitled *La Société française en 1789: Semaur-en-Auxois* (Paris, 1970). Another good one is D. Ligou's study of *Montauban à la fin de l'Ancien Régime et aux débuts de la Révolution* (Paris, 1958). Also see M. Courtier's *Recherches sur les structures sociales de Chateaudun* (Paris, 1969). Unfortunately hundreds more like them are needed.

Since probably at least 80 percent of the population of France in the eighteenth century depended directly on agriculture for their livelihood, that aspect of social and economic history has received considerable attention. This has been especially true since 1924 when Georges Lefebvre published his monumental and now classic study of the peasants of the *département* du Nord during the Revolution: *Les paysans du Nord pendant la Révolution* (Lille, 1924). The other classic in the field was published in 1931 by Marc Bloch. It has since been translated into English as *French Rural History: An Essay on Its Basic Characteristics* (Berkeley, 1966). Continuing this tradition, several fine studies have appeared since World War II. These include Paul Bois, *Paysans de l'Ouest: Des structures économiques et sociales aux options politiques depuis l'époque révolutionnaire dans le Sarthe* (Paris–La Haye, 1960), which in spite of its title includes a large amount of information about the prerevolutionary period. A comparable work but dealing specifically with the Old Regime is *Les Paysans de la Bourgogne du Nord au dernier siècle de l'ancien régime* (Paris, 1960), by Pierre de Saint-Jacob. Another similar work is that of A. Poitrineau, *La Vie rurale en Basse-Auvergne au XVIIIe siècle, 1726–1789* (Paris, 1965). Another recent general study that deals with the difficult and controversial problem of agriculture and population growth in the eighteenth century is M. Morineau, *Les Faux-Semblants d'un démarrage économique: agriculture et demographie au XVIIIe siècle* (Paris, 1971).

Of particular importance because it is one of the few discussions of the subject by Albert Soboul available in English, is his article "The French Rural Community in the Eighteenth and Nineteenth Centuries," *Past and Present,* No. 10 (1956). Other useful articles in English include R. R. Palmer, "Georges Lefebvre: The Peasants and the French Revolution," *Journal of Modern History* 31 (December 1959), and Alan Davies, "The Origins of the French Peasant Revolution of 1789," *History* 49 (February 1964). On that particular subject the definitive work remains that of Georges Lefebvre now translated into English, *The Great Fear of 1789* (New York, 1973). E. Le Roy Ladurie's excellent study of the peasants, *Les Paysans du Languedoc* (Paris, 1966) also belongs in this group.

Certainly of significance for the social history of the eighteenth century but difficult to classify under the scheme developed for these suggestions are two books by Shelby T. McCloy. The first of these was *Government Assistance in Eighteenth-Century France* (Durham, N.C., 1946), which contains valuable information about the enlargement of government welfare activity during the century, and a broader consideration of the same theme in his *The Humanitarian Movement in Eighteenth-Century France* (Lexington, Ky., 1957).

1 2 3 4 5 6 7 8 9